PHP and MySQL®
Create-Modify-Reuse

PHP and MySQL®
Create-Modify-Reuse

Tim Boronczyk

with

Martin E. Psinas

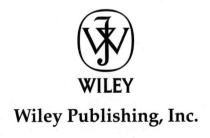

WILEY

Wiley Publishing, Inc.

PHP and MySQL® : Create-Modify-Reuse

Published by
Wiley Publishing, Inc.
10475 Crosspoint Boulevard
Indianapolis, IN 46256
www.wiley.com

Copyright © 2008 by Wiley Publishing, Inc., Indianapolis, Indiana

Published simultaneously in Canada

ISBN: 978-0-470-19242-9

Manufactured in the United States of America

10 9 8 7 6 5 4 3 2 1

Library of Congress Cataloging-in-Publication Data

Boronczyk, Tim, 1979-
    PHP and MySQL : create-modify-reuse / Tim Boronczyk with Martin E. Psinas.
        p.   cm.
    Includes index.
    ISBN 978-0-470-19242-9 (paper/website)
        1. MySQL (Electronic resource)   2. PHP (Computer program language)   3. Web sites—Design.
I. Psinas, Martin E.   II. Title.
QA76.73.P224B64   2008
006.7'6—dc22
                                                                    2008011996

About the Author

Timothy Boronczyk is a native of Syracuse, NY, where he works as a freelance developer, programmer and technical editor. He has been involved in web design since 1998 and over the years has written several articles and tutorials on PHP programming. Timothy holds a degree in software application programming and recently started his first business venture, Salt City Tech (www.saltcitytech.com). In his spare time, he enjoys photography, hanging out with friends, and sleeping with his feet hanging off the end of his bed. He's easily distracted by shiny objects.

About the Contributor

Martin E. Psinas is a recognized security expert and valued member of the open-source community. He has been contracted as a technical editor, code auditor, and is a published author with Pearson Education as well as the #1 PHP magazine, *PHP | Architect*. In his free time, he maintains his personal web site and is a volunteer administrator/contributor at codewalkers.com — a resource for PHP & MySQL developers. Martin interacts frequently with the leaders of the PHP project as well as PHP User's Groups.

Credits

Acquisitions Editor
Jenny Watson

Development Editor
Ed Connor

Technical Editor
Graham Christensen

Production Editor
Daniel Scribner

Copy Editor
Michael Koch

Editorial Manager
Mary Beth Wakefield

Production Manager
Tim Tate

Vice President and Executive Group Publisher
Richard Swadley

Vice President and Executive Publisher
Joseph B. Wikert

Project Coordinator, Cover
Lynsey Stanford

Proofreader
Corina Copp

Indexer
Ron Strauss

Contents

Contents

Contents

Introduction

I'm especially amazed at how the Internet has grown and evolved over the past decade or so. It has grown from a collection of static text documents connected by a few hyperlinks to a platform for delivering rich, distributed applications. And when it comes time to develop these web-based applications, many programmers are choosing PHP and MySQL.

In this book, I present basic code for 12 PHP-powered projects that you can use and extend however you wish. I have tried to write them so the code can be easily reused in future applications, but in some instances the entire application can be reused as well!

I've enjoyed the opportunity to write and share with you this information and I hope you have just as much fun reading it and learning from it. More importantly, I hope you find good, practical uses for the projects found within this book.

Who This Book Is For

I present basic yet functional projects for you to implement and extend in any way you see fit. That very fact assumes you know the fundamentals of programming in PHP and general web development. This book is not a textbook. Still, you do not need to be an advanced PHP programmer to gain much by reading it. New programmers should find this book helpful as it will give them guidance in how to program different applications. The 12 projects may even serve to ignite their curiosity and spur them to write 12 more projects of their own. Intermediate and more experienced programmers will find this book helpful because they are able to take the projects I present, modify them and apply them to their real-world needs.

Some projects build upon previous projects, so while you don't have to read the book from cover to cover, I do suggest reading all relevant chapters (or at least the pertinent sections) regardless of your skill level. For example, in Chapter 7, I present an online photo album, but pictures are uploaded using the AJAX file manager presented in Chapter 6. Both projects are laid out in the manner presented in Chapter 1.

What This Book Covers

The code in this book was written for MySQL 5.0 Community Server and PHP version 5.2.5, so essentially I am covering those releases or greater. Additional modification may be necessary if you plan on using earlier releases.

How This Book Is Structured

Each chapter is organized so following projects can build upon earlier projects. Here's a brief rundown of what you can look forward to in the following chapters:

Chapter 1: User Registration
Create a basic user registration system
Reusable components: configuration/include files, 401.php, User class

Chapter 2: Community Forum
Expand on user registration system to create a community forum with user privileges and threaded posts
Reusable components: JpegThumbnail class, BBCode class

Chapter 3: Mailing List
Create a mailing list with control address and digest mailings
Reusable components: POP3Client class

Chapter 4: Search Engine
Build a custom search engine for your own site
Reusable components: entire application

Chapter 5: Personal Calendar
Write a personal calendar utility to keep yourself organized
Reusable components: entire application

Chapter 6: AJAX File Manager
Create an AJAX-ified file upload and directory viewer
Reusable components: entire application (this project introduces AJAX which will be used in subsequent projects)

Chapter 7: Online Photo Album
Create a file-based image gallery with automatically generated thumbnails that supports JPEG and QuickTime formats.
Reusable components: MovThumbnail class

Chapter 8: Shopping Cart
Write a categorized shopping cart
Reusable components: ShoppingCart class

Chapter 9: Web Site Statistics
Log site traffic and collect information about site visitors to make better business decisions
Reusable components: PieChart class, BarChart class

Chapter 10: News/Blog system
Build a news or blog system with comments and RSS feed
Reusable components: entire application (project also introduces reusable components such as YUI calendar and TinyMCE rich text control)

Chapter 11: Shell Scripts

Write and run management scripts

Reusable components: `CommandLine` class, `recurs_copy()` function

Chapter 12: Security and Logging

Learn about SQL injection, path traversal, weak authentication, and XSS and how to avoid them

Reusable components: `write_log()` function, `view_log.php`, record delete script

What You Need to Use This Book

Since you'll be writing PHP code, you'll need an editor to do so. Whichever you choose to use is a matter of preference. Additionally, you will also need a server running PHP and MySQL to host your applications and a web browser to access them. What you use is a matter of choice. I've provided instructions for setting up applications on both Unix and Windows platforms when necessary, for example the Mailing List application in Chapter 3, which runs as a scheduled job.

Personally, I used vi to write code, hosted the projects on a server running Slackware Linux and accessed them from a Windows XP computer using Firefox.

Some of the projects make use of special extensions to PHP, although I have tried to keep this to a minimum. For example, the Search Engine application presented in Chapter 4 uses the pspell extension. If additional functionality was needed which could only be provided by an extension, I avoided third-party extensions so that if you want to install a particular extension you only need to look as far as the official documentation at `www.php.net`. The relevant extensions are mentioned in the appropriate chapters.

Conventions

To help you get the most from the text and keep track of what's happening, I've used a number of conventions throughout the book.

As for styles in the text:

❑ We *highlight* new terms and important words when we introduce them.

❑ We show keyboard strokes like this: Ctrl+A.

❑ We show file names, URLs, and code within the text like so: `persistence.properties`.

❑ We present code in two different ways:

```
We use a monofont type with no highlighting for most code examples.
We use gray highlighting to emphasize code that's particularly important
in the present context.
```

Source Code

As you work through the examples in this book, you may choose either to type in all the code manually or to use the source code files that accompany the book. All of the source code used in this book is available for download at `www.wrox.com`. When at the site, simply locate the book's title (either by using the Search box or by using one of the title lists) and click the Download Code link on the book's detail page to obtain all the source code for the book.

> *Because many books have similar titles, you may find it easiest to search by ISBN; this book's ISBN is 978-0-470-19242-9.*

Once you download the code, just decompress it with your favorite compression tool. Alternately, you can go to the main Wrox code download page at `www.wrox.com/dynamic/books/download.aspx` to see the code available for this book and all other Wrox books.

Errata

We make every effort to ensure that there are no errors in the text or in the code. However, no one is perfect, and mistakes do occur. If you find an error in one of our books, like a spelling mistake or faulty piece of code, we would be very grateful for your feedback. By sending in errata you may save another reader hours of frustration and at the same time you will be helping us provide even higher quality information.

To find the errata page for this book, go to `www.wrox.com` and locate the title using the Search box or one of the title lists. Then, on the book details page, click the Book Errata link. On this page you can view all errata that has been submitted for this book and posted by Wrox editors. A complete book list including links to each book's errata is also available at `www.wrox.com/misc-pages/booklist.shtml`.

If you don't spot "your" error on the Book Errata page, go to `www.wrox.com/contact/techsupport .shtml` and complete the form there to send us the error you have found. We'll check the information and, if appropriate, post a message to the book's errata page and fix the problem in subsequent editions of the book.

p2p.wrox.com

For author and peer discussion, join the P2P forums at `p2p.wrox.com`. The forums are a web-based system for you to post messages relating to Wrox books and related technologies and interact with other readers and technology users. The forums offer a subscription feature to e-mail you topics of interest of your choosing when new posts are made to the forums. Wrox authors, editors, other industry experts, and your fellow readers are present on these forums.

At p2p.wrox.com you will find a number of different forums that will help you not only as you read this book, but also as you develop your own applications. To join the forums, just follow these steps:

1. Go to p2p.wrox.com and click the Register link.

2. Read the terms of use and click Agree.

3. Complete the required information to join as well as any optional information you wish to provide and click Submit.

4. You will receive an e-mail with information describing how to verify your account and complete the joining process.

You can read messages in the forums without joining P2P but in order to post your own messages, you must join.

Once you join, you can post new messages and respond to messages other users post. You can read messages at any time on the Web. If you would like to have new messages from a particular forum e-mailed to you, click the Subscribe to this Forum icon by the forum name in the forum listing.

For more information about how to use the Wrox P2P, be sure to read the P2P FAQs for answers to questions about how the forum software works as well as many common questions specific to P2P and Wrox books. To read the FAQs, click the FAQ link on any P2P page.

1

User Registration

Offering account registration and user logins is a great way of giving users a sense of individuality and serving tailored content. Such authentication is often at the very heart of many community-oriented and e-commerce web sites. Because this functionality is so useful, the first application I present is a user registration system.

From a functional perspective, the system will allow users to create accounts. Members must provide an e-mail address that they can use to validate their registration. Users should also be able to update their passwords and e-mail addresses and reset forgotten passwords. This is pretty standard functionality and what the web users of today have come to expect.

From an architectural standpoint, the directory holding your code should be logically organized. For example, support and include files should be kept outside of a publically accessible directory. Also, user records should be stored in a database. Since there are a large number of tools designed to view and work with data stored in relational databases such as MySQL, this affords transparency and flexibility.

Plan the Directory Layout

The first step is to plan the directory structure for the application. I'm going to recommend you create three main folders: One named `public_files` from which all publicly accessible files will be served, another named `lib` to store include files to be shared by any number of other files, and finally a `templates` folder to store presentation files. Although PHP will be able to reference files from anywhere in your setup, the web server should only serve files from the `public_files` folder. Keeping support files outside of the publicly accessible directory increases security.

Inside the `public_files` I also create `css` to store any style sheets, `js` for JavaScript source files and `img` for graphic files. You may want to create other folders to keep yourself organized. One named `sql` to store MySQL files would be a good idea, `doc` for documentation and development notes and `tests` to store smoke test or unit testing files.

Planning the Database

In addition to planning the directory layout, thought needs to be given to the database layout as well. The information you choose to collect from your users will depend on what type of service your site offers. In turn, this affects how your database tables will look. At the very least a unique user ID, username, password hash, and e-mail address should be stored. You will also need a mechanism to track which accounts have been verified or are pending verification.

```
CREATE TABLE WROX_USER (
    USER_ID     INTEGER UNSIGNED   NOT NULL   AUTO_INCREMENT,
    USERNAME    VARCHAR(20)        NOT NULL,
    PASSWORD    CHAR(40)           NOT NULL,
    EMAIL_ADDR  VARCHAR(100)       NOT NULL,
    IS_ACTIVE   TINYINT(1)         DEFAULT 0,

    PRIMARY KEY (USER_ID)
)
ENGINE=MyISAM DEFAULT CHARACTER SET latin1
    COLLATE latin1_general_cs AUTO_INCREMENT=0;

CREATE TABLE WROX_PENDING (
    USER_ID        INTEGER UNSIGNED   NOT NULL,
    TOKEN          CHAR(10)           NOT NULL,
    CREATED_DATE   TIMESTAMP          DEFAULT   CURRENT_TIMESTAMP,

    FOREIGN KEY (USER_ID)
        REFERENCES WROX_USER(USER_ID)
)
ENGINE=MyISAM DEFAULT CHARACTER SET latin1
    COLLATE latin1_general_cs;
```

I have allocated 40 characters of storage for the password hash in WROX_USER as I will use the sha1() function which returns a 40-character hexadecimal string. You should never store the original password in the database — a good security precaution. The idea here is that a hash is generated when the user provides his or her password for the first time. The password given subsequently is hashed using the same function and the result is compared with what's stored to see if they match.

I set the maximum storage length for an e-mail address at 100 characters. Technically the standards set the maximum length for an e-mail address at 320 (64 characters are allowed for the username, one for the @ symbol and then 255 for the hostname). I don't know anyone that has such a long e-mail address though and I have seen plenty of database schemas that use 100 and work fine.

Some other information you may want to store are first and last name, address, city, state/province, postal code, phone numbers, and the list goes on.

The WROX_PENDING table has an automatically initializing timestamp column, which lets you go back to the database and delete pending accounts that haven't been activated after a certain amount of time. The table's columns could be merged with WROX_USER, but I chose to separate them since the pending token is only used once. User data is considered more permanent and the WROX_USER table isn't cluttered with temporary data.

Writing Shared Code

Code that is shared by multiple files should be set aside in its own file and included using `include` or `require` so it's not duplicated, which makes maintaining the application easier. Where possible, code that might be useful in future applications should be collected separately as functions or classes to be reused. It's a good idea to write code with reusability in mind. `common.php` contains shared code to be included in other scripts in the application to establish a sane baseline environment at runtime. Since it should never be called directly by a user, it should be saved in the `lib` directory.

```php
<?php
// set true if production environment else false for development
define ('IS_ENV_PRODUCTION', true);

// configure error reporting options
error_reporting(E_ALL | E_STRICT);
ini_set('display_errors', !IS_ENV_PRODUCTION);
ini_set('error_log', 'log/phperror.txt');

// set time zone to use date/time functions without warnings
date_default_timezone_set('America/New_York');

// compensate for magic quotes if necessary
if (get_magic_quotes_gpc())
{
    function _stripslashes_rcurs($variable, $top = true)
    {
        $clean_data = array();
        foreach ($variable as $key => $value)
        {
            $key = ($top) ? $key : stripslashes($key);
            $clean_data[$key] = (is_array($value)) ?
                stripslashes_rcurs($value, false) : stripslashes($value);
        }
        return $clean_data;
    }
    $_GET = _stripslashes_rcurs($_GET);
    $_POST = _stripslashes_rcurs($_POST);
    // $_REQUEST = _stripslashes_rcurs($_REQUEST);
    // $_COOKIE = _stripslashes_rcurs($_COOKIE);
}
?>
```

You may not always have control over the configuration of your server so it is wise to specify some common directives to make your applications more portable. Setting error reporting options, for example, lets you display errors while in development or redirect them in a production environment so they don't show to the user.

Magic quotes is a configuration option where PHP can automatically escape single quotes, double quotes, and backslashes in incoming data. Although this might seem useful, assuming whether this directive is on or not can lead to problems. It's better to normalize the data first and then escape it with `addslashes()` or `mysql_real_escape_string()` (preferably the latter if it's going to be stored in the database) when necessary. Compensating for magic quotes ensures data is properly escaped *how* you want and *when* you want despite how PHP is configured, making development easier and less error-prone.

Establishing a connection to a MySQL database is a common activity which makes sense to move out to its own file. db.php holds configuration constants and code to establish the connection. Again, as it is meant to be included in other files and not called directly, it should be saved in lib.

```php
<?php
// database connection and schema constants
define('DB_HOST', 'localhost');
define('DB_USER', 'username');
define('DB_PASSWORD', 'password');
define('DB_SCHEMA', 'WROX_DATABASE');
define('DB_TBL_PREFIX', 'WROX_');

// establish a connection to the database server
if (!$GLOBALS['DB'] = mysql_connect(DB_HOST, DB_USER, DB_PASSWORD))
{
    die('Error: Unable to connect to database server.');
}
if (!mysql_select_db(DB_SCHEMA, $GLOBALS['DB']))
{
    mysql_close($GLOBALS['DB']);
    die('Error: Unable to select database schema.');
}
?>
```

The DB_HOST, DB_USER, DB_PASSWORD and DB_SCHEMA constants represent the values needed to establish a successful connection to the database. If the code is put into production in an environment where the database server is not running on the same host as PHP and the web server, you might also want to provide a DB_PORT value and adjust the call to mysql_connect() appropriately.

The connection handle for the database is then stored in the $GLOBALS super global array so it is available in any scope of any file that includes db.php (or that is included in the file that has referenced db.php).

Prefixing table names helps prevent clashes with other programs' tables that might be stored in the same schema and providing the prefix as a constant makes the code easier to update later if it should change, since the value appears just in one place.

Common functions can also be placed in their own files. I plan to use this random_text() function, for example, to generate a CAPTCHA string and validation token so it can be saved in a file named functions.php.

```php
<?php
// return a string of random text of a desired length
function random_text($count, $rm_similar = false)
{
    // create list of characters
    $chars = array_flip(array_merge(range(0, 9), range('A', 'Z')));
```

```php
    // remove similar looking characters that might cause confusion
    if ($rm_similar)
    {
        unset($chars[0], $chars[1], $chars[2], $chars[5], $chars[8],
            $chars['B'], $chars['I'], $chars['O'], $chars['Q'],
            $chars['S'], $chars['U'], $chars['V'], $chars['Z']);
    }

    // generate the string of random text
    for ($i = 0, $text = ''; $i < $count; $i++)
    {
        $text .= array_rand($chars);
    }

    return $text;
}
?>
```

An important rule when programming no matter what language you're using is to never trust user input. People can (and will) provide all sorts of crazy and unexpected input. Sometimes this is accidental, at other times it's malicious. PHP's `filter_input()` and `filter_var()` functions can be used to scrub incoming data, though some people still prefer to write their own routines, as the filter extension may not be available in versions prior to 5.2.0. If you're one of those people, then they can be placed in `functions.php` as well.

User Class

The majority of the code written maintaining a user's account can be encapsulated into one data structure, making it easy to extend or reuse in future applications. This includes the database interaction logic, which will make storing and retrieving information easier. Here's `User.php`:

```php
<?php
class User
{
    private $uid;      // user id
    private $fields;   // other record fields

    // initialize a User object
    public function __construct()
    {
        $this->uid = null;
        $this->fields = array('username' => '',
                              'password' => '',
                              'emailAddr' => '',
                              'isActive' => false);
    }

    // override magic method to retrieve properties
    public function __get($field)
```

(continued)

5

(continued)

```
    {
        if ($field == 'userId')
        {
            return $this->uid;
        }
        else
        {
            return $this->fields[$field];
        }
    }

    // override magic method to set properties
    public function __set($field, $value)
    {

        if (array_key_exists($field, $this->fields))
        {
            $this->fields[$field] = $value;
        }
    }

    // return if username is valid format
    public static function validateUsername($username)
    {
        return preg_match('/^[A-Z0-9]{2,20}$/i', $username);
    }

    // return if email address is valid format
    public static function validateEmailAddr($email)
    {
        return filter_var($email, FILTER_VALIDATE_EMAIL);
    }

    // return an object populated based on the record's user id
    public static function getById($user_id)
    {
        $user = new User();
        $query = sprintf('SELECT USERNAME, PASSWORD, EMAIL_ADDR, IS_ACTIVE ' .
            'FROM %sUSER WHERE USER_ID = %d', DB_TBL_PREFIX, $user_id);
        $result = mysql_query($query, $GLOBALS['DB']);
        if (mysql_num_rows($result))
        {
            $row = mysql_fetch_assoc($result);
            $user->username = $row['USERNAME'];
            $user->password = $row['PASSWORD'];
            $user->emailAddr = $row['EMAIL_ADDR'];
            $user->isActive = $row['IS_ACTIVE'];
            $user->uid = $user_id;
        }
        mysql_free_result($result);
        return $user;
    }
```

```php
    // return an object populated based on the record's username
    public static function getByUsername($username)
    {
        $user = new User();
        $query = sprintf('SELECT USER_ID, PASSWORD, EMAIL_ADDR, IS_ACTIVE ' .
            'FROM %sUSER WHERE USERNAME = "%s"', DB_TBL_PREFIX,
            mysql_real_escape_string($username, $GLOBALS['DB']));
        $result = mysql_query($query, $GLOBALS['DB']);
        if (mysql_num_rows($result))
        {
            $row = mysql_fetch_assoc($result);
            $user->username = $username;
            $user->password = $row['PASSWORD'];
            $user->emailAddr = $row['EMAIL_ADDR'];
            $user->isActive = $row['IS_ACTIVE'];
            $user->uid = $row['USER_ID'];
        }
        mysql_free_result($result);
        return $user;
    }


    // save the record to the database
    public function save()
    {
        if ($this->uid)
        {
            $query = sprintf('UPDATE %sUSER SET USERNAME = "%s", ' .
                'PASSWORD = "%s", EMAIL_ADDR = "%s", IS_ACTIVE = %d ' .
                'WHERE USER_ID = %d', DB_TBL_PREFIX,
                mysql_real_escape_string($this->username, $GLOBALS['DB']),
                mysql_real_escape_string($this->password, $GLOBALS['DB']),
                mysql_real_escape_string($this->emailAddr, $GLOBALS['DB']),
                $this->isActive, $this->userId);
            return mysql_query($query, $GLOBALS['DB']);
        }
        else
        {
            $query = sprintf('INSERT INTO %sUSER (USERNAME, PASSWORD, ' .
                'EMAIL_ADDR, IS_ACTIVE) VALUES ("%s", "%s", "%s", %d)',
                DB_TBL_PREFIX,
                mysql_real_escape_string($this->username, $GLOBALS['DB']),
                mysql_real_escape_string($this->password, $GLOBALS['DB']),
                mysql_real_escape_string($this->emailAddr, $GLOBALS['DB']),
                $this->isActive);
            if (mysql_query($query, $GLOBALS['DB']))
            {
                $this->uid = mysql_insert_id($GLOBALS['DB']);
                return true;
            }
```

(continued)

(continued)

```
            else
            {
                return false;
            }
        }
    }

    // set the record as inactive and return an activation token
    public function setInactive()
    {
        $this->isActive = false;
        $this->save(); // make sure the record is saved

        $token = random_text(5);
        $query = sprintf('INSERT INTO %sPENDING (USER_ID, TOKEN) ' .
            'VALUES (%d, "%s")', DB_TBL_PREFIX, $this->uid, $token);
        return (mysql_query($query, $GLOBALS['DB'])) ? $token : false;
    }

    // clear the user's pending status and set the record as active
    public function setActive($token)
    {
        $query = sprintf('SELECT TOKEN FROM %sPENDING WHERE USER_ID = %d ' .
            'AND TOKEN = "%s"', DB_TBL_PREFIX, $this->uid,
            mysql_real_escape_string($token, $GLOBALS['DB']));
        $result = mysql_query($query, $GLOBALS['DB']);
        if (!mysql_num_rows($result))
        {
            mysql_free_result($result);
            return false;
        }
        else
        {
            mysql_free_result($result);
            $query = sprintf('DELETE FROM %sPENDING WHERE USER_ID = %d ' .
                'AND TOKEN = "%s"', DB_TBL_PREFIX, $this->uid,
                mysql_real_escape_string($token, $GLOBALS['DB']));
            if (!mysql_query($query, $GLOBALS['DB']))
            {
                return false;
            }
            else
            {
                $this->isActive = true;
                return $this->save();
            }
        }
    }
}
?>
```

The class has two private properties: $uid which maps to the WROX_USER table's USER_ID column and the array $fields which maps to the other columns. They are exposed in an intuitive manner by overriding the __get() and __set() magic methods, but I still protect $uid from accidental change.

The static getById() and getByUsername() methods contain code responsible for retrieving the record from the database and populating the object. save() writes the record to the database and is smart enough to know when to execute an INSERT query or an UPDATE query based on if the user ID is set. All that's necessary to create a new user account is to obtain a new instance of a User object, set the record's fields, and call save().

```php
<?php
$u = new User();
$u->username = 'timothy';
$u->password = sha1('secret');
$u->emailAddr = 'timothy@example.com';
$u->save();
?>
```

It's the same logic to update an account; I retrieve the existing account, make my changes, and again save it to the database with save().

```php
<?php
$u = User::getByUsername('timothy');
$u->password = sha1('new_password');
$u->save();
?>
```

The setInactive() and setActive() methods handle the account activation. Calling setInactive() marks the account inactive, generates, an activation token, stores, the information in the database, and returns, the token. When the user activates their account, you accept the token and provide it to setActive(). The method will remove the token record and set the account active.

CAPTCHA

The word CAPTCHA stands for *Completely Automated Public Turing Test to Tell* **C***omputers and Humans Apart*. Besides being a painfully contrived acronym, CAPTCHAs are often used as a deterrent to keep spammers and other malicious users from automatically registering user accounts.

The user is presented with a challenge, oftentimes as a graphical image containing letters and numbers. He or she then has to read the text and enter it in an input field. If the two values match, then it is assumed an intelligent human being and not a computer is requesting the account sign-up.

It's not a perfect solution, however. CAPTCHAs cause problems for legitimate users with special accessibility needs, and some modern software can read the text in CAPTCHA images (see www.cs.sfu.ca/~mori/research/gimpy/). There are other types of challenges which can be presented to a user. For example, there are audio CAPTCHAs where the user enters the letters and numbers after hearing them recited in an audio file. Some even present math problems to the user.

CAPTCHAs should be considered a tool in the web master's arsenal to deter lazy miscreants and not a replacement for proper monitoring and security. Inconvenience to the visitor increases with the complexity of the challenge method, so I'll stick with a simple image-based CAPTCHA example here.

```php
<?php
include '../../lib/functions.php';

// must start or continue session and save CAPTCHA string in $_SESSION for it
// to be available to other requests
if (!isset($_SESSION))
{
    session_start();
    header('Cache-control: private');
}

// create a 65x20 pixel image
$width = 65;
$height = 20;
$image = imagecreate(65, 20);

// fill the image background color
$bg_color = imagecolorallocate($image, 0x33, 0x66, 0xFF);
imagefilledrectangle($image, 0, 0, $width, $height, $bg_color);

// fetch random text
$text = random_text(5);

// determine x and y coordinates for centering text
$font = 5;
$x = imagesx($image) / 2 - strlen($text) * imagefontwidth($font) / 2;
$y = imagesy($image) / 2 - imagefontheight($font) / 2;

// write text on image
$fg_color = imagecolorallocate($image, 0xFF, 0xFF, 0xFF);
imagestring($image, $font, $x, $y, $text, $fg_color);

// save the CAPTCHA string for later comparison
$_SESSION['captcha'] = $text;

// output the image
header('Content-type: image/png');
imagepng($image);

imagedestroy($image);
?>
```

I recommend saving the script in the `public_files/img` folder (since it needs to be publically accessible and outputs a graphic image) as `captcha.php`. The image it creates is a 65×20 pixel PNG graphic with blue background and a white random text string five characters long, as seen in Figure 1-1. The string must be stored as a `$_SESSION` variable so you can check later to see if the user enters it correctly. To make the image more complex, you can use different fonts, colors, and background images.

```
AM421
```

Figure 1-1

Templates

Templates make it easier for developers to maintain a consistent look and feel across many pages, they help keep your code organized, and they move presentation logic out of your code, making both your PHP *and* HTML files more readable. There are a lot of different templating products available — some big (like Smarty, http://smarty.php.net) and some small (TinyButStrong, www.tinybutstrong .com). Each have their own benefits and drawbacks regardless if the solution is commercial, open source, or home-brewed. Sometimes the choice of which one to use will boil down to a matter of personal preference.

Speaking of personal preference, although I love the spirit of templating, I'm not a fan of most implementations. Despite all the benefits, modern templating systems complicate things. Some have their own special syntax to learn and almost all incur additional processing overhead. Truth be told, most projects don't need a dedicated template engine; PHP can be considered a template engine itself and can handle templating for even moderately large web projects with multiple developers if proper planning and organization is in place.

The setup that works best for me is to keep the core of my presentation in specific HTML files in a templates folder. This folder is usually outside of the web-accessible base (though the CSS, JavaScript and image files referenced in the HTML do need to be publically accessible) since I don't want a visitor or search engine to stumble upon a slew of content-less pages.

For now, here's a basic template that's suitable for the needs of this project:

```
<!DOCTYPE html PUBLIC "-//W3C//DTD XHTML 1.0 Strict//EN"
 "http://www.w3.org/TR/xhtml1/DTD/xhtml1-strict.dtd">
<html xmlns="http://www.w3.org/1999/xhtml" xml:lang="en" lang="en">
 <head>
  <title>
<?php
if (!empty($GLOBALS['TEMPLATE']['title']))
{
    echo $GLOBALS['TEMPLATE']['title'];
}
?>
</title>
  <link rel="stylesheet" type="text/css" href="css/styles.css"/>
<?php
if (!empty($GLOBALS['TEMPLATE']['extra_head']))
{
    echo $GLOBALS['TEMPLATE']['extra_head'];
}
?>
 </head>
 <body>
  <div id="header">
```

(continued)

(continued)

```php
<?php
if (!empty($GLOBALS['TEMPLATE']['title']))
{
    echo $GLOBALS['TEMPLATE']['title'];
}
?>
  </div>
  <div id="content">
<?php
if (!empty($GLOBALS['TEMPLATE']['content']))
{
    echo $GLOBALS['TEMPLATE']['content'];
}
?>
  </div>
  <div id="footer">Copyright &copy;<?php echo date('Y'); ?></div>
  </div>
  </body>
</html>
```

There should be some conventions in place to keep things sane. For starters, content will be stored in the $GLOBALS array in the requested script so it will be available in any scope within the included template file. I commonly use the following keys:

- ❑ title — Page title

- ❑ description — Page description

- ❑ keywords — Page keywords (the page's title, description and keywords can all be stored in a database)

- ❑ extra_head — A means to add additional HTML headers or JavaScript code to a page

- ❑ content — The page's main content

Occasionally I'll also include a menu or sidebar key depending on the project and planned layout, though your exact variables will depend on the template. So long as there are standard conventions written down and faithfully adhered to, a development team of any size can work successfully with such a template solution.

Registering a New User

With the directory structure laid out and enough of the support code written, the focus can now move to registering a new user. The following code can be saved in the public_files folder as register.php. Figure 1-2 shows the page viewed in a browser.

Figure 1-2

```php
<?php
// include shared code
include '../lib/common.php';
include '../lib/db.php';
include '../lib/functions.php';
include '../lib/User.php';

// start or continue session so the CAPTCHA text stored in $_SESSION is
// accessible
session_start();
header('Cache-control: private');

// prepare the registration form's HTML
ob_start();
?>
<form method="post"
 action="<?php echo htmlspecialchars($_SEVER['PHP_SELF']); ?>">
 <table>
  <tr>
   <td><label for="username">Username</label></td>
   <td><input type="text" name="username" id="username"
    value="<?php if (isset($_POST['username']))
    echo htmlspecialchars($_POST['username']); ?>"/></td>
  </tr><tr>
   <td><label for="password1">Password</label></td>
   <td><input type="password" name="password1" id="password1"
    value=""/></td>
  </tr><tr>
```

(continued)

(continued)

```
    <td><label for="password2">Password Again</label></td>
    <td><input type="password" name="password2" id="password2"
    value=""/></td>
  </tr><tr>
    <td><label for="email">Email Address</label></td>
    <td><input type="text" name="email" id="email"
    value="<?php if (isset($_POST['email']))
    echo htmlspecialchars($_POST['email']); ?>"/></td>
  </tr><tr>
    <td><label for="captcha">Verify</label></td>
    <td>Enter text seen in this image<br/ >
    <img src="img/captcha.php?nocache=<?php echo time(); ?>" alt=""/><br />
    <input type="text" name="captcha" id="captcha"/></td>
  </tr><tr>
    <td> </td>
    <td><input type="submit" value="Sign Up"/></td>
    <td><input type="hidden" name="submitted" value="1"/></td>
  </tr><tr>
 </table>
</form>
<?php
$form = ob_get_clean();

// show the form if this is the first time the page is viewed
if (!isset($_POST['submitted']))
{
    $GLOBALS['TEMPLATE']['content'] = $form;
}

// otherwise process incoming data
else
{
    // validate password
    $password1 = (isset($_POST['password1'])) ? $_POST['password1'] : '';
    $password2 = (isset($_POST['password2'])) ? $_POST['password2'] : '';
    $password = ($password1 && $password1 == $password2) ?
        sha1($password1) : '';

    // validate CAPTCHA
    $captcha = (isset($_POST['captcha']) &&
        strtoupper($_POST['captcha']) == $_SESSION['captcha']);

    // add the record if all input validates
    if (User::validateUsername($_POST['username']) && password &&
        User::validateEmailAddr($_POST['email']) && $captcha)
    {
        // make sure the user doesn't already exist
        $user = User::getByUsername($_POST['username']);
        if ($user->userId)
        {
            $GLOBALS['TEMPLATE']['content'] = '<p><strong>Sorry, that ' .
                'account already exists.</strong></p> <p>Please try a ' .
```

```
                'different username.</p>';
            $GLOBALS['TEMPLATE']['content'] .= $form;
        }
        else
        {
            // create an inactive user record
            $user = new User();
            $user->username = $_POST['username'];
            $user->password = $password;
            $user->emailAddr = $_POST['email'];
            $token = $user->setInactive();

            $GLOBALS['TEMPLATE']['content'] = '<p><strong>Thank you for ' .
                'registering.</strong></p> <p>Be sure to verify your ' .
                'account by visiting <a href="verify.php?uid=' .
                $user->userId . '&token=' . $token . '">verify.php?uid=' .
                $user->userId . '&token=' . $token . '</a></p>';
        }
    }
    // there was invalid data
    else
    {
        $GLOBALS['TEMPLATE']['content'] .= '<p><strong>You provided some ' .
            'invalid data.</strong></p> <p>Please fill in all fields ' .
            'correctly so we can register your user account.</p>';
        $GLOBALS['TEMPLATE']['content'] .= $form;
    }
}

// display the page
include '../templates/template-page.php';
?>
```

The first thing `register.php` does is import the shared code files it depends on. Some programmers prefer to place all the `include` statements in one common header file and include that for shorter code. Personally, however, I prefer to include them individually as I find it easier to maintain.

Other programmers may use `chdir()` to change PHP's working directory so they don't have to repeatedly backtrack in the file system to include a file. Again, this is a matter of personal preference. Be careful with this approach, however, when targeting older installations of PHP that use safe mode. `chdir()` may fail without generating any kind of error message if the directory is inaccessible.

```
<?php
// include shared code
chdir('../');
include 'lib/common.php';
include 'lib/db.php';
include 'lib/functions.php';
include 'lib/User.php';
...
?>
```

After importing the shared code files I call `session_start()`. HTTP requests are stateless, which means the web server returns each page without tracking what was done before or anticipating what might happen next. PHP's session tracking gives you an easy way to maintain state across requests and carry values from one request to the next. A session is required for keeping track of the CAPTCHA value generated by `captcha.php`.

I like to use output buffering when preparing large blocks of HTML such as the registration form, for greater readability. Others may prefer to maintain a buffer variable and repeatedly append to it throughout the script, like so:

```php
<?php
$GLOBALS['TEMPLATE']['content'] = '<form action="'.
    htmlspecialchars(currentFile()) . '" method="post">';
$GLOBALS['TEMPLATE']['content'] .= '<table>';
$GLOBALS['TEMPLATE']['content'] .= '<tr>';
$GLOBALS['TEMPLATE']['content'] .= '<td><label for="username">Username</label>' .
 '</td>';
...
?>
```

I find that approach becomes rather cumbersome relatively fast. With output buffering, all I need to do is start the capturing with `ob_start()`, retrieve the buffer's contents with `ob_get_contents()`, and stop capturing with `ob_end_clean()`. `ob_get_clean()` combines `ob_get_contents()` and `ob_end_clean()` in one function call. It's also easier for the engine to fall in and out of PHP mode so such code with large blocks of output would theoretically run faster than with the buffer concatenation method.

No `$_POST` values should be received the first time a user views the page so the code just outputs the registration form. When the user submits the form, the `$_POST['submitted']` variable is set and it knows to start processing the input.

The validation code to check the use rname and password are part of the `User` class. The two password values are compared against each other and then the password's hash is saved for later storage. Finally, the user's CAPTCHA input is checked with what was previously stored in the session by `captcha.php`. If everything checks out, the record is added to the database.

The `verify.php` script referenced in the HTML code is responsible for taking in a user ID and activation token, checking the corresponding values in the database, and then activating the user's account. It must be saved in the publically accessible directory as well.

```php
<?php
// include shared code
include '../lib/common.php';
include '../lib/db.php';
include '../lib/functions.php';
include '../lib/User.php';

// make sure a user id and activation token were received
if (!isset($_GET['uid']) || !isset($_GET['token']))
{
    $GLOBALS['TEMPLATE']['content'] = '<p><strong>Incomplete information ' .
        'was received.</strong></p> <p>Please try again.</p>';
```

```php
    include '../templates/template-page.php';
    exit();
}

// validate userid
if (!$user = User::getById($_GET['uid']))
{
    $GLOBALS['TEMPLATE']['content'] = '<p><strong>No such account.</strong>' .
        '</p> <p>Please try again.</p>';
}
// make sure the account is not active
else
{
    if ($user->isActive)
    {
        $GLOBALS['TEMPLATE']['content'] = '<p><strong>That account ' .
            'has already been verified.</strong></p>';
    }
    // activate the account
    else
    {
        if ($user->setActive($_GET['token']))
        {
            $GLOBALS['TEMPLATE']['content'] = '<p><strong>Thank you ' .
                'for verifying your account.</strong></p> <p>You may ' .
                'now <a href="login.php">login</a>.</p>';
        }
        else
        {
            $GLOBALS['TEMPLATE']['content'] = '<p><strong>You provided ' .
                'invalid data.</strong></p> <p>Please try again.</p>';
        }
    }
}

// display the page
include '../templates/template-page.php';
?>
```

E-mailing a Validation Link

Right now `register.php` provides a direct link to verify the account, though in a production environment it's typical to send the link in an e-mail to the address provided. The hope is that legitimate users will supply legitimate e-mail accounts and actively confirm their accounts, and bulk spammers wouldn't.

The `mail()` function is used to send e-mails from within PHP. The first argument is the user's e-mail address, the second is the e-mail's subject, and the third is the message. The use of @ to suppress warning messages is generally discouraged, though in this case it is necessary because `mail()` will return false *and* generate a warning if it fails.

The code you integrate into `register.php` to send a message instead of displaying the validation link in the browser window might look something like this:

```php
<?php
...
// create an inactive user record
$user = new User();
$user->username = $_POST['username'];
$user->password = $password;
$user->emailAddr = $_POST['email'];
$token = $user->setInactive();

$message = 'Thank you for signing up for an account!  Before you '.
    ' can login you need to verify your account. You can do so ' .
    'by visiting http://www.example.com/verify.php?uid=' .
    $user->userId . '&token=' . $token . '.';

if (@mail($user->emailAddr, 'Activate your new account', $message))
{
    $GLOBALS['TEMPLATE']['content'] = '<p><strong>Thank you for ' .
        'registering.</strong></p> <p>You will be receiving an ' .
        'email shortly with instructions on activating your ' .
        'account.</p>';
}
else
{
    $GLOBALS['TEMPLATE']['content'] = '<p><strong>There was an ' .
        'error sending you the activation link.</strong></p> ' .
        '<p>Please contact the site administrator at <a href="' .
        'mailto:admin@example.com">admin@example.com</a> for ' .
        'assistance.</p>';
}
...
?>
```

Figure 1-3 shows the confirmation message sent as an e-mail viewed in an e-mail program.

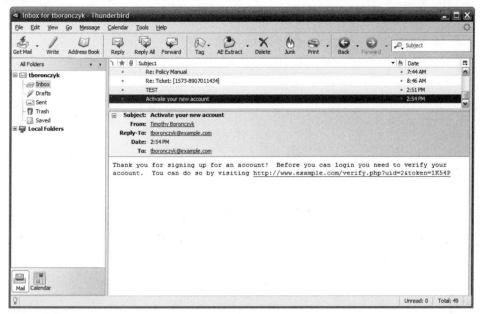

Figure 1-3

Sending the message as a plain text e-mail is simple, while sending an HTML-formatted message is a bit more involved. Each have their own merits: plain text messages are more accessible and less likely to get blocked by a user's spam filter while HTML-formatted messages appear friendlier, less sterile and can have clickable hyperlinks to make validating the account easier.

An HTML-formatted e-mail message might look like this:

```html
<html>
<p>Thank you for signing up for an account!</p>
<p>Before you can login you need to verify your account. You can do so by
visiting <a href="http://www.example.com/verify.php?uid=###&amp;token=xxxxx">
http://www.example.com/verify.php?uid=###&amp;token=xxxxx</a>.</p>
<p>If your mail program doesn't allow you to click on hyperlinks in a
message, copy it and paste it into the address bar of your web browser to
visit the page.</p>
</html>
```

However, if you sent it as the previous example then the e-mail would still be received as plain text even though it contains HTML markup. The proper MIME and Content-Type headers also need to be sent as well to inform the e-mail client how to display the message. These additional headers are given to mail()'s optional fourth parameter.

```php
<?php
// assume the formatted message is stored as $html_message

// formatted mail requires a MIME and Content-Type header
$headers = array('MIME-Version: 1.0',
                 'Content-Type: text/html; charset="iso-8859-1"');

// additional headers are supplied as the 4th argument to mail()
mail($user->emailAddr, 'Please activate your new account', $html_message,
    join("\n", $headers));
?>
```

It's possible to have the best of both e-mail worlds by sending a mixed e-mail message. A mixed e-mail contains both plain-text and HTML-formatted messages and then it becomes the mail client's job to decide which portion it should display. Here's an example of such a multi-part message:

```
--==A.BC_123_XYZ_678.9
Content-Type: text/plain; charset="iso-8859-1"

Thank you for signing up for an account!

Before you can login you need to verify your account. You can do so by visiting
http://www.example.com/verify.php?uid=##&token=xxxxx.

--==A.BC_123_XYZ_678.9
Content-Type: text/plain; charset="iso-8859-1"

<html>
<p>Thank you for signing up for an account!</p>
<p>Before you can login you need to verify your account. You can do so by
visiting <a href="http://www.example.com/verify.php?uid=###&amp;token=xxxxx">
http://www.example.com/verify.php?uid=###&amp;token=xxxxx</a>.</p>
<p>If your mail program doesn't allow you to click on hyperlinks in a
message, copy it and paste it into the address bar of your web browser to
visit the page.</p>
</html>

--==A.BC_123_XYZ_678.9--
```

The correct headers to use when sending the message would be:

```
MIME-Version: 1.0
Content-Type: multipart/alternative; boundary="==A.BC_123_XYZ_678.9"
```

Note that a special string is used to mark boundaries of different message segments. There's no significance to ==A.BC_123_XYZ_678.9 as I've used — it just needs to be random text which doesn't appear in the body of any of the message parts. When used to separate message blocks, the string is preceded by two dashes and is followed by a blank line. Trailing dashes mark the end of the message.

Logging In and Out

With the ability to create new user accounts and verify them as belonging to a real people with valid e-mail addresses in place, the next logical step is to provide a mechanism for these users to log in and out. Much of the dirty work tracking the session will be done by PHP so all you need to do is store some identifying information in $_SESSION. Save this code as login.php.

```php
<?php
// include shared code
include '../lib/common.php';
include '../lib/db.php';
include '../lib/functions.php';
include '../lib/User.php';

// start or continue the session
session_start();
header('Cache-control: private');

// perform login logic if login is set
if (isset($_GET['login']))
{
    if (isset($_POST['username']) && isset($_POST['password']))
    {
        // retrieve user record
        $user = (User::validateUsername($_POST['username'])) ?
            User::getByUsername($_POST['username']) : new User();

        if ($user->userId && $user->password == sha1($_POST['password']))
        {
            // everything checks out so store values in session to track the
            // user and redirect to main page
            $_SESSION['access'] = TRUE;
            $_SESSION['userId'] = $user->userId;
            $_SESSION['username'] = $user->username;
            header('Location: main.php');
        }
        else
        {
            // invalid user and/or password
            $_SESSION['access'] = FALSE;
            $_SESSION['username'] = null;
            header('Location: 401.php');
        }
    }
    // missing credentials
    else
    {
        $_SESSION['access'] = FALSE;
        $_SESSION['username'] = null;
        header('Location: 401.php');
    }
    exit();
}
```

(continued)

(continued)

```php
// perform logout logic if logout is set
// (clearing the session data effectively logsout the user)
else if (isset($_GET['logout']))
{
    if (isset($_COOKIE[session_name()]))
    {
        setcookie(session_name(), '', time() - 42000, '/');
    }

    $_SESSION = array();
    session_unset();

    session_destroy();
}

// generate login form
ob_start();
?>
<form action="<?php echo htmlspecialchars($_SERVER['PHP_SELF']); ?>?login"
 method="post">
 <table>
  <tr>
   <td><label for="username">Username</label></td>
   <td><input type="text" name="username" id="username"/></td>
  </tr><tr>
   <td><label for="password">Password</label></td>
   <td><input type="password" name="password" id="password"/></td>
  </tr><tr>
   <td> </td>
   <td><input type="submit" value="Log In"/></td>
  </tr>
 </table>
</form>
<?php
$GLOBALS['TEMPLATE']['content'] = ob_get_clean();

// display the page
include '../templates/template-page.php';
?>
```

The code encapsulates the logic to both process logins and logouts by passing a parameter in the page address. Submitting a login form to `login.php?login` would processes the login logic. Linking to `login.php?logoff` will effectively log out the user by clearing all session data. The login form is shown in Figure 1-4.

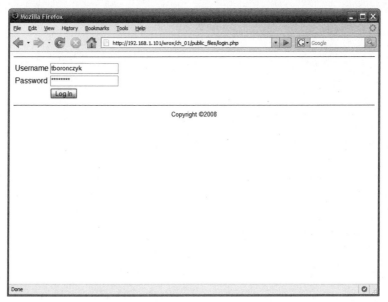

Figure 1-4

To log a user in, the script accepts a username and password. The supplied username is passed to the getByUsername() method so the record can be retrieved from the database and the supplied password is hashed for comparison. If the credentials match, the user provided the correct username and password and is logged in by storing identifying information in the session and redirecting the browser to the main page. The session is cleared and the user is redirected to an error page (404.php) if authentication fails.

The script outputs HTML code for a login form if called without any parameters. This is convenient if you want to link to it from another page, or redirect back to the login form from the error page. But you're not restricted to using this form. Because an exit statement has been strategically placed after the login code, you can use the script to process any login form, whether it's in a page template or elsewhere. Just remember to pass the login parameter in the address.

The user is redirected to 401.php if the login is not successful:

```php
<?php
// include shared code
include '../lib/common.php';

// start or join the session
session_start();
header('Cache-control: private');

// issue 401 error if the user has not been authenticated
if (!isset($_SESSION['access']) || $_SESSION['access'] != TRUE)
{
    header('HTTP/1.0 401 Authorization Error');
```

(continued)

23

(continued)

```php
        ob_start();
?>
<script type="text/javascript">
window.seconds = 10;
window.onload = function()
{
    if (window.seconds != 0)
    {
        document.getElementById('secondsDisplay').innerHTML = '' +
            window.seconds + ' second' + ((window.seconds > 1) ? 's' : '');
        window.seconds--;
        setTimeout(window.onload, 1000);
    }
    else
    {
        window.location = 'login.php';
    }
}
</script>
<?php
        $GLOBALS['TEMPLATE']['extra_head'] = ob_get_contents();
        ob_clean();

?>
<p>The resource you've requested requires user authentication. Either you have
not supplied the necessary credentials or the credentials you have supplied
do not authorize you for access.</p>

<p><strong>You will be redirected to the login page in
<span id="secondsDisplay">10 seconds</span>.</strong></p>

<p>If you are not automatically taken there, please click on the following
link: <a href="login.php">Log In</a></p>
<?php
        $GLOBALS['TEMPLATE']['content'] = ob_get_clean();

        include '../templates/template-page.php';
        exit();
}
?>
```

The 401 response is shown in Figure 1-5. The primary responsibility of the script is to send an authorization error to the browser and redirect the user back to the login form (the response code for an HTTP authorization error is 401). Because session_start() is called and $_SESSION['access'] is checked, the error is only sent if the user hasn't been authenticated. To protect any page you only need to include this file at the top of the document. If the user has logged in then he or she will see the intended content.

Figure 1-5

There are different ways to perform a client-side redirect for a user. Here I've mixed a little bit of JavaScript code in with the script's output to count down 10 seconds (1,000 microseconds) — enough time for the user to see he or she is being denied access — and actively updates the time remaining until it performs the redirect by setting the `window.location` property. Another way to redirect the client is by outputting an HTML meta element:

```
<meta http-equiv="refresh"
  content="10;URL=http://www.example.com/login.php" />
```

Regardless of the method you choose to employ, you should always provide a link in case the browser doesn't redirect the user properly.

Changing Information

People may want to change their names, passwords, and e-mail addresses and it makes sense to allow this in your applications. I've already shown you an example of changing a user record earlier when I first discussed the `User` class. It's the same process here — simply set the object's properties to new values and call the `save()` method.

I've saved this code as `main.php` for the simple fact that `login.php` redirects the user to `main.php` after a successful login. In your own implementation, you may want to name it something like `editmember.php` and have `main.php` offer some interesting content instead. Either way, the form is shown in Figure 1-6.

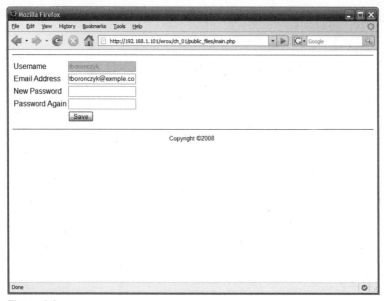

Figure 1-6

```php
<?php
// include shared code
include '../lib/common.php';
include '../lib/db.php';
include '../lib/functions.php';
include '../lib/User.php';

// 401 file referenced since user should be logged in to view this page
include '401.php';

// generate user information form
$user = User::getById($_SESSION['userId']);

ob_start();
?>
<form action="<?php echo htmlspecialchars($_SERVER['PHP_SELF']); ?>"
 method="post">
 <table>
  <tr>
   <td><label>Username</label></td>
   <td><input type="text" name="username" disabled="disabled"
    readonly="readonly"value="<?php echo $user->username; ?>"/></td>
  </tr><tr>
   <td><label for="email">Email Address</label></td>
   <td><input type="text" name="email" id="email"
    value="<?php echo (isset($_POST['email']))? htmlspecialchars(
$_POST['email']) : $user->emailAddr; ?>"/></td>
  </tr><tr>
```

```
    <td><label for="password">New Password</label></td>
    <td><input type="password" name="password1" id="password1"/></td>
   </tr><tr>
    <td><label for="password2">Password Again</label></td>
    <td><input type="password" name="password2" id="password2"/></td>
   </tr><tr>
   <td> </td>
    <td><input type="submit" value="Save"/></td>
    <td><input type="hidden" name="submitted" value="1"/></td>
   </tr><tr>
  </table>
</form>
<?php
$form = ob_get_clean();

// show the form if this is the first time the page is viewed
if (!isset($_POST['submitted']))
{
    $GLOBALS['TEMPLATE']['content'] = $form;
}
// otherwise process incoming data
else
{
    // validate password
    $password1 = (isset($_POST['password1']) && $_POST['password1']) ?
        sha1($_POST['password1']) : $user->password;
    $password2 = (isset($_POST['password2']) && $_POST['password2']) ?
        sha1($_POST['password2']) : $user->password;
    $password = ($password1 == $password2) ? $password1 : '';

    // update the record if the input validates
    if (User::validateEmailAddr($_POST['email']) && $password)
    {
        $user->emailAddr = $_POST['email'];
        $user->password = $password;
        $user->save();

        $GLOBALS['TEMPLATE']['content'] = '<p><strong>Information ' .
            'in your record has been updated.</strong></p>';
    }
    // there was invalid data
    else
    {
        $GLOBALS['TEMPLATE']['content'] .= '<p><strong>You provided some ' .
            'invalid data.</strong></p>';
        $GLOBALS['TEMPLATE']['content'] .= $form;
    }
}

// display the page
include '../templates/template-page.php';
?>
```

You may want to modify the code to verify the user's password before processing any changes to his or her user record. It's also common to set the account inactive and reverify the e-mail address if the user updates it.

Forgotten Passwords

Sometimes users will forget their passwords and not be able to log in. Since the actual password is never stored, there's no way to retrieve it for them. Instead, a new password must be generated and sent to the user's e-mail address on file. Code to accomplish this can be saved as `forgotpass.php`:

```php
<?php
// include shared code
include '../lib/common.php';
include '../lib/db.php';
include '../lib/functions.php';
include '../lib/User.php';

// construct password request form HTML
ob_start();
?>
<form action="<?php echo htmlspecialchars($_SEVER['PHP_SELF']); ?>"
 method="post">
<p>Enter your username. A new password will be sent to the email address on
 file.</p>
<table>
<tr>
 <td><label for="username">Username</label></td>
 <td><input type="text" name="username" id="username"
  value="<?php if (isset($_POST['username']))
  echo htmlspecialchars($_POST['username']); ?>"/></td>
</tr><tr>
 <td> </td>
 <td><input type="submit" value="Submit"/></td>
 <td><input type="hidden" name="submitted" value="1"/></td>
</tr><tr>
</table>
</form>
<?php
$form = ob_get_clean();

// show the form if this is the first time the page is viewed
if (!isset($_POST['submitted']))
{
    $GLOBALS['TEMPLATE']['content'] = $form;
}
// otherwise process incoming data
```

```
else
{
    // validate username
    if (User::validateUsername($_POST['username']))
    {
        $user = User::getByUsername($_POST['username']);
        if (!$user->userId)
        {
            $GLOBALS['TEMPLATE']['content'] = '<p><strong>Sorry, that ' .
                'account does not exist.</strong></p> <p>Please try a ' .
                'different username.</p>';
            $GLOBALS['TEMPLATE']['content'] .= $form;
        }
        else
        {
            // generate new password
            $password = random_text(8);

            // send the new password to the email address on record
            $message = 'Your new password is: ' . $password;
            mail($user->emailAddr, 'New password', $message);

            $GLOBALS['TEMPLATE']['content'] = '<p><strong>A new ' .
                'password has been emailed to you.</strong></p>';

            // store the new password
            $user->password = $password;
            $user->save();
        }
    }
    // there was invalid data
    else
    {
        $GLOBALS['TEMPLATE']['content'] .= '<p><strong>You did not ' .
            'provide a valid username.</strong></p> <p>Please try ' .
            'again.</p>';
        $GLOBALS['TEMPLATE']['content'] .= $form;
    }
}

// display the page
include '../templates/template-page.php';
?>
```

Figure 1-6 shows the page viewed in a web browser.

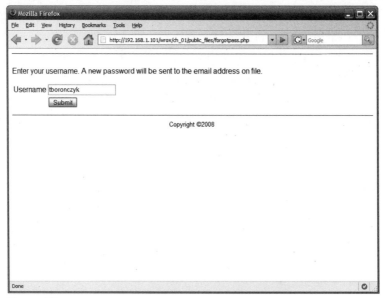

Figure 1-7

Summary

Voilà! You now have a basic user-registration framework to extend anyway you like. Perhaps you want to collect more information from your users, such as their cell phone numbers for SMS messaging, mailing addresses, or even internet messenger screen names.

You've also learned how to establish a well-organized directory structure for your applications and seen some of the benefits of writing reusable code. The directory layout and many of the support files will be used throughout the rest of this book.

In the next chapter you'll build upon what you've written so far and program a basic community bulletin board, more commonly known as a *forum*.

2

Community Forum

In the last chapter you saw what's necessary to put a user registration and account login system in place and came away with two pieces of reusable code: the `User` class and the `401.php` include. In this chapter you'll see how they can be used as part of a larger project as you build a community forum. I'll also show you how to easily restrict different activities users can perform by incorporating permissions.

What you create in this chapter will not be a full-featured forum product capable of competing with other popular software available freely such as phpBB and Invision Power Board or commercially such as vBulletin. It's a basic foundation you can build on to create a custom forum expressly tailored to your needs.

Design of the Forum

A *forum* is a site where users can interact with one another by posting messages organized in threads by topic. Generally anyone is able to read messages, but only users who have registered and logged in are able to post and interact in the discussions. So, the first requirement is that only those who have registered and logged in will be able to post.

The second requirement is to implement a way for certain users to administer the forums without granting such access to all users. Oftentimes these activities include adding new forums and moderating other users' messages.

Typically forums allow users to associate a small, thumbnail-sized graphic with their account which then appears alongside their messages. These graphics are called *avatars* and add a touch of personalization. The forum will allow for these as well.

Designing the Database

This project will make use of the WROX_USER table from the previous project, though you are required to add an additional column too. It will be used to store which permissions the user has been granted. The column should be an unsigned integer.

Two new tables are then needed to store forum data. The table WROX_FORUM stores the names and descriptions of the different forums under which messages are collected. The WROX_FORUM_MESSAGE stores each post and organizational information to keep everything in the right order. I choose not to add a column specifying an avatar since I can name the images the same as the username. As the username must be a unique alphanumeric value, storing the value in an extra column would be a redundant effort anyway.

Field	Type	Null	Key	Default	Extra
USER_ID	int(10) unsigned	NO	PRI	NULL	auto_increment
USERNAME	varchar(20)	NO			
PASSWORD	char(40)	NO			
EMAIL_ADDR	varchar(100)	NO			
IS_ACTIVE	tinyint(1)	YES		0	
PERMISSION	**int(10) unsigned**	**NO**		0	

Field	Type	Null	Key	Default	Extra
FORUM_ID	int(10) unsigned	NO	PRI	NULL	auto_increment
FORUM_NAME	varchar(50)	NO			
DESCRIPTION	varchar(100)	NO			

Field	Type	Null	Key	Default	Extra
MSG_ID	bigint(20) unsigned	NO	PRI	NULL	auto_increment
PARENT_ID	bigint(20) unsigned	NO	MUL	0	
FORUM_ID	int(10) unsigned	NO			
USER_ID	int(10) unsigned	NO	MUL		
SUBJECT	varchar(100)	NO			
MSG_TEXT	text	NO			
MSG_DATE	timestamp	NO		CURRENT_TIMESTAMP	

Here is the SQL:

```
ALTER TABLE WROX_USER
    ADD PERMISSION INTEGER UNSIGNED NOT NULL DEFAULT 0
AFTER
    IS_ACTIVE;

CREATE TABLE WROX_FORUM (
```

```
        FORUM_ID           INTEGER UNSIGNED  NOT NULL  AUTO_INCREMENT,
        FORUM_NAME         VARCHAR(50)       NOT NULL,
        DESCRIPTION        VARCHAR(100)      NOT NULL,


    PRIMARY KEY (FORUM_ID)
)
ENGINE=MyISAM DEFAULT CHARACTER SET latin1
    COLLATE latin1_general_cs AUTO_INCREMENT=0;

CREATE TABLE WROX_FORUM_MESSAGE (
        MESSAGE_ID         BIGINT UNSIGNED   NOT NULL  AUTO_INCREMENT,
        PARENT_MESSAGE_ID  BIGINT UNSIGNED   NOT NULL DEFAULT 0,
        FORUM_ID           INTEGER UNSIGNED  NOT NULL,
        USER_ID            INTEGER UNSIGNED  NOT NULL,
        SUBJECT            VARCHAR(100)      NOT NULL,
        MESSAGE_TEXT       TEXT              NOT NULL,
        MESSAGE_DATE       TIMESTAMP         NOT NULL  DEFAULT CURRENT_TIMESTAMP,


    PRIMARY KEY (MESSAGE_ID),

    FOREIGN KEY (PARENT_MESSAGE_ID)
        REFERENCES WROX_FORUM_MESSAGE(MESSAGE_ID),

    FOREIGN KEY (USER_ID)
        REFERENCES WROX_USER(USER_ID)
)
ENGINE=MyISAM DEFAULT CHARACTER SET latin1
    COLLATE latin1_general_cs AUTO_INCREMENT=0;
```

Notice WROX_FORUM_MESSAGE references itself from the PARENT_MESSAGE_ID column to allow us to organize the messages in a thread — any post with a PARENT_MESSAGE_ID value of 0 will be considered the thread's start. Also note we store the user ID instead of the full username as the post's author. Storing the integer instead of the username saves space in the database and helps preserve the integrity of our data. We can join WROX_FORUM_MESSAGE and WROX_USER to retrieve the username or pass the ID to User::getById() later.

Working with Permissions and Bitwise Operators

A basic understanding of bit operators and how computers store information is all it takes to understand how our permission scheme will work. The operators I'll focus on are the bitwise-and (&) and bitwise-or (|) operators.

Think of a standard light switch; the circuit can have two states. It's either closed with electricity flowing through it or open so no charge can flow. Each byte that makes up a number stored in a computer is ultimately nothing more than a series of tiny electrical switches, with on (closed) and off (open) values. The computer interprets a series of the consecutive on/off values into something interesting for us humans, such as a letter or a number.

Bitwise operators such as bitwise-and and bitwise-or can compare specific bits in the sequences and flip them on or off. If a sequence of switches or bits changes, then the meaning does as well. It's customary to represent the on state with the number 1 and off with 0. Take a brief look at how the following numbers 0 through 24 are represented:

0	1	2	3	4
0000 0000	0000 0001	0000 0010	0000 0011	0000 0100
5	6	7	8	9
0000 0101	0000 0110	0000 0111	0000 1000	0000 1001
10	11	12	13	14
0000 1010	0000 1011	0000 1100	0000 1101	0000 1110
14	16	17	18	19
0000 1111	0001 0000	0001 0001	0001 0010	0001 0011
20	21	22	23	24
0001 0100	0001 0101	0001 0110	0001 0111	0001 1000

Notice there is something special about the numbers 1, 2, 4, 8 and 16. In each of these values the left-most 1-bit advances a placeholder. These are powers of 2 (2^0=1, 2^1=2, 2^2=4, 2^3=8, 2^4=16 and so forth). This is the reason why they are the integer values for the permission constants. Let's take a closer look to see why these numbers work.

If you stack the binary representations of two numbers atop each other you can compare the bit values and obtain a new number. With bitwise-or, the placement results in a 1 if at least one of the compared bits is on (just like logical operator counterparts where the return will be true if at least one of the test conditions is true).

```
1 | 2 = 3           2 | 8 = 10          4 | 8 | 16 = 28

1        0 0001     2        0 0010     4        0 0100
2        0 0010     8        0 1000     8        0 1000
3        0 0011     10       0 1010     16       1 0000
                                        28       1 1100
```

It's also possible to go the other way and mask out a value. With bitwise-and the resulting bit is 1 only if all compared bits are 1 (again this is just like its logical operator counterpart where the return value will be true only if all test conditions are true).

```
30 & 16 = 16        12 & 2 = 0          30 & 16 & 4 = 0

30       1 1110     12       0 1100     31       1 1111
16       1 0000     2        0 0010     21       1 0101
16       1 0000     0        0 0000     5        0 0101
                                        5        0 0101
```

Pretty nifty, eh? You can assign multiple permissions to a user by or'ing them together:

```
// user can create forums and move and delete messages
$user->permission = User::CREATE_FORUM | User::MOVE_MESSAGE |
    User::DELETE_MESSAGE;
```

To see if the user has been granted a particular permission, you mask out the value you're looking for with bitwise-and:

```
// but the same would not be able to delete a forum
if ($user->permission & User::DELETE_FORUM)
{
    // delete forum code here
    ...
}
```

Updating the User Class

To support the permissions requirements, the User class needs to be updated. First, the various permissions are identified as constants whose values increment in powers of 2. As the constructor initializes the object's internal fields property to a new empty user, it must be modified to include the permissions field.

```
const CREATE_FORUM = 2;
const MOVE_MESSAGE = 4;
const DELETE_MESSAGE = 8;
const DELETE_FORUM = 16;

public function __construct()
{
    $this->uid = null;
    $this->fields = array('username' => '',
                          'password' => '',
                          'emailAddr' => '',
                          'isActive' => false,
                          'permission' => 0);
}
```

The three methods getById(), getByUsername() and save() all work with the underlying WROX_USER database table. Since the table's definition has changed, they too must be modified to take into account the new permissions field.

```
public static function getById($userId)
{
    $u = new User();
    $query = sprintf('SELECT USERNAME, PASSWORD, EMAIL_ADDR, ' .
        'IS_ACTIVE, PERMISSION FROM %sUSER WHERE USER_ID = %d',
        DB_TBL_PREFIX, $userId);
    $result = mysql_query($query, $GLOBALS['DB']);
    if (mysql_num_rows($result))
    {
        $row = mysql_fetch_assoc($result);
        $u->username = $row['USERNAME'];
        $u->password = $row['PASSWORD'];
        $u->emailAddr = $row['EMAIL_ADDR'];
        $u->isActive = $row['IS_ACTIVE'];
```

(continued)

(continued)

```php
            $u->permission = $row['PERMISSION'];
            $u->uid = $userId;
        }
        mysql_free_result($result);
        return $u;
    }

    public static function getByUsername($username)
    {
        $u = new User();
        $query = sprintf('SELECT USER_ID, PASSWORD, EMAIL_ADDR, ' .
            'IS_ACTIVE, PERMISSION FROM %sUSER WHERE USERNAME = "%s"',
            DB_TBL_PREFIX,
            mysql_real_escape_string($username, $GLOBALS['DB']));
        $result = mysql_query($query, $GLOBALS['DB']);
        if (mysql_num_rows($result))
        {
            $row = mysql_fetch_assoc($result);
            $u->username = $username;
            $u->password = $row['PASSWORD'];
            $u->emailAddr = $row['EMAIL_ADDR'];
            $u->isActive = $row['IS_ACTIVE'];
            $u->permission = $row['PERMISSION'];
            $u->uid = $row['USER_ID'];
        }
        mysql_free_result($result);
        return $u;
    }

    public function save()
    {
        if ($this->uid)
        {
            $query = sprintf('UPDATE %sUSER SET USERNAME = "%s", ' .
                'PASSWORD = "%s", EMAIL_ADDR = "%s", IS_ACTIVE = %d, ' .
                'PERMISSION = %d WHERE USER_ID = %d', DB_TBL_PREFIX,
                mysql_real_escape_string($this->username, $GLOBALS['DB']),
                mysql_real_escape_string($this->password, $GLOBALS['DB']),
                mysql_real_escape_string($this->emailAddr, $GLOBALS['DB']),
                $this->isActive, $this->permission, $this->uid);
            return mysql_query($query, $GLOBALS['DB']);
        }
        else
        {
            $query = sprintf('INSERT INTO %sUSER (USERNAME, PASSWORD, ' .
                'EMAIL_ADDR, IS_ACTIVE, PERMISSION) VALUES ("%s", "%s", ' .
                '"%s", %d, %d)', DB_TBL_PREFIX,
                mysql_real_escape_string($this->username, $GLOBALS['DB']),
                mysql_real_escape_string($this->password, $GLOBALS['DB']),
                mysql_real_escape_string($this->emailAddr, $GLOBALS['DB']),
                $this->isActive, $this->permission);
```

```
        if (mysql_query($query, $GLOBALS['DB']))
        {
            $this->uid = mysql_insert_id($GLOBALS['DB']);
            return true;
        }
        else
        {
            return false;
        }
    }
}
```

Here is the complete code for the updated User object definition:

```php
<?php
class User
{
    // Permission levels
    const CREATE_FORUM = 2;
    const MOVE_MESSAGE = 4;
    const DELETE_MESSAGE = 8;
    const DELETE_FORUM = 16;

    private $uid;     // user id
    private $fields;  // other record fields


    // initialize a User object
    public function __construct()
    {
        $this->uid = null;
        $this->fields = array('username' => '',
                              'password' => '',
                              'emailAddr' => '',
                              'isActive' => false,
                              'permission' => 0);
    }

    // override magic method to retrieve properties
    public function __get($field)
    {
        if ($field == 'userId')
        {
            return $this->uid;
        }
        else
        {
            return $this->fields[$field];
        }
    }

    // override magic method to set properties
    public function __set($field, $value)
```

(continued)

(continued)

```
    {
        if (array_key_exists($field, $this->fields))
        {
            $this->fields[$field] = $value;
        }
    }

    // return if username is valid format
    public static function validateUsername($username)
    {
        return preg_match('/^[A-Z0-9]{2,20}$/i', $username);
    }

    // return if email address is valid format
    public static function validateEmailAddr($email)
    {
        return filter_var($email, FILTER_VALIDATE_EMAIL);
    }

    // return an object populated based on the record's user id
    public static function getById($userId)
    {
        $u = new User();
        $query = sprintf('SELECT USERNAME, PASSWORD, EMAIL_ADDR, ' .
            'IS_ACTIVE, PERMISSION FROM %sUSER WHERE USER_ID = %d',
            DB_TBL_PREFIX, $userId);
        $result = mysql_query($query, $GLOBALS['DB']);
        if (mysql_num_rows($result))
        {
            $row = mysql_fetch_assoc($result);
            $u->username = $row['USERNAME'];
            $u->password = $row['PASSWORD'];
            $u->emailAddr = $row['EMAIL_ADDR'];
            $u->isActive = $row['IS_ACTIVE'];
            $u->permission = $row['PERMISSION'];
            $u->uid = $userId;
        }
        mysql_free_result($result);
        return $u;
    }

    // return an object populated based on the record's username
    public static function getByUsername($username)
    {
        $u = new User();
        $query = sprintf('SELECT USER_ID, PASSWORD, EMAIL_ADDR, ' .
            'IS_ACTIVE, PERMISSION FROM %sUSER WHERE USERNAME = "%s"',
            DB_TBL_PREFIX,
            mysql_real_escape_string($username, $GLOBALS['DB']));
        $result = mysql_query($query, $GLOBALS['DB']);
```

```
        if (mysql_num_rows($result))
        {
            $row = mysql_fetch_assoc($result);
            $u->username = $username;
            $u->password = $row['PASSWORD'];
            $u->emailAddr = $row['EMAIL_ADDR'];
            $u->isActive = $row['IS_ACTIVE'];
            $u->permission = $row['PERMISSION'];
            $u->uid = $row['USER_ID'];
        }
        mysql_free_result($result);
        return $u;
    }

    // save the record to the database
    public function save()
    {
        if ($this->uid)
        {
            $query = sprintf('UPDATE %sUSER SET USERNAME = "%s", ' .
                'PASSWORD = "%s", EMAIL_ADDR = "%s", IS_ACTIVE = %d, ' .
                'PERMISSION = %d WHERE USER_ID = %d', DB_TBL_PREFIX,
                mysql_real_escape_string($this->username, $GLOBALS['DB']),
                mysql_real_escape_string($this->password, $GLOBALS['DB']),
                mysql_real_escape_string($this->emailAddr, $GLOBALS['DB']),
                $this->isActive, $this->permission, $this->uid);
            return mysql_query($query, $GLOBALS['DB']);
        }
        else
        {
            $query = sprintf('INSERT INTO %sUSER (USERNAME, PASSWORD, ' .
                'EMAIL_ADDR, IS_ACTIVE, PERMISSION) VALUES ("%s", "%s", ' .
                '"%s", %d, %d)', DB_TBL_PREFIX,
                mysql_real_escape_string($this->username, $GLOBALS['DB']),
                mysql_real_escape_string($this->password, $GLOBALS['DB']),
                mysql_real_escape_string($this->emailAddr, $GLOBALS['DB']),
                $this->isActive, $this->permission);
            if (mysql_query($query, $GLOBALS['DB']))
            {
                $this->uid = mysql_insert_id($GLOBALS['DB']);
                return true;
            }
            else
            {
                return false;
            }
        }
    }

    // set the record as inactive and return an activation token
    public function setPending()
```

(continued)

(continued)

```
        {
            $this->isActive = false;
            $this->save(); // make sure the record is saved

            $token = random_text(5);
            $query = sprintf('INSERT INTO %sPENDING (USER_ID, TOKEN) ' .
                'VALUES (%d, "%s")', DB_TBL_PREFIX, $this->uid, $token);
            return (mysql_query($query, $GLOBALS['DB'])) ? $token : false;
        }

        // clear the user's pending status and set the record as active
        public function clearPending($token)
        {
            $query = sprintf('SELECT TOKEN FROM %sPENDING WHERE USER_ID = %d ' .
                'AND TOKEN = "%s"', DB_TBL_PREFIX, $this->uid,
                mysql_real_escape_string($token, $GLOBALS['DB']));
            $result = mysql_query($query, $GLOBALS['DB']);
            if (!mysql_num_rows($result))
            {
                mysql_free_result($result);
                return false;
            }
            else
            {
                mysql_free_result($result);
                $query = sprintf('DELETE FROM %sPENDING WHERE USER_ID = %d ' .
                    'AND TOKEN = "%s"', DB_TBL_PREFIX, $this->uid,
                    mysql_real_escape_string($token, $GLOBALS['DB']));
                if (!mysql_query($query, $GLOBALS['DB']))
                {
                    return false;
                }
                else
                {
                    $this->isActive = true;
                    return $this->save();
                }
            }
        }
    }
}
?>
```

Code and Code Explanation

The majority of the code that builds the forum application is contained in x files. `add_forum.php` is the administrative interface to add new forums. It should be protected from unauthorized use by including the `401.php file`. The files to provide user functionality are `add_post.php` and `view.php`.

Adding Forums

It makes sense to start writing code for the project with the file responsible for creating forums. It's important the script be only shown to users who are logged in and have permissions to create new forums. Ensuring the script is made available only to users who have logged in is done by including the `401.php` file from Chapter 1. You can then decide whether to offer, show or process the form by checking the if the appropriate permission bit is set in `$user->permission`. If it isn't, the script terminates with a suitable error message.

```php
include '401.php';

$user = User::getById($_SESSION['userId']);
if (~$user->permission & User::CREATE_FORUM)
{
    die('<p>Sorry, you do not have sufficient privileges to create new ' .
        'forums.</p>');
}
```

The script then goes on to collect the name and brief description from the user through a form and creates the forum record in the database.

```html
<form action="<?php htmlspecialchars($_SERVER['PHP_SELF']); ?>"
 method="post">
 <div>
  <label for="forum_name">Forum Name:</label>
  <input type="input" id="forum_name" name="forum_name"/><br/>
  <label for="forum_desc">Description:</label>
  <input type="input" id="forum_desc" name="forum_desc"/>
  <br/>
  <input type="hidden" name="submitted" value="true"/>
  <input type="submit" value="Create"/>
 </div>
</form>
```

When the form is submitted, the information is validated and added to the database. If it isn't, then a message can be displayed back to the user stating the values should be corrected and resubmitted. The form can be modified to repopulate the files in this case, even if the data is invalid, so the user doesn't have to type it all again, making it easier to correct the entries.

Here is the complete code for `public_files/add_forum.php`:

```php
<?php
// include shared code
include '../lib/common.php';
include '../lib/db.php';
include '../lib/functions.php';
include '../lib/User.php';

// 401 file included because user should be logged in to access this page
include '401.php';
```

(continued)

(continued)

```php
// user must have appropriate permissions to use this page
$user = User::getById($_SESSION['userId']);
if (~$user->permission & User::CREATE_FORUM)
{
    die('<p>Sorry, you do not have sufficient privileges to create new ' .
        'forums.</p>');
}

// validate incoming values
$forum_name = (isset($_POST['forum_name'])) ? trim($_POST['forum_name']) : '';
$forum_desc = (isset($_POST['forum_desc'])) ? trim($_POST['forum_desc']) : '';

// add entry to the database if the form was submitted and the necessary
// values were supplied in the form
if (isset($_POST['submitted']) && $forum_name && $forum_desc)
{
    $query = sprintf('INSERT INTO %sFORUM (FORUM_NAME, DESCRIPTION) ' .
        'VALUES ("%s", "%s")', DB_TBL_PREFIX,
        mysql_real_escape_string($forum_name, $GLOBALS['DB']),
        mysql_real_escape_string($forum_desc, $GLOBALS['DB']));
    mysql_query($query, $GLOBALS['DB']);

    // redirect user to list of forums after new record has been stored
    header('Location: view.php');
}

// form was submitted but not all the information was correctly filled in
else if (isset($_POST['submitted']))
{
    $message = '<p>Not all information was provided. Please correct ' .
        'and resubmit.</p>';
}

// generate the form
ob_start();
if (isset($message))
{
    echo $message;
}
?>
<form action="<?php htmlspecialchars($_SERVER['PHP_SELF']); ?>"
 method="post">
 <div>
  <label for="forum_name">Forum Name:</label>
  <input type="input" id="forum_name" name="forum_name" value="<?php
   echo htmlspecialchars($forum_name); ?>"/><br/>
  <label for="forum_desc">Description:</label>
  <input type="input" id="forum_desc" name="forum_desc" value="<?php
   echo htmlspecialchars($forum_desc); ?>"/>
  <br/>
```

```
     <input type="hidden" name="submitted" value="true"/>
     <input type="submit" value="Create"/>
   </div>
 </form>
 <?php
 $GLOBALS['TEMPLATE']['content'] = ob_get_clean();

 // display the page
 include '../templates/template-page.php';
 ?>
```

Figure 2-1 shows the adding of a new forum through the form.

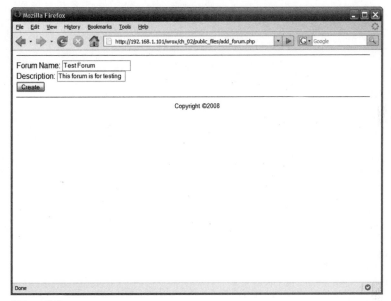

Figure 2-1

Adding Posts

The next thing that needs to be provided for is a way for users to post new messages to the forums and have them saved in the database. This is the purpose of add_post.php. Again, it should only be made available to users who have logged in.

Two parameters may be passed in the URL when calling the script. Minimally, you should provide the id of the forum (fid). If the id of a parent message is also passed (mid) then it will be aggregated as a thread. Otherwise the parent message id will default to 0 marking the post as the start of a new thread.

```
include '401.php';

$user = User::getById($_SESSION['userId']);
if (!$user->userId)
{
    die('<p>Sorry, you must be logged in to post.</p>');
}

$forum_id = (isset($_GET['fid'])) ? (int)$_GET['fid'] : 0;
$query = sprintf('SELECT FORUM_ID FROM %sFORUM WHERE FORUM_ID = %d',
    DB_TBL_PREFIX, $forum_id);
$result = mysql_query($query, $GLOBALS['DB']);
if (!mysql_num_rows($result))
{
    mysql_free_result($result);
    mysql_close($GLOBALS['DB']);
    die('<p>Invalid forum id.</p>');
}
mysql_free_result($result);

$msg_id = (isset($_GET['mid'])) ? (int)$_GET['mid'] : 0;
$query = sprintf('SELECT MESSAGE_ID FROM %sFORUM_MESSAGE WHERE ' .
    'MESSAGE_ID = %d', DB_TBL_PREFIX, $msg_id);
$result = mysql_query($query, $GLOBALS['DB']);
if ($msg_id && !mysql_num_rows($result))
{
    mysql_free_result($result);
    mysql_close($GLOBALS['DB']);
    die('<p>Invalid forum id.</p>');
}
mysql_free_result($result);
```

The displayed form should collect the message information from the user.

```
<form method="post"
 action="<?php echo htmlspecialchars($_SERVER['PHP_SELF']) . '?fid=' .
 $forum_id . '&mid=' . $msg_id; ?>">
 <div>
  <label for="msg_subject">Subject:</label>
  <input type="input" id="msg_subject" name="msg_subject"/></br>
  <label for="msg_text">Post:</label>
  <textarea id="msg_text" name="msg_text"><textarea>
  <br/>
  <input type="hidden" name="submitted" value="true"/>
  <input type="submit" value="Create"/>
 </div>
</form>
```

Once the form has been submitted back to add_post.php, the incoming values are validated to make sure they exist and added to the database. The user is then redirected back to the forum to view his or her recently posted message.

Here is the full code for `public_files/add_post.php`:

```php
<?php
// include shared code
include '../lib/common.php';
include '../lib/db.php';
include '../lib/functions.php';
include '../lib/User.php';

// include 401 file because user should be logged in to access this page
include '401.php';

// retrieve user information
$user = User::getById($_SESSION['userId']);
if (!$user->userId)
{
    die('<p>Sorry, you must be logged in to post.</p>');
}

// validate incoming values
$forum_id = (isset($_GET['fid'])) ? (int)$_GET['fid'] : 0;
$query = sprintf('SELECT FORUM_ID FROM %sFORUM WHERE FORUM_ID = %d',
    DB_TBL_PREFIX, $forum_id);
$result = mysql_query($query, $GLOBALS['DB']);
if (!mysql_num_rows($result))
{
    mysql_free_result($result);
    mysql_close($GLOBALS['DB']);
    die('<p>Invalid forum id.</p>');
}
mysql_free_result($result);

$msg_id = (isset($_GET['mid'])) ? (int)$_GET['mid'] : 0;
$query = sprintf('SELECT MESSAGE_ID FROM %sFORUM_MESSAGE WHERE ' .
    'MESSAGE_ID = %d', DB_TBL_PREFIX, $msg_id);
$result = mysql_query($query, $GLOBALS['DB']);
if ($msg_id && !mysql_num_rows($result))
{
    mysql_free_result($result);
    mysql_close($GLOBALS['DB']);
    die('<p>Invalid forum id.</p>');
}
mysql_free_result($result);

$msg_subject = (isset($_POST['msg_subject'])) ?
    trim($_POST['msg_subject']) : '';
$msg_text = (isset($_POST['msg_text'])) ? trim($_POST['msg_text']) : '';

// add entry to the database if the form was submitted and the necessary
// values were supplied in the form
```

(continued)

45

(continued)

```php
    if (isset($_POST['submitted']) && $msg_subject && $msg_text)
    {
        $query = sprintf('INSERT INTO %sFORUM_MESSAGE (SUBJECT, ' .
            'MESSAGE_TEXT, PARENT_MESSAGE_ID, FORUM_ID, USER_ID) VALUES ' .
            '("%s", "%s", %d, %d, %d)', DB_TBL_PREFIX,
            mysql_real_escape_string($msg_subject, $GLOBALS['DB']),
            mysql_real_escape_string($msg_text, $GLOBALS['DB']),
            $msg_id, $forum_id, $user->userId);
        mysql_query($query, $GLOBALS['DB']);
        // redirect
        header('Location: view.php?fid=' . $forum_id . (($msg_id) ?
            '&mid=' . $msg_id : ''));
    }

    // form was submitted but not all the information was correctly filled in
    else if (isset($_POST['submitted']))
    {
        $message = '<p>Not all information was provided. Please correct ' .
            'and resubmit.</p>';
    }

    // generate the form
    ob_start();
    if (isset($message))
    {
        echo $message;
    }
?>
<form method="post"
 action="<?php echo htmlspecialchars($_SERVER['PHP_SELF']) . '?fid=' .
 $forum_id . '&mid=' . $msg_id; ?>">
 <div>
  <label for="msg_subject">Subject:</label>
  <input type="input" id="msg_subject" name="msg_subject" value="<?php
   echo htmlspecialchars($msg_subject); ?>"/><br/>
  <label for="msg_text">Post:</label>
  <textarea id="msg_text" name="msg_text"><?php
   echo htmlspecialchars($msg_text); ?></textarea>
  <br/>
  <input type="hidden" name="submitted" value="true"/>
  <input type="submit" value="Create"/>
 </div>
</form>
<?php
$GLOBALS['TEMPLATE']['content'] = ob_get_clean();

// display the page
include '../templates/template-page.php';
?>
```

Displaying Forums and Posts

Both `add_forum.php` and `add_post.php` redirect the user to `view.php` after saving their data to the database. There are three different displays this file can generate: a list of all forums, a list of message threads that make up a particular forum and finally the contents of the messages. By passing parameters in the URL and analyzing them, you are able to determine which display should be generated. Briefly consider these examples:

❏   `view.php` displays the list of all available forums.

❏   `view.php?fid=1` displays the threads in whatever forum has a primary key 1 in the database.

❏   `view.php?fid=1&mid2` displays the actual messages that make up thread 2 in forum 1.

Both `fid` and `mid` should be validated with each page call, but the database queries can also retrieve information at the same time, such as the forum name and how to construct back-links, if the parameters are valid to show to the user.

```php
$forum_id = (isset($_GET['fid'])) ? (int)$_GET['fid'] : 0;
$msg_id = (isset($_GET['mid'])) ? (int)$_GET['mid'] : 0;

if ($forum_id)
{
    $query = sprintf('SELECT FORUM_NAME FROM %sFORUM WHERE FORUM_ID = %d',
        DB_TBL_PREFIX, $forum_id);
    $result = mysql_query($query, $GLOBALS['DB']);

    if (!mysql_num_rows($result))
    {
        die('<p>Invalid forum id.</p>');
    }
    $row = mysql_fetch_assoc($result);
    echo '<h1>' . htmlspecialchars($row['FORUM_NAME']) . '</h1>';
    mysql_free_result($result);

    if ($msg_id)
    {
        $query = sprintf('SELECT MESSAGE_ID FROM %sFORUM_MESSAGE ' .
            'WHERE MESSAGE_ID = %d', DB_TBL_PREFIX, $msg_id);
        $result = mysql_query($query, $GLOBALS['DB']);

        if (!mysql_num_rows($result))
        {
            mysql_free_result($result);
            die('<p>Invalid forum id.</p>');
        }
        mysql_free_result($result);

        // link back to thread view
        echo '<p><a href="view.php?fid=' . $forum_id . '">Back to forum ' .
            'threads.</a></p>';
    }
```

(continued)

(continued)

```
        else
        {
            // link back to forum list
            echo '<p><a href="view.php">Back to forum list.</a></p>';
        }
    }
    else
    {
        echo '<h1>Forums</h1>';
    }
```

The $_SESSION array can be checked to see if a user has logged on, and if so then a link to
add_post.php should be provided so he or she can add new messages. Additionally, the user's
permissions can be tested to see if the User::CREATE_FORUM permission bit is set. If he or she is allowed
to create new forums, then a link to add_forum.php should also be generated.

```
if (isset($_SESSION['access']))
{
    echo '<p><a href="add_post.php?fid=' . $forum_id . '">Post new ' .
        'message.</a></p>';
}

if (isset($_SESSION['userId']))
{
    $user = User::getById($_SESSION['userId']);
    if ($user->permission & User::CREATE_FORUM)
    {
        echo '<p><a href="add_forum.php">Create new forum.</a></p>';
    }
}
```

However you decide to style the display is your decision, but ultimately, generating the forum view is as
simple as displaying a list of all available forums and their descriptions as links to the user.

```
$query = sprintf('SELECT FORUM_ID, FORUM_NAME, DESCRIPTION FROM %sFORUM ' .
        'ORDER BY FORUM_NAME ASC, FORUM_ID ASC', DB_TBL_PREFIX);
$result = mysql_query($query, $GLOBALS['DB']);

echo '<ul>';
while ($row = mysql_fetch_assoc($result))
{
    echo '<li><a href="' . htmlspecialchars($_SERVER['PHP_SELF']);
    echo '?fid=' . $row['FORUM_ID'] . '">';
    echo htmlspecialchars($row['FORUM_NAME']) . ': ';
    echo htmlspecialchars($row['DESCRIPTION']) . '</li>';
}
echo '</ul>';
mysql_free_result($result);
```

Similarly, the thread view should retrieve a list of messages whose record has a PARENT_MESSAGE_ID of 0 for the selected forum.

```
$query = sprintf('SELECT MESSAGE_ID, SUBJECT, ' .
    'UNIX_TIMESTAMP(MESSAGE_DATE) AS MESSAGE_DATE FROM %sFORUM_MESSAGE ' .
    'WHERE PARENT_MESSAGE_ID = 0 AND FORUM_ID = %d ORDER BY ' .
    'MESSAGE_DATE DESC', DB_TBL_PREFIX, $forum_id);
$result = mysql_query($query, $GLOBALS['DB']);

if (mysql_num_rows($result))
{
    echo '<ul>';
    while ($row = mysql_fetch_assoc($result))
    {
        echo '<li><a href="view.php?fid=' . $forum_id . '&mid=' .
            $row['MESSAGE_ID'] . '">';
        echo date('m/d/Y', $row['MESSAGE_DATE']) . ': ';
        echo htmlspecialchars($row['SUBJECT']) . '</li>';
    }
    echo '</ul>';
}
else
{
    echo '<p>This forum contains no messages.</p>';
}
mysql_free_result($result);
```

The message view shows all the messages that make up a particular thread. The query is a bit more complex than those used in the other views because it contains a JOIN clause to join the WROX_USER table to retrieve the message's author information as well.

```
$query = sprintf('
SELECT
    USERNAME, FORUM_ID, MESSAGE_ID, PARENT_MESSAGE_ID,
    SUBJECT, MESSAGE_TEXT, UNIX_TIMESTAMP(MESSAGE_DATE) AS MESSAGE_DATE
FROM
    %sFORUM_MESSAGE M JOIN %sUSER U
        ON M.USER_ID = U.USER_ID
WHERE
    MESSAGE_ID = %d OR
    PARENT_MESSAGE_ID = %d
ORDER BY
    MESSAGE_DATE ASC',
    DB_TBL_PREFIX,
    DB_TBL_PREFIX,
    $msg_id,
    $msg_id);

$result = mysql_query($query, $GLOBALS['DB']);

echo '<table border=1>';
```

(continued)

(continued)

```php
while ($row = mysql_fetch_assoc($result))
{
    echo '<tr>';
    echo '<td style="text-align:center; vertical-align:top; width:150px;">';
    if (file_exists('avatars/' . $row['USERNAME'] . 'jpg')
    {
        echo '<img src="avatars/' . $row['USERNAME'] . '.jpg" />';
    }
    else
    {
        echo '<img src="img/default_avatar.jpg" />';
    }
    echo '<br/><strong>' . $row['USERNAME'] . '</strong><br/>';
    echo date('m/d/Y<\b\r/>H:i:s', $row['MESSAGE_DATE']) . '</td>';
    echo '<td style="vertical-align:top;">';
    echo '<div><strong>' . htmlspecialchars($row['SUBJECT']) .
        '</strong></div>';
    echo '<div>' . htmlspecialchars($row['MESSAGE_TEXT']) . '</div>';
    echo '<div style="text-align: right;">';
    echo '<a href="add_post.php?fid=' . $row['FORUM_ID'] . '&mid=' .
        (($row['PARENT_MESSAGE_ID'] != 0) ? $row['PARENT_MESSAGE_ID'] :
        $row['MESSAGE_ID']) . '">Reply</a></div></td>';
    echo '</tr>';
}
echo '</table>';
mysql_free_result($result);
```

Here is the complete code for `view.php`:

```php
<?php
// include shared code
include '../lib/common.php';
include '../lib/db.php';
include '../lib/functions.php';
include '../lib/User.php';

// start or continue session
session_start();

// validate incoming values
$forum_id = (isset($_GET['fid'])) ? (int)$_GET['fid'] : 0;
$msg_id = (isset($_GET['mid'])) ? (int)$_GET['mid'] : 0;

ob_start();
if ($forum_id)
{
    // display forum name as header
    $query = sprintf('SELECT FORUM_NAME FROM %sFORUM WHERE FORUM_ID = %d',
        DB_TBL_PREFIX, $forum_id);
    $result = mysql_query($query, $GLOBALS['DB']);

    if (!mysql_num_rows($result))
```

```
    {
        die('<p>Invalid forum id.</p>');
    }
    $row = mysql_fetch_assoc($result);
    echo '<h1>' . htmlspecialchars($row['FORUM_NAME']) . '</h1>';
    mysql_free_result($result);

    if ($msg_id)
    {
        $query = sprintf('SELECT MESSAGE_ID FROM %sFORUM_MESSAGE ' .
            'WHERE MESSAGE_ID = %d', DB_TBL_PREFIX, $msg_id);
        $result = mysql_query($query, $GLOBALS['DB']);

        if (!mysql_num_rows($result))
        {
            mysql_free_result($result);
            die('<p>Invalid forum id.</p>');
        }
        mysql_free_result($result);

        // link back to thread view
        echo '<p><a href="view.php?fid=' . $forum_id . '">Back to forum ' .
            'threads.</a></p>';
    }
    else
    {
        // link back to forum list
        echo '<p><a href="view.php">Back to forum list.</a></p>';

        // display option to add new post if user is logged in
        if (isset($_SESSION['access']))
        {
            echo '<p><a href="add_post.php?fid=' . $forum_id . '">Post new ' .
                'message.</a></p>';
        }
    }
}
else
{
    echo '<h1>Forums</h1>';
    if (isset($_SESSION['userId']))
    {
        // display link to create new forum if user has permissions to do so
        $user = User::getById($_SESSION['userId']);
        if ($user->permission & User::CREATE_FORUM)
        {
            echo '<p><a href="add_forum.php">Create new forum.</a></p>';
        }
    }
}

// generate message view
```

(continued)

(continued)

```
if ($forum_id && $msg_id)
{
    $query = sprintf('
SELECT
    USERNAME, FORUM_ID, MESSAGE_ID, PARENT_MESSAGE_ID,
    SUBJECT, MESSAGE_TEXT, UNIX_TIMESTAMP(MESSAGE_DATE) AS MESSAGE_DATE
FROM
    %sFORUM_MESSAGE M JOIN %sUSER U
        ON M.USER_ID = U.USER_ID
WHERE
    MESSAGE_ID = %d OR
    PARENT_MESSAGE_ID = %d
ORDER BY
    MESSAGE_DATE ASC',
    DB_TBL_PREFIX,
    DB_TBL_PREFIX,
    $msg_id,
    $msg_id);

    $result = mysql_query($query, $GLOBALS['DB']);

    echo '<table border=1>';
    while ($row = mysql_fetch_assoc($result))
    {
        echo '<tr>';
        echo '<td style="text-align:center; vertical-align:top; width:150px;">';
        if (file_exists('avatars/' . $row['USERNAME'] . 'jpg')
        {
            echo '<img src="avatars/' . $row['USERNAME'] . '.jpg" />';
        }
        else
        {
            echo '<img src="img/default_avatar.jpg" />';
        }
        echo '<br/><strong>' . $row['USERNAME'] . '</strong><br/>';
        echo date('m/d/Y\b\r/>H:i:s', $row['MESSAGE_DATE']) . '</td>';
        echo '<td style="vertical-align:top;">';
        echo '<div><strong>' . htmlspecialchars($row['SUBJECT']) .
            '</strong></div>';
        echo '<div>' . htmlspecialchars($row['MESSAGE_TEXT']) . '</div>';
        echo '<div style="text-align: right;">';
        echo '<a href="add_post.php?fid=' . $row['FORUM_ID'] . '&mid=' .
            (($row['PARENT_MESSAGE_ID'] != 0) ? $row['PARENT_MESSAGE_ID'] :
            $row['MESSAGE_ID']) . '">Reply</a></div></td>';
        echo '</tr>';
    }
    echo '</table>';
    mysql_free_result($result);
}
```

```php
// generate thread view
else if ($forum_id)
{

    $query = sprintf('SELECT MESSAGE_ID, SUBJECT, ' .
        'UNIX_TIMESTAMP(MESSAGE_DATE) AS MESSAGE_DATE FROM %sFORUM_MESSAGE ' .
        'WHERE PARENT_MESSAGE_ID = 0 AND FORUM_ID = %d ORDER BY ' .
        'MESSAGE_DATE DESC', DB_TBL_PREFIX, $forum_id);
    $result = mysql_query($query, $GLOBALS['DB']);

    if (mysql_num_rows($result))
    {
        echo '<ul>';
        while ($row = mysql_fetch_assoc($result))
        {
            echo '<li><a href="view.php?fid=' . $forum_id . '&mid=' .
                $row['MESSAGE_ID'] . '">';
            echo date('m/d/Y', $row['MESSAGE_DATE']) . ': ';
            echo htmlspecialchars($row['SUBJECT']) . '</li>';
        }
        echo '</ul>';
    }
    else
    {
        echo '<p>This forum contains no messages.</p>';
    }
    mysql_free_result($result);
}
// generate forums view
else
{
    $query = sprintf('SELECT FORUM_ID, FORUM_NAME, DESCRIPTION FROM %sFORUM ' .
            'ORDER BY FORUM_NAME ASC, FORUM_ID ASC', DB_TBL_PREFIX);
    $result = mysql_query($query, $GLOBALS['DB']);

    echo '<ul>';
    while ($row = mysql_fetch_assoc($result))
    {
        echo '<li><a href="' . htmlspecialchars($_SERVER['PHP_SELF']);
        echo '?fid=' . $row['FORUM_ID'] . '">';
        echo htmlspecialchars($row['FORUM_NAME']) . ': ';
        echo htmlspecialchars($row['DESCRIPTION']) . '</li>';
    }
    echo '</ul>';
    mysql_free_result($result);
}
$GLOBALS['TEMPLATE']['content'] = ob_get_lean();

// display the page
include '../templates/template-page.php';
?>
```

Figure 2-2 shows the first view, a list of all available forums, Figure 2-3 shows the list of threads in a particular forum and Figure 2-4 shows the contents of the messages.

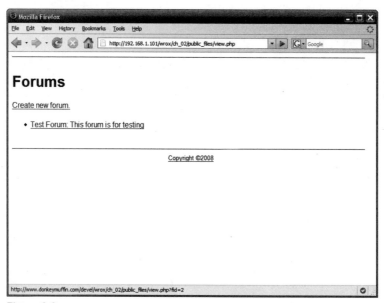

Figure 2-2

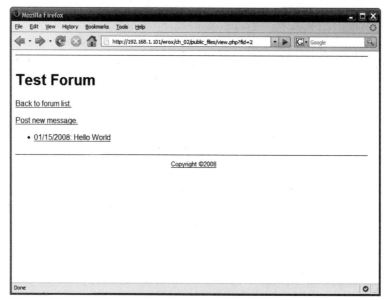

Figure 2-3

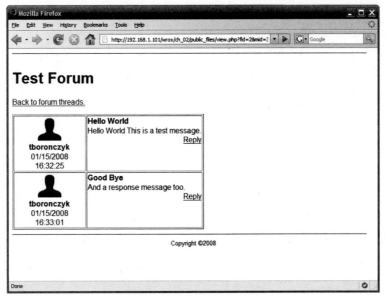

Figure 2-4

Pagination

Using the forum will become cumbersome as the number of threads and messages grows. To keep things manageable, you may want to implement some sort of pagination.

There are essentially two steps to add pagination. First, an additional parameter needs to be passed in the URL to identify the starting offset in the record set. Then links are generated, which allows the user to navigate to the next or previous pages. Either `mysql_data_seek()` can be used to move the result cursor to the appropriate offset, or a `LIMIT` clause can be appended to the SQL statement.

Most tutorials teach the `LIMIT` method, but keep in mind that 1) `LIMIT` is non-standard SQL and 2) if you choose to use `LIMIT` then you'll need to send a query to the database beforehand to determine the total number of records so you can create the appropriate links. I much prefer fetching the records, finding the total number of results using `mysql_num_rows()` and then moving to the appropriate offset with `mysql_data_seek()`, which saves me from making an additional query.

```
$display = 25;  // paginate showing 25 entries per page

$query = sprintf('SELECT MESSAGE_ID, SUBJECT, ' .
    'UNIX_TIMESTAMP(MESSAGE_DATE) AS MESSAGE_DATE FROM %sFORUM_MESSAGE ' .
    'WHERE PARENT_MESSAGE_ID = 0 AND FORUM_ID = %d ORDER BY ' .
    'MESSAGE_DATE DESC', DB_TBL_PREFIX, $forum_id);
$result = mysql_query($query, $GLOBALS['DB']);

if ($total = mysql_num_rows($result))
```

(continued)

(continued)

```
{
    // accept the display offset
    $start = (isset($_GET['start']) && ctype_digit($_GET['start']) &&
        $_GET['start'] <= $total) ? $_GET['start'] : 0;

    // move the data pointer to the appropriate starting record
    mysql_data_seek($start);

    // display entries
    echo '<ul>';
    $count = 0;
    while ($row = mysql_fetch_assoc($result) && $count++ < $display)
    {
        echo '<li><a href="view.php?fid=' . $forum_id . '&mid=' .
            $row['MESSAGE_ID'] . '">';
        echo date('m/d/Y', $row['MESSAGE_DATE']) . ': ';
        echo htmlspecialchars($row['SUBJECT']) . '</li>';
    }
    echo '</ul>';

    // Generate the paginiation menu.
    echo '<p>';
    if ($start > 0)
    {
        echo '<a href="view.php?fid=' . $form_id . '&start=0">' .
            'FIRST</a> ';
        echo '<a href="view.php?fid=' . $forum_id . '&start=' .
            ($start - $display) . '">&lt;PREV</a>';
    }
    if ($total > ($start + $display))
    {
        echo '<a href="view.php?fid=' . $forum_id . '&start=' .
            ($start + $display) . '">NEXT&gt;</a> ';
        echo '<a href="view.php?fid=' . $form_id . '&start=' .
            ($total - $display) . '">LAST</a>';
    }
    echo '</p>';
}
else
{
    echo '<p>This forum contains no messages.</p>';
}
mysql_free_result($result);
```

Avatars

I'm taking advantage of the fact that each user must have a unique alphanumeric username. When saving an uploaded graphic for the avatar with the username as the filename, you don't have to worry about overwriting files. If a file does get overwritten, it's because the user is uploading a newer file for his or her avatar. This also spares you from tracking additional information in the database as mentioned earlier.

To upload a file through an HTML form, the `form` element must have the `enctype` attribute set to `multipart/form-data`. Then the user can specify the file through an input element:

```
<form action=upload_avatar.php" method="post" enctype="multipart/form-data">
  <div>
    <input type="file" name="avatar"/>
    <input type="submit" value="upload"/>
  </div>
</form>
```

Information about uploaded files is available to PHP in the `$_FILES` superglobal array. It's a multidimensional array with the name assigned to the HTML form's `input` element as the first index (useful when uploading multiple files) and the following for the second:

- ❑   `name` — the original filename
- ❑   `tmp_name` — the name of the file as it is stored temporarily on the server
- ❑   `size` — the size of the file (reported in bytes)
- ❑   `type` — the file's mime-type
- ❑   `error` — an error code indicating the reason for failure of an upload (the value will be 0 if the upload was successful)

The uploaded file is temporarily stored and will be deleted once the script is done running, so usually it is necessary to copy the file to a permanent location using `move_uploaded_file()`. I'm going to take a different approach though because there's no telling what type of image the user will submit, or if the file will even be an image at all. And if it is a file, you want to make sure the dimensions aren't gigantic. I'll instead open the uploaded image and save a resized copy in the permanent location so I can guarantee its size and format.

The functionality of resizing the image can be encapsulated into a class for the purpose of reusability. Table 2-1 shows the publically available methods for `JpegThumbnail`.

Table 2-1: `JpegThumbnail` Properties and Methods

Property	Description
`height`	The specified height of the thumbnail image
`width`	The specified width of the thumbnail image
Method	**Description**
`__construct(width, height)`	Initialize a new `JpegThumbnail` object with the specified `width` and `height`
`generate(image, [filename])`	Resize `image` and send it to the browser or save to a file if `filename` is provided

Here is the code for `lib/JpegThumbnail.php`:

```php
<?php
class JpegThumbnail
{
    public $width;  // maximum thumbnail width
    public $height; // maximum thumbnail height

    // intialize a new Thumbnail object
    public function __construct($width = 50, $height = 50)
    {
        $this->width = $width;
        $this->height = $height;

    }
    // accept a source file location and return an open image handle or
    // save to disk if destination provided
    public function generate($src, $dest = '')
    {
        // retrive image dimensions
        list($width, $height) = getimagesize($src);

        // determine if resize is necessary
        if(($lowest = min($this->width / $width, $this->height / $height)) < 1)
        {
            $tmp = imagecreatefromjpeg($src);

            // resize
            $sm_width = floor($lowest * $width);
            $sm_height = floor($lowest * $height);
            $img = imagecreatetruecolor($sm_width, $sm_height);
            imagecopyresized($img, $tmp, 0,0, 0,0, $sm_width, $sm_height,
                $width, $height);
            imagedestroy($tmp);
        }
        // image is already thumbnail size and resize not necessary
        else
        {
            $img = imagecreatefromjpeg($src);
        }

        // save to disk or return the open image handle
        if ($dest)
        {
            imagejpeg($img, $dest, 100);
            imagedestroy($img);
        }
        else
        {
            return $img;
        }
    }
}
?>
```

The `upload_avatar.php` code to handle the upload would then make use of the `JpegThumbnail` class:

```php
<?php
// include shared code
include '../lib/common.php';
include '../lib/db.php';
include '../lib/functions.php';
include '../lib/User.php';
include '../lib/JpegThumbnail.php';
include '401.php';

$user = User::getById($_SESSION['userId']);

if (!$_FILES['avatar']['error'])
{
    // create a thumbnail copy of the image
    $img = new JpegThumbnail();
    $img->generate($_FILES['avatar']['tmp_name'],
        'avatars/' . $user->username . '.jpg');
}
?>
```

But what happens if the user hasn't upload an avatar yet? It makes sense to have a default avatar to show for those users so `view.php` will not show a broken image link. You could modify the account creation script to copy a default icon into the avatar directory for the user, but this would needlessly waste hard disk space by having multiple copies of the same file. It would be better to check if the file exists and if it doesn't, then serve a default image.

BBCode

Our forum currently uses a plain HTML `textarea` box to allow a user to submit his or her post and filters out HTML characters using `htmlspecialchars()` before display for security purposes. In effect, users may only post plain text messages. There are different options available if you wanted to allow users to format their messages—you could remove filtering with `htmlspecialchars()` and replace the input field with a JavaScript powered rich text editor (I'll show you this in Chapter 10) or you could allow the user to enter special BBCode markup tags.

BBCode (short for Bullet Board Code) is a markup language similar to HTML. While not standardized like HTML, it is in widespread use in many forum applications. You would accept a post marked-up with BBCode tags and then translate them into a subset of allowed HTML tags before displaying it.

Here is some code written to convert BBCode-formatted text to HTML, which I've saved as
lib/BBCode.php:

```php
<?php
// Class to format text marked up with BBCode tags to HTML-- see
// http://www.phpbb.com/community/faq.php?mode=bbcode for more information.
Class BBCode
{
    // private method to replace BBCode tags with suitable HTML
    private static function _format_bbcode($string)
    {
        // use regular expression to identify and break apart BBCode tags
        while (preg_match('|\[([a-z]+)=?(.*?)\](.*?)\[/\1\]|', $string, $part,
            PREG_OFFSET_CAPTURE))
        {
            $part[2][0] = str_replace('"', "", $part[2][0]);
            $part[2][0] = str_replace("'", "", $part[2][0]);
            $part[3][0] = _format_bbcode($part[3][0]);
            switch ($part[1][0])
            {
                // process bold, italic and underline elements
                case 'b':
                case 'i':
                case 'u':
                    $replace = sprintf('<%s>%s</%s>', $part[1][0], $part[3][0],
                        $part[1][0]);
                    break;

                // process code element
                case 'code':
                    $replace = '<pre>' . $part[3][0] . '</pre>';
                    break;

                // process color styling
                case 'color':
                    $replace = sprintf('<span style="color: %s">%s</span>',
                        $part[2][0], $part[3][0]);
                    break;

                // process email element
                case 'email':
                    $replace = sprintf('<a href="mailto:%s">%s<\a>',
                        $part[3][0], $part[3][0]);
                    break;

                // process size styling
                case 'size':
                    $replace = sprintf('<span style="font-size: %s">%s</span>',
                        $part[2][0], $part[3][0]);
                    break;

                // process quotes
                case 'quote':
                    $replace = (empty($part[2][0])) ?
```

```
                        ('<blockquote><p>' . $part[3][0] .
                            '</p></blockquote>') :
                        sprintf('<blockquote><p>%s wrote:<br />%s</p>' .
                            '</blockquote>', $part[2][0], $part[3][0]);
                break;

            // process image element
            case 'img':
                $replace = '<img src="' . $part[3][0] . '" alt=""/>';
                break;

            // process hyperlink
            case 'url':
                $replace = sprintf('<a href="%s">%s</a>',
                    (!empty($part[2][0])) ? $part[2][0] : $part[3][0],
                    $part[3][0]));
                break;

            // process bulleted lists
            case 'list':
                $replace = str_replace('[*]', '</li><li>', $part[3][0]);
                $replace = '<x>' . $replace;
                switch ($part[2][0])
                {
                    case '1':
                        $replace = str_replace('<x></li>',
                            '<ol style="list-style-type: decimal">',
                            $replace . '</ol>');
                        break;

                    case 'A':
                        $replace = str_replace('<x></li>',
                            '<ol style="list-style-type: upper-alpha">',
                            $replace . '</ol>');
                        break;

                    case 'a':
                        $replace = str_replace('<x></li>',
                            '<ol style="list-style-type: lower-alpha">',
                            $replace . '</ol>');
                        break;

                    default:
                        $replace = str_replace('<x></li>',
                            '<ul>', $replace . '</ul>');
                        break;
                }
                break;

        default:
            $replace = $part[3][0];
            break;
    }
```

(continued)

(continued)

```
            $string = substr_replace($string, $replace, $part[0][1],
                strlen($part[0][0]));
        }
        return $string;
    }

    public static format($string)
    {
        // replace tags
        $string = BBCode::_format_bbcode($string);

        // clean up line endings and add paragraph and line break tags
        $string = str_replace("\r\n\r\n", '</p><p>', $string);
        $string = str_replace("\n\n", '</p><p>', $string);
        $string = str_replace("\r\n", '<br />', $string);
        $string = str_replace("\n", '<br />', $string);
        $string = '<p>' . $string . '</p>';

        return $string;
    }
}
?>
```

Note that the class doesn't preclude the inclusion of HTML in the string—it just converts the BBCode elements to HTML elements (which is how it should be as each function should have *one* clearly defined purpose). To prevent any other HTML elements from appearing in the string you may want to process it through PHP's `strip_tags()` function first.

```
<?php
include '../lib/BBCode.php';

$message = strip_tags($_GET['message']);
$message = BBCode::format($message);
echo $message;
?>
```

Summary

In this chapter I've put together the basic foundation upon which you can build a custom form tailored expressly to your needs. In doing so, you've learned how to integrate permissions and even resize uploaded images and convert BBCode markup to HTML.

In the next chapter I'll shift our focus from the web to e-mail as you write a set of scripts that coordinate together to provide a basic mailing list service.

3

Mailing List

E-mail is one of the oldest and most prolific members of the Internet family. In fact, some estimates show over 60 billion e-mail messages are sent every day . . . an estimate that I suspect is somewhat on the conservative side! E-mail is used by business executives to schedule meetings and close deals, by grandparents to share digital photos of their grandchildren, and by students to exchange class notes and homework assignments. There's no denying people have found e-mail to be a great way to exchange ideas and information regardless of whatever the exact number is.

In this chapter you'll build an e-mail–driven discussion list powered by PHP. The finished project is a basic implementation that you can tailor to your specific needs. Perhaps more importantly, you will come away with reusable code to connect to a POP3 server and an understanding of how PHP scripts can be run outside of the realm of web pages.

Design of the Mailing List

A mailing list allows users to send one message to multiple recipients. A user who has registered with the service is able to send a message to a special e-mail address and all other subscribed members will receive a copy of it. This application will allow participants to:

❑   Subscribe and unsubscribe from the list

❑   Configure their accounts to receive individual messages as they are sent to the list throughout the day or to receive a daily digest e-mail aggregating all the individual messages

❑   Send messages to one central address and have it forward to all members on the list

This project makes use of two e-mail accounts — one to which messages for redistribution will be sent and another where specially crafted messages can be sent for users to manage their membership preferences. Administrative messages will be nothing more than a blank e-mail but with the appropriate command provided in the subject line. The commands that will be available are:

SUBSCRIBE   Subscribe the e-mail address to the mailing list

UNSUBSCRIBE   Remove the address from the mailing list

SET +DIGEST   Set the member's preference to receive the daily digest message

SET –DIGEST   Set the member's preference to receive individual messages

HELP   Reply with a list of available commands and other helpful information

Chapter 1 shows how an e-mail message may contain multiple parts. For the sake of simplicity, the mailing list will only accept plain text messages from subscribers. It will extract the plain-text portion of any multi-part message it receives and the rest may be discarded. You may want to modify this behavior when the basic project is complete, depending on your needs.

Choosing POP3

You're probably asking yourself how to accept incoming messages and run the PHP scripts since you're now working in the realm of e-mail. There are no HTTP requests and you won't be receiving $_GET and $_POST variables from the user. Instead, the scripts will be scheduled to run automatically and emulate a person using an e-mail client to connect to a mail server and retrieve messages from the account's inbox.

Most people's exposure to the e-mail is limited to the mail client program they use, such as Thunderbird or Outlook. Few care about the path a message takes so long as it is received by the intended recipient. Behind the scenes, several different servers coordinate the delivery, and the "life" of an e-mail message can be quite exciting as it is passed along.

An e-mail message starts at the mail client, which sends it off to an SMTP (Simple Mail Transfer Protocol) server. The SMTP server is responsible for routing mail across the Internet to other mail servers. The final server in the chain delivers the message to the account's maildrop directory where it waits to be retrieved by the recipient. The recipient uses his or her mail client to connect to a POP3 (Post Office Protocol version 3) or IMAPv4 (Internet Message Access Protocol version 4) server, which in turn reads the maildrop and presents the message. This is shown in Figure 3-1.

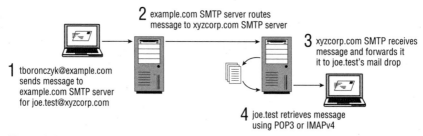

1 tboronczyk@example.com sends message to example.com SMTP server for joe.test@xyzcorp.com

2 example.com SMTP server routes message to xyzcorp.com SMTP server

3 xyzcorp.com SMTP receives message and forwards it it to joe.test's mail drop

4 joe.test retrieves message using POP3 or IMAPv4

Figure 3-1

There are different options available to you to retrieve e-mail with PHP:

❑ Write a stand-alone SMTP server in PHP to listen for incoming mail, accept the messages, and process them.

❑ Have an SMTP mail server such as sendmail, exim, or qmail deliver incoming messages to a dedicated maildrop folder and write scripts to process them directly from there.

❑ Let the SMTP server deliver the messages and write scripts to connect to a POP3 or IMAPv4 service, retrieve and process the messages from the account's inbox through them.

Each approach has its own merits and drawbacks, but I'm in favor of the last one . . . particularly using the POP3 option. Obviously some sort of queuing mechanism must be put in place to hold incoming messages, but why should you have to reinvent the wheel? A queue is already set up with the interaction of the different servers and POP3 offers an easy way to access the maildrop.

POP3 is considerably less complex than IMAPv4 and only supports basic message retrieval, but that's all this project requires anyway. If you're interested in the differences between the two protocols, a dated but still relevant comparison is available at `www.imap.org/papers/imap.vs.pop.brief.html`.

Designing the Database

All of the mailing list subscribers can be stored in a MySQL database, although the table will be pretty simple because all you need to store is the e-mail address and digest preference. This is what the table will look like:

```
+-------------+-------------------+------+-----+---------+
| Field       | Type              | Null | Key | Default |
+-------------+-------------------+------+-----+---------+
| EMAIL_ADDR  | varchar(100)      | NO   | PRI |         |
| IS_DIGEST   | tinyint(1)        | NO   |     | 0       |
+-------------+-------------------+------+-----+---------+
```

Members who have a 0 in their IS_DIGEST column will be those who want to receive individual messages. Otherwise, the value should be 1 and members will receive the digest message at the end of the day instead.

If you want to have users activate their membership after subscribing, then you will need to also add an IS_ACTIVE column and a table to track validation tokens as you did in Chapter 1.

Here's the SQL code for WROX_MAILLIST_USER:

```
CREATE TABLE WROX_MAILLIST_USER (
    EMAIL_ADDR   VARCHAR(100)      NOT NULL,
    IS_DIGEST    TINYINT(1)        NOT NULL  DEFAULT 0,

    PRIMARY KEY (EMAIL_ADDR)
)
ENGINE=MyISAM DEFAULT CHARACTER SET latin1
    COLLATE latin1_general_cs;
```

Code and Code Explanation

With POP3 decided upon and the database schema provided, I will now continue with the code. First I will discuss the POP3Client class, and then the remaining files that work together to provide the mailing list service.

The POP3 Client

The code needed to connect and communicate with the POP3 service is a prime candidate for OOP structuring. As a class, it will be easy to reuse the code in future projects. Besides the necessary constructor and connect methods, if each publically exposed method corresponds to a POP3 command, then the class's interface becomes intuitive to use as well.

POP3 was designed to be simple from its inception. There are only a few commands required to access a user's maildrop directory and retrieve messages. Table 3-1 lists the minimum commands that need to be implemented for a functional client.

Table 3-1: POP3 Commands

Command	Description
USER username	Provides the username needed in order to log into the mail account on the server
PASS password	Provides the password needed in order to log into the mail account on the server
STAT	Retrieves the mail box's drop listing; the response indicates the number of messages in the inbox and their aggregate size
LIST (message id)	Retrieves a scan listing for all messages in the inbox (or for a particular message if an optional message id is provided); the response gives message ids and sizes
RETR message id	Retrieves a specific message from the server
DELE message id	Marks a message to be deleted
RSET	Resets the state of the inbox; flags on any messages marked for deletion are cleared so they will not be deleted when the connection to the server is closed
NOOP	No operation — this does nothing but return +OK (this is useful for testing)
QUIT	Closes the connection and deletes all marked messages

The protocol also offers a few optional commands — APOP, which provides an alternate method of authenticating to the server, and TOP and UDIL, which pertain to message retrieval. You may implement them if you want, but they aren't necessary for this project. The full POP3 specification is available at http://rfc.net/rfc1939.html.

The POP3Client class needs two properties: a private one to store the connection handle with the server and a public one to store the last response received from the server. Because server responses start either with +OK if a command is successful or −ERR if there is a problem, an isOk() method can check for +OK in the response string and returns a Boolean so one can easily tell if something is wrong or not.

```
class POP3Client
{
    private $server;
    public $response;

    public function __construct()
    {
        $this->server = null;
        $this->response = '';
    }

    private function isOk()
    {
        return substr($this->response, 0, 3) == '+OK';
    }
    ...
}
```

A method encapsulating the connection logic is also needed. connect() accepts the server name and an optional port as arguments (POP3 traditionally uses port 110 for incoming connections). The fsockopen() function is used to establish the socket connection between the code and the server and returns the resource handle. This handle will be used later with file functions such as fwrite() and fgets() to communicate with the server.

```
public function connect($server, $port = 110)
{
    if (!$this->server = @fsockopen('tcp://' . $server, 110))
    {
        return false;
    }

    $this->response = trim(fgets($this->server, 512));
    if (!$this->isOk())
    {
        fclose($this->server);
        return false;
    }
    return true;
}
```

The protocol pairs carriage return and new line characters (\r\n) to denote line ending, so you will need to make sure this is sent with any data you send through the connection. Conversely, you'll need to trim them from any data read in. Responses that span multiple lines such as inbox listings end with a single period (and of course the trailing \r\n).

Note that the LIST and STAT commands share the same name of existing PHP functions so their corresponding method names will need to be mangled to avoid any conflicts. (Technically list() is a language construct and is the only one that causes a problem. I've chosen to mangle stat() as well for the sake of consistency.) I precede the affected names with an underscore.

Code for each method will almost be cookie-cutter: send the appropriate message to the server, read its response into $this->response, and return $this->isOk() so the calling code knows if there is an error.

```php
public function noop()
{
    fwrite($this->server, 'NOOP' . "\r\n");
    $this->response = trim(fgets($this->server, 512));
    return $this->isOk();
}
```

The _list() and retr() methods will be required to perform slightly more work, though. Given no arguments, _list() will read in the scan listing of message IDs and their sizes and return the information back to the caller as an array. _list() will instead provide information about the targeted message if an ID is provided. retr() will fetch a particular e-mail message.

```php
public function _list()
{
    if (func_num_args())
    {
        $args = func_get_args();
        fwrite($this->server, 'LIST ' . $args[0] . "\r\n");
        $this->response = trim(fgets($this->server, 512));
        if (!$this->isOk())
        {
            return false;
        }
        else
        {
            $message = explode(' ', $this->response);
            array_shift($message);  // drop +OK
            $message[1] = trim($message[1]);  // trim trailing \r\n
            return $message;
        }
    }
    else
    {
        fwrite($this->server, 'LIST' . "\r\n");
        $this->response = trim(fgets($this->server, 512));
        if (!$this->isOk())
        {
            return false;
        }
        else
        {
            $messages = array();
            while (($line = fgets($this->server, 512)) != '.' . "\r\n")
            {
                list($id, $size) = explode(' ', $line);
                $messages[$id] = trim($size);
            }
            return $messages;
        }
    }
```

```
        }
    }

    public function retr($id)
    {
        fwrite($this->server, 'RETR ' . $id . "\r\n");
        $this->response = trim(fgets($this->server, 512));
        if (!$this->isOk())
        {
            return false;
        }
        else
        {
            $message = '';
            while (($line = fgets($this->server, 512)) != '.' . "\r\n")
            {
                $message .= $line;
            }
            return $message;
        }
    }
}
```

Using the POP3Client class is as simple as creating a new object, connecting to the server, and issuing the appropriate commands.

```php
<?php
$p = new POP3Client();

// connect to mail.example.com POP3 server
if (!$p->connection('mail.example.com'))
{
    echo $p->response;
    die();
}

// login using the desired account credentials
if (!$p->user('tboronczyk') || !$p->password('secret'))
{
    echo $p->response;
    $p->quit();
    die();
}

// test the connection
$p->noop();
echo $p->response;

$p->quit();
?>
```

If you like, you may combine the user() and password() methods into a single login() method that accepts the username and password as its arguments. It is arguably more convenient to authenticate to the server with one method call instead of two, though you would then lose the ability to review the server's response to the USER command.

Here is the complete code for `lib/POP3Client.php`:

```php
<?php
class POP3Client
{
    private $server;
    public $response;

    // initialize a new POP3Client object
    public function __construct()
    {
        $this->server = null;
        $this->response = '';
    }

    // return true if +OK response received
    private function isOk()
    {
        return substr($this->response, 0, 3) == '+OK';
    }

    // open a connection to the POP3 server
    public function connect($server, $port = 110)
    {
        if (!$this->server = @fsockopen('tcp://' . $server, 110))
        {
            return false;
        }

        $this->response = trim(fgets($this->server, 512));
        if (!$this->isOk())
        {
            fclose($this->server);
            return false;
        }
        return true;
    }

    // send USER command to server
    public function user($username)
    {
        fwrite($this->server, 'USER ' . $username . "\r\n");
        $this->response = trim(fgets($this->server, 512));
        return $this->isOk();
    }

    // send PASS command to server
    public function pass($password)
    {
        fwrite($this->server, 'PASS ' . $password . "\r\n");
        $this->response = trim(fgets($this->server, 512));
        return $this->isOk();
    }

    // send NOOP command to server (should always return true
```

```php
    // or else something is seriously wrong with the POP3 server!)
    public function noop()
    {
        fwrite($this->server, 'NOOP' . "\r\n");
        $this->response = trim(fgets($this->server, 512));
        return $this->isOk();
    }

    // send STAT command to server
    public function _stat()
    {
        fwrite($this->server, 'STAT' . "\r\n");
        $this->response = trim(fgets($this->server, 512));
        return $this->isOk();
    }

    // send LIST command to server, may accept message id
    public function _list()
    {
        if (func_num_args())
        {
            $args = func_get_args();
            fwrite($this->server, 'LIST ' . $args[0] . "\r\n");
            $this->response = trim(fgets($this->server, 512));
            if (!$this->isOk())
            {
                return false;
            }
            else
            {
                $message = explode(' ', $this->response);
                array_shift($message);  // drop +OK
                $message[1] = trim($message[1]);  // trim trailing \r\n
                return $message;
            }
        }
        else
        {
            fwrite($this->server, 'LIST' . "\r\n");
            $this->response = trim(fgets($this->server, 512));
            if (!$this->isOk())
            {
                return false;
            }
            else
            {
                $messages = array();
                while (($line = fgets($this->server, 512)) != '.' . "\r\n")
                {
                    list($id, $size) = explode(' ', $line);
                    $messages[$id] = trim($size);
                }
```

(continued)

(continued)

```php
                return $messages;
            }
        }
    }

    // send RETR command to server
    public function retr($id)
    {
        fwrite($this->server, 'RETR ' . $id . "\r\n");
        $this->response = trim(fgets($this->server, 512));
        if (!$this->isOk())
        {
            return false;
        }
        else
        {
            $message = '';
            while (($line = fgets($this->server, 512)) != '.' . "\r\n")
            {
                $message .= $line;
            }
            return $message;
        }
    }

    // send DELE command to server
    public function dele($id)
    {
        fwrite($this->server, 'DELE ' . $id . "\r\n");
        $this->response = trim(fgets($this->server, 512));
        return $this->isOk();
    }

    // send RSET command to server
    public function rset()
    {
        fwrite($this->server, 'RSET' . "\r\n");
        $this->response = trim(fgets($this->server, 512));
        return $this->isOk();
    }

    // send QUIT command to server
    public function quit()
    {
        fwrite($this->server, 'QUIT' . "\r\n");
        $this->response = trim(fgets($this->server, 512));
        fclose($this->server);
        return $this->isOk();
    }
}
?>
```

The Configuration File

It makes sense to store common configuration values in a specific configuration file, such as the location of directories important to the application and login credentials for the required POP3 accounts. I've saved the following as `lib/config.php`:

```php
<?php
// set time zone to use date/time functions without warnings
date_default_timezone_set('America/New_York');

// local support directories
define('QUEUE_DIR', '/srv/apache/wrox/ch_03/queue');
define('REPLY_DIR', '/srv/apache/wrox/ch_03/replies');

// address and port for POP3 server
define('POP3_SERVER', 'mail.example.com');
define('POP3_PORT', 110);

// account information for list activity address
define('LIST_EMAIL', 'list@example.com');
define('LIST_USER', 'list');
define('LIST_PASSWORD', 'secret');

// account information for list management address
define('MANAGE_EMAIL', 'manage@example.com');
define('MANAGE_USER', 'manage');
define('MANAGE_PASSWORD', 'pa55w0rd');
?>
```

The directory indicated by the QUEUE_DIR constant will be used to aggregate individual messages into the digest mailing. The REPLY_DIR directory will hold various administrative messages saved as text files. It makes sense for the possible responses to the commands to be stored within individual text files in a separate directory to keep things organized and make future maintenance of the application easier. The POP3_SERVER, POP3_PORT and account information constants will be used to log into the appropriate mail accounts.

Account Management

Messages sent to the special administrative address must be processed so members can subscribe to the mailing list and manage their preferences. First a connection to the POP3 server will be established using the appropriate credentials provided in the configuration file. Then, each message that may exist in the inbox will be retrieved, the sender's e-mail address and the subject line from its headers will be extracted and the appropriate action is performed based on the request. The message must be marked for deletion after the requested action has been performed so it is not erroneously processed the next time the management script runs.

```
$pop = new POP3Client();
$pop->connect(POP3_SERVER, POP3_PORT);
$pop->user(MANAGE_USER) && $pop->pass(MANAGE_PASSWORD);

foreach (array_keys($pop->_list()) as $id)
{
    $message = $pop->retr($id);

    preg_match_all('/From: (.+)|Subject: (.+)/i', $message, $matches);
    $from = trim($matches[1][0]);
    $subject = trim($matches[2][1]);


    ...

    $pop->dele($id);
}

$pop->quit();
```

The project requirements specify SUBSCRIBE, UNSUBSCRIBE, SET [+|-]DIGEST and HELP as supported commands. After a user's command is processed, the contents of the appropriate response file will be sent back confirming the success or failure of the action. Some responses may have placeholders for the list and management e-mail addresses, which will be replaced with the values stored in the configuration constants by the management script. These files will be stored in the REPLY_DIR directory.

subscribe.txt   Sent when a new member subscribes to the list
                                       using SUBSCRIBE

```
You have subscribed.

List messages should be sent to <list_email>.

For information on managing your list subscription, send an email
with the subject HELP to <manage_email>.
```

unsubscribe.txt   Sent when a member unsubscribes from the list
                                       using UNSUBSCRIBE

```
You have been unsubscribed. Thank you for participating.
```

already_subscribed.txt   Sent when a member tries to subscribe to the list
                                       using SUBSCRIBE from an already registered
                                       e-mail address

```
This address was already found in the mailing list membership. You
cannot re-subscribe a currently registered address.

For information on managing your list subscription, send an email
with the subject HELP to <manage_email>.
```

not_subscribed.txt

Sent when a member tries to unsubscribe from the list using UNSUBSCRIBE from an address which was not registered

```
This address was not found in the mailing list membership. You
cannot unsubscribe unless you have previously subscribed.

For information on managing your list subscription, send an email
with the subject HELP to <manage_email>.
```

digest_on.txt

Sent when a member chooses to receive a daily digest message using SET +DIGEST instead of individual messages throughout the day

```
You have set your preferences to receive postings as one aggregated
digest message instead of individual emails. You can change this by
sending a message with SET -DIGEST in the subject line to
<manage_email>.

For other available commands, send HELP.
```

digest_off.txt

Sent when a member chooses to receive messages throughout the day using SET -DIGEST

```
You have set your preferences to receive individual email postings
instead of a single daily digest message. You can change this by
sending a message with SET +DIGEST in the subject line to
<manage_email>.

For other available commands, send HELP.
```

error.txt

Sent when an error is encountered while attempting to fulfill the request

```
An error occurred while processing your request. Please try again
later.

For information on managing your list subscription, send an email
with the subject HELP to <manage_email>.
```

help.txt

Sent when the user requests assistance using HELP

```
List messages should be sent to <list_email>.

You can manage your list subscription by sending commands in the
subject line of your message to <manage_email>.

Available commands are:

    SUBSCRIBE        Subscribe to the mailing list

    UNSUBSCRIBE      Remove yourself from the mailing list

    SET +DIGEST      Set preferences to receive postings as one
                     aggregated digest message instead of individual
                     emails

    SET -DIGEST      Set preferences to receive individual email
                     postings instead of digest

    HELP             Receive this message
```

`unknown.txt`   Sent when the user provides an unrecognized command

```
You have sent an unknown command. Available commands are:

    SUBSCRIBE        Subscribe to the mailing list

    UNSUBSCRIBE      Remove yourself from the mailing list

    SET +DIGEST      Set preferences to receive postings as one
                     aggregated digest message instead of individual
                     emails

    SET -DIGEST      Set preferences to receive individual email
                     postings instead of digest

    HELP             Receive this message
```

On unix-type platforms, the very first line of the script file must be `#! /usr/bin/php` (or whichever path points to the location of the PHP interpreter). This is a special type of comment interpreted by the shell that allows the file to be run as a stand-alone shell script. The script's execute permission must also be set for the system to be able to run it. This can be done from the command line by issuing the command `chmod +x` *filename*.

The following is the complete code for `manage.php`:

```php
#! /usr/bin/php
<?php
// include shared code
include '../lib/config.php';
include '../lib/db.php';
include '../lib/POP3Client.php';

// establish a connection to the POP3 server
$pop = new POP3Client();
$pop->connect(POP3_SERVER, POP3_PORT);
$pop->user(MANAGE_USER)
$pop->pass(MANAGE_PASSWORD);

// process each message in inbox
foreach (array_keys($pop->_list()) as $id)
{
    // fetch message
    $message = $pop->retr($id);

    // retrieve the email address and subject headers
    preg_match_all('/From: (.+)|Subject: (.+)/i', $message, $matches);
    $from = trim($matches[1][0]);
    $subject = trim($matches[2][1]);

    // determine if the email address exists
    $query = sprintf('SELECT EMAIL_ADDR FROM %sMAILLIST_USER WHERE ' .
        'EMAIL_ADDR = "%s"', DB_TBL_PREFIX,
        mysql_real_escape_string($from, $GLOBALS['DB']));
    $result = mysql_query($query, $GLOBALS['DB']);
    $exists = (mysql_num_rows($result));
    mysql_free_result($result);

    // send appropriate response
    switch (strtoupper($subject))
    {
        // subscribe email address to list
        case 'SUBSCRIBE':
            if ($exists)
            {
                // address already exists
                $response_file = 'already_subscribed.txt';
            }
            else
            {
                $query = sprintf('INSERT INTO %sMAILLIST_USER ' .
                    '(EMAIL_ADDR) VALUES ("%s")', DB_TBL_PREFIX,
                    mysql_real_escape_string($from, $GLOBALS['DB']));

                $response_file = (mysql_query($query, $GLOBALS['DB'])) ?
                    'subscribe.txt' : 'error.txt';
            }
```

(continued)

(continued)

```
            break;

        // remove email address from list
        case 'UNSUBSCRIBE':
            if ($exists)
            {
                $query = sprintf('DELETE FROM %sMAILLIST_USER WHERE ' .
                    'EMAIL_ADDR = "%s"', DB_TBL_PREFIX,
                    mysql_real_escape_string($from, $GLOBALS['DB']));

                $response_file = (mysql_query($query, $GLOBALS['DB'])) ?
                    'unsubscribe.txt' : 'error.txt';
            }
            else
            {
                // address does not exist
                $response_file = 'not_subscribed.txt';
            }
            break;

        // set preference for digest
        case 'SET +DIGEST':
            if ($exists)
            {
                $query = sprintf('UPDATE %sMAILLIST_USER SET ' .
                    'IS_DIGEST = 1 WHERE EMAIL_ADDR = "%s"', DB_TBL_PREFIX,
                    mysql_real_escape_string($from, $GLOBALS['DB']));

                $response_file = (mysql_query($query, $GLOBALS['DB'])) ?
                    'digest_on.txt' : 'error.txt';
            }
            else
            {
                // address does not exist
                $response_file = 'not_subscribed.txt';
            }
            break;

        // set preference for individual messages
        case 'SET -DIGEST':
            if ($exists)
            {
                $query = sprintf('UPDATE %sMAILLIST_USER SET ' .
                    'IS_DIGEST = 0 WHERE EMAIL_ADDR = "%s"', DB_TBL_PREFIX,
                    mysql_real_escape_string($from, $GLOBALS['DB']));

                $response_file = (mysql_query($query, $GLOBALS['DB'])) ?
                    'digest_off.txt' : 'error.txt';
            }
            else
            {
                // address does not exist
                $response_file = 'not_subscribed.txt';
            }
```

```
            break;

        // use help message
        case 'HELP':
            $response_file = 'help.txt';

        // unknown command was received
        default:
            $response_file = 'unknown.txt';
    }
    // Read the data
    $response = file_get_contents(REPLY_DIR . '/' . $response_file);

    // these placeholders will be swapped in the message templates
    $replace = array('<list_email>' => LIST_EMAIL,
                    '<manage_email>' => MANAGE_EMAIL);
    $response = str_replace(array_keys($replace), array_values($replace),
        $response);

    // send message
    mail($from, 'RE: ' . $subject, $response,
        'From: ' . LIST_EMAIL . "\r\n" .
        'Reply-To: ' . LIST_EMAIL . "\r\n");

    // mark message for delete
    $pop->dele($id);
}

$pop->quit();
mysql_close($GLOBALS['DB']);
?>
```

Processing Messages

Individual messages received by the mailing list address will be forwarded to other list members and the digest file will be constructed for those opting to receive only the daily mailing. The script responsible for this will begin by logging on to the POP3 server using the client code developed earlier in the chapter and act on each message in the account's inbox. The most complex part of this process will be processing the message itself.

For the sake of simplicity, the requirements allow you to only accept plain text messages. If the list receives a multi-part message then the script will parse out the plain-text message and use that (how such messages are constructed was discussed in Chapter 1). If you wanted to accept HTML messages, accept and archive attachments or anything else, then you would need to write the appropriate logic to handle it.

```
$message = $pop->retr($id);

preg_match_all('/Date: (.+)|From: (.+)|Subject: (.+)|boundary="(.+)"/',
    $message, $matches);
$date = trim($matches[1][0]);
$from = trim($matches[2][1]);
```

(continued)

(continued)

```php
$subject = trim($matches[3][2]);
$boundary = (isset($matches[4][3])) ? $matches[4][3] : false;

if (!$boundary)
{
    list($header, $body) = explode("\r\n\r\n", $message, 2);
}
else
{
    $chunks = preg_split('/' . $boundary . '/', $message);
    array_shift($chunks); // drop headers before MIME boundary
    array_shift($chunks); // again to drop headers after MIME boundary
    array_pop($chunks);   // drop trailing --

    foreach ($chunks as $chunk)
    {
        list($header, $body) = explode("\r\n\r\n", $chunk, 2);
        if (strpos($header, 'Content-Type: text/plain;') !== false)
        {
            break;
        }
    }
}
```

After a message has been retrieved, a list of the mail recipients who are receiving individual messages must be fetched from the database. The message will then be forwarded to them.

The message will also be appended to a growing file in the QUEUE_DIR to be sent to daily digest subscribers. The name of the digest file should include the date to avoid any confusion later if there happens to be stale or archived files in the directory.

```php
$digest = fopen(QUEUE_DIR . '/digest-' . date('Ymd') . '.txt', 'a+');

fwrite($digest, $subject . "\r\n");
fwrite($digest, $from . "\r\n");
fwrite($digest, $date . "\r\n\r\n");
fwrite($digest, $body . "\r\n");
fwrite($digest, str_repeat('-', 70) . "\r\n");
```

Here is the complete code for the script responsible for processing incoming mailing list messages. I've saved it as `individual.php`:

```php
#! /usr/bin/php
<?php
// include shared code
include '../lib/config.php';
include '../lib/db.php';
include '../lib/POP3Client.php';

// open digest file for append, create if it doesn't exist
$digest = fopen(QUEUE_DIR . '/digest-' . date('Ymd') . '.txt', 'a+');
```

```
// establish a connection to the POP3 server
$pop = new POP3Client();
$pop->connect(POP3_SERVER, POP3_PORT);
$pop->user(LIST_USER) && $pop->pass(LIST_PASSWORD);

// process each message in inbox
foreach (array_keys($pop->_list()) as $id)
{
    // fetch message
    $message = $pop->retr($id);

    // retrieve the Date, From and Subject headers and multipart boundary
    // marker from the message headers
    preg_match_all('/Date: (.+)|From: (.+)|Subject: (.+)|boundary="(.+)"/',
        $message, $matches);
    $date = trim($matches[1][0]);
    $from = trim($matches[2][1]);
    $subject = trim($matches[3][2]);
    $boundary = (isset($matches[4][3])) ? $matches[4][3] : false;

    // discard messages not from subscribed users
    $query = sprintf('SELECT EMAIL_ADDR FROM %sMAILLIST_USER WHERE ' .
        'EMAIL_ADDR = "%s"', DB_TBL_PREFIX,
        mysql_real_escape_string($from, $GLOBALS['DB']));
    $result = mysql_query($query, $GLOBALS['DB']);
    if (!mysql_num_rows($result))
    {
        mysql_free_result($result);

        $pop->dele($id);
        continue;
    }
    mysql_free_result($result);

    // multipart messages
    if ($boundary)
    {
        // split the message into chunks
        $chunks = preg_split('/' . $boundary . '/', $message);
        array_shift($chunks); // drop headers before MIME boundary
        array_shift($chunks); // again to drop headers after MIME boundary
        array_pop($chunks);   // drop trailing --

        // use just the text/plain chunk
        foreach ($chunks as $chunk)
        {
            list($header, $body) = explode("\r\n\r\n", $chunk, 2);
            if (strpos($header, 'Content-Type: text/plain;') !== false)
            {
                break;
            }
        }
    }
}
```

(continued)

(continued)

```
        else
        {
            // plain text email
            list($header, $body) = explode("\r\n\r\n", $message, 2);
        }

        // retrieve users to receive individual messages
        $query = sprintf('SELECT EMAIL_ADDR FROM %sMAILLIST_USER WHERE ' .
            'IS_DIGEST = 0', DB_TBL_PREFIX);
        $result = mysql_query($query, $GLOBALS['DB']);

        // forward a copy of the mail
        while ($user = mysql_fetch_assoc($result))
        {
            mail($user['EMAIL_ADDR'], $subject, $body,
                'From: ' . LIST_EMAIL . "\r\n" .
                'Reply-To: ' . LIST_EMAIL . "\r\n");
        }
        mysql_free_result($result);

        // append message to digest
        fwrite($digest, $subject . "\r\n");
        fwrite($digest, $from . "\r\n");
        fwrite($digest, $date . "\r\n\r\n");
        fwrite($digest, $body . "\r\n");
        fwrite($digest, str_repeat('-', 70) . "\r\n");

        // mark message for delete
        $pop->dele($id);
    }

    $pop->quit();
    fclose($digest);
    mysql_close($GLOBALS['DB']);
?>
```

The script may run a bit slow because it repeatedly queries the database for the same user information, though I intentionally chose to organize my script this way. I could have retrieved the addresses and stored them in an array at the start of the script but then I risk exhausting PHP's allocated memory if the number of subscribers is too large. Depending on the configuration of your MySQL database, it may realize the same query is executing repeatedly and begin caching the records to return, which makes this concern moot.

Another option would be to open two connections to the database and use one of them to retrieve the membership list. At the end of each loop, the resource's internal pointer would be reset using `mysql_data_seek()`. This is probably the most optimal method since the dataset isn't repeatedly retrieved or stored in PHP. You may want to optimize it depending on your needs. I felt in the interest of clarity it would be best to present the code as I did.

Processing the Digest

The final processing step will be to forward the contents of the aggregated digest file to the remaining list members at the end of the day. You may delete it afterwards since it is no longer needed (which I chose to do here) or keep it for archival purposes.

Here is the complete code for digest.php:

```
#! /usr/bin/php
<?php
// include shared code
include '../lib/config.php';
include '../lib/db.php';
include '../lib/POP3Client.php';

// retrieve users to receive digest messages
$query = sprintf('SELECT EMAIL_ADDR FROM %sMAILLIST_USER WHERE IS_DIGEST = 1',
    DB_TBL_PREFIX);
$result = mysql_query($query, $GLOBALS['DB']);

// open digest file
$time = strtotime('-1 day');
$digest = QUEUE_DIR . '/digest-' . date('Ymd', $time) . '.txt';
if (!file_exists($digest))
{
    // no digest file
    mysql_free_result($result);
    exit();
}
$body = file_get_contents($digest);

// send mail to each recipient
while ($row = mysql_fetch_assoc($result))
{
    mail($row['EMAIL_ADDR'], 'List Digest for ' . date('m/d/Y', $time),
        $body,
        'From: ' . LIST_EMAIL . "\r\n" .
        'Reply-To: ' . LIST_EMAIL . "\r\n");
}
mysql_free_result($result);
mysql_close($GLOBALS['DB']);

// delete digest file
unlink($digest);
?>
```

Setting Up the Mailing List

The project scripts in this chapter aren't meant to be run by a user visiting a web page, but rather periodically scheduled and executed automatically by the system. The digest.php script should run once a day to send the daily digest message, probably sometime late at night or during early morning.

The best way to schedule individual.php depends on the membership size and the amount of messages your list will be receiving. Exactly how scheduling is accomplished depends on which operating system is installed on the server.

On servers running a unix-variant operating system, you'll be adding entries to a crontab file to schedule their runs and the cron daemon will execute them when it's time. To add entries to your crontab file, call crontab -e from the command line.

Each entry in the crontab file is made up of a series of fields separated by a space. Normally there are seven fields per entry, and each entry is on its own line. An asterisk (*) may be used in any field with no specified value and some versions of cron allow you to specify multiple values for a field by separating them with a comma.

Table 3-2 shows the expected fields.

Table 3-2: crontab File Fields

Field	Description
Minute	What minute (0 through 59) the command will run
Hour	Hour of the day in 24-hour format (0 through 23 with 0 as midnight)
Date	Day of the month (0 through 31)
Month	Month, may either be numeric (0 through 12) or textual (January through December)
Day	Day of the week, may either be numeric (0 through 6) or textual (Sun through Sat)
User	The user account to run the job under
Command	The command to run

As an example, this entry runs the individual.php script every 15 minutes:

```
0,15,30,45 * * * * nobody /srv/apache/wrox/ch_03/scripts/individual.php
```

This entry runs manage.php every 5 minutes, except when the individual.php script is set to run:

```
5,10,20,25,35,40,50,55 * * * * nobody /srv/apache/wrox/ch_03/scripts/manage.php
```

This entry for digest.php runs it every night at 5 minutes after midnight:

```
5 0 * * * nobody /srv/apache/wrox/ch_03/scripts/digest.php
```

On the Windows platform, tasks are scheduled using the Scheduled Tasks applet. To open the applet, go to Start > Control Panel and double-click the Scheduled Tasks icon (if your using Category View, the icon can be found under Performance and Maintenance). Then double-click the Add Scheduled Task entry to launch the Scheduled Task Wizard, shown in Figure 3-2.

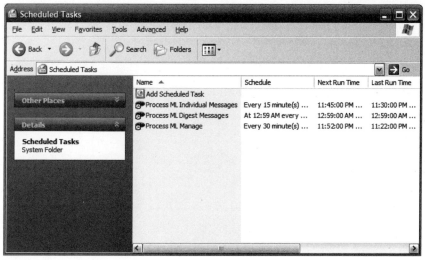

Figure 3-2

The wizard will guide you through setting up automated runs. When asked which program you want Windows to run, browse and locate the PHP interpreter and at the final screen check the option to open Advanced Properties when you click Finish.

In the options windows under the Tasks tab, add the appropriate script name in the Run field after the interpreter. An example is shown in Figure 3-3. Then progress to the Schedule tab and click the Advanced button. For digest message processing, the example configures the Advanced Schedule Options to repeat the task every 15 minutes for a duration of 23 hours, 59 minutes. This is shown in Figure 3-4. The script will now run daily and repeat every 15 minutes for 24 hours. At the end of the 24 hours it will be a new day and the task will start over.

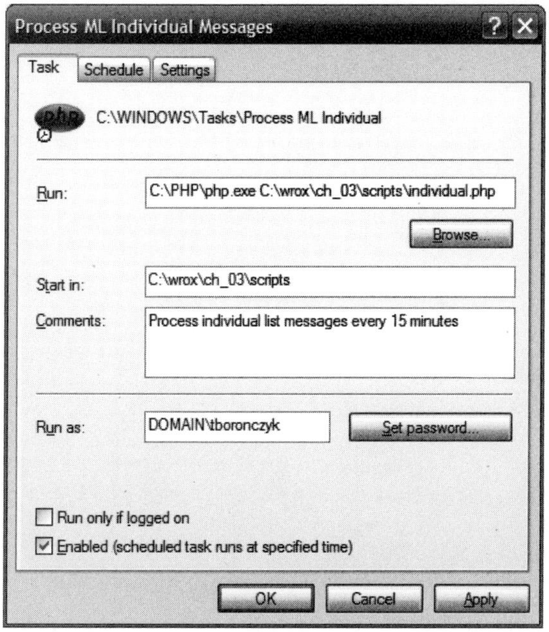

Figure 3-3

Figure 3-4

Summary

With just a few simple scripts, you can provide a basic mailing list service where members can correspond with one another as a group and discuss topics relevant to their interests. Granted the service written in this chapter may not be as feature-rich as popular mailing list mangers like Mailman, LISTSERV, and EZMLM, but it's a great starting point. You now have a basic foundation to build upon in whatever direction your individual needs dictate. Perhaps you might want to allow HTML messages, allow attachments, or archive individual messages and integrate a web-based front-end to what you've written to build something like Google Groups or Yahoo! Groups.

The idea of processing e-mail messages doesn't stop at just mailing lists. Perhaps you may want to write a blogging application that allows its posts to be updated via e-mail. Or, maybe you need a community photo album that updates its images from e-mail attachments. Think creatively!

In the next chapter you'll explore building a custom search engine.

4

Search Engine

The amount of information available online today is absolutely mind-boggling. It's no wonder why so many of us have become dependent on search engines such as Google and Yahoo! to help us find what we're looking for. We just type in some terms and click a button and seemingly, as if by magic, the desired results appear. It's doubtful, however, that many of us have stopped to think about what happens behind the scenes when we click that search button.

In this chapter, I will guide you through building a basic search engine, which you can implement on your own web site. The result of this project won't make you the next Yahoo! or Google, but it serves two goals: to help visitors quickly find the information they're looking for on your site and to give you some important insight into how search engines work in the process.

Designing the Search Engine

Dissecting the typical search engine reveals the anatomy of a simple beast in three parts: a crawler, an indexer, and a front end. A crawler goes out looking for fresh content to queue up for the indexer. In larger search engines, the crawler may actually download these pages and scan them for links to still more pages. The indexer in turn takes content, analyzes it, and formulates a searchable index. A front-end component of the search engine then accepts a query, uses it to search the index and presents the results back to the user. The devil, as always, is in the details.

The best algorithms to create an efficient index or rank results by perceived relevancy are closely guarded secrets in the search engine industry, and developing these is where a few lucky programmers have earned millions of dollars.

The full text-searching capabilities of MySQL make it possible to build low-grade search engines for small amounts of content, but this approach has some drawbacks as I will discuss. Instead, this project will have a crawler/indexer and front end.

The functionality of the crawler and indexer components will be combined in the same code file for this project. The document will be indexed to an inverted-index in a MySQL database immediately after it is retrieved. It will be written to run as a stand-alone `cron` job or scheduled task, the same way the scripts in the mailing list project from the previous chapter work.

The front end of the search engine will take in search terms from the user, query the index and return links to the appropriate documents. I will show you how to offer suggested alternatives for any misspelled words in the query to help make things more user-friendly, although this will require the `pspell` extension to be loaded in PHP.

The project will also have an administrative back end where an administrator can adjust the configuration of the crawler/indexer. Specifically, the admin will have the ability to define which documents are placed in the index and provide a list of stop words — common words such as *a*, *is*, and *but* that have little relevancy in a search query and should not be included in the index.

Problems with Full-Text Search

MySQL introduced full-text indexing and searching capabilities back in version 3.23.23. The implementation is straightforward and easy to use — define a FULLTEXT index and use MATCH/AGAINST in the query. Consider this example:

```
CREATE TABLE WROX_SOCIAL_EVENT (
    EVENT_ID        INTEGER UNSIGNED   NOT NULL   AUTO_INCREMENT,
    USER_ID         INTEGER UNSIGNED   NOT NULL,
    HEADLINE        TEXT               NOT NULL,
    EVENT_TEXT      TEXT               NOT NULL,
    EVENT_DATE      TIMESTAMP          NOT NULL,

    PRIMARY KEY (EVENT_ID),

    FOREIGN KEY (USER_ID)
        REFERENCES WROX_SOCIAL_USER(USER_ID),

    FULLTEXT INDEX (HEADLINE, EVENT_TEXT)
)
ENGINE=MyISAM DEFAULT CHARACTER SET latin1
    COLLATE latin1_general_cs AUTO_INCREMENT=0;
```

Assume this table is for a social networking web site where users post upcoming events and visitors want searches against information in the HEADLINE and EVENT_TEXT columns to find events of interest to them. A full-text search query might look like this:

```
SELECT
    EVENT_ID, U.USER_ID, U.USERNAME, HEADLINE, EVENT_TEXT, EVENT_DATE
FROM
    WROX_SOCIAL_EVENT E JOIN WROX_SOCIAL_USER U
        ON E.USER_ID = U.USER_ID
WHERE
    MATCH (HEADLINE, EVENT_TEXT) AGAINST ('<search term>');
```

Unfortunately, there are some drawbacks to depending on MySQL's full-text search functionality. Full-text indexes can only be used with the MyISAM engine, which doesn't strictly enforce foreign key constraints or perform row-level locking like InnoDB does. Many times MyISAM is a good choice, but if your application depends on InnoDB features, then you won't be able to perform full-text searching.

Another problem is that the list of stop words MySQL uses is directly compiled in to the binary. Suppose a new event is added for a one-day workshop titled "Help Me Look Sensible" designed to help recent college graduates learn how to dress professionally before they go out into the workplace. Each word in the title appears on MySQL's stop list, so even searching for the event by name would return zero results! To modify the list, you must edit the `myisam/ft_static.c` source file and then recompile MySQL. This may not be a viable option for you depending on your hosting situation.

As a third point, MySQL only indexes words that are four characters or greater in length. This might pose a problem if the same college graduate wants to search for *PHP* (thankfully, *beer* is four letters long).

There are also some logistical/performance implications for using full-text searching. The entire document must be stored in the database which leads to needless wasted space. (An inverted index doesn't store stop words and condenses duplicate words to one-to-many relationships with integer keys.) This wasted space isn't necessarily an issue with a small number of documents, but may become one as the number of pages increases. Search performance can decrease exponentially, making the user wait needless seconds or minutes for the results to be returned.

Designing the Database

Five database tables are used for the project. The first two store the search engine's configuration options.

```
+--------------+--------------+------+
| Field        | Type         | Null |
+--------------+--------------+------+
| DOCUMENT_URL | varchar(255) | NO   |
+--------------+--------------+------+


+--------------+--------------+------+
| Field        | Type         | Null |
+--------------+--------------+------+
| TERM_VALUE   | varchar(255) | NO   |
+--------------+--------------+------+
```

The `WROX_SEARCH_CRAWL` table collects the addresses for the indexer to retrieve and include in the index. Essentially, this is a list of all files a user may search through using the search engine. `WROX_SEARCH_STOP_WORD` stores a list of stop words that should not be included in the index. Typically these are articles, pronouns, prepositions, and other words that have little value as search terms.

It would be nice if MySQL exposed its internal list of stop words using a special SHOW or SELECT query because then an INSERT-SELECT statement could pre-populate the table with data. You could then use this list as a starting point to add or filter various words as needed. However, this isn't the case so you must develop your own list of stop words.

The next three tables construct the inverted index to be fed by the indexer and searched by the front end of the search engine. An inverted index is a common data structure used in search algorithms to optimize the speed of the query. The trade-off between this and other indexing schemes is that populating and maintaining the index is slower but searching is faster. The user doesn't have to wait forever for the results of a simple query.

```
+-----------------+-------------------+------+-----+---------+----------------+
| Field           | Type              | Null | Key | Default | Extra          |
+-----------------+-------------------+------+-----+---------+----------------+
| DOCUMENT_ID     | int(10) unsigned  | NO   | PRI | NULL    | auto_increment |
| DOCUMENT_URL    | varchar(255)      | NO   | UNI |         |                |
| DOCUMENT_TITLE  | varchar(255)      | YES  |     | NULL    |                |
| DESCRIPTION     | varchar(255)      | YES  |     | NULL    |                |
+-----------------+-------------------+------+-----+---------+----------------+


+------------+-------------------+------+-----+---------+----------------+
| Field      | Type              | Null | Key | Default | Extra          |
+------------+-------------------+------+-----+---------+----------------+
| TERM_ID    | int(10) unsigned  | NO   | PRI | NULL    | auto_increment |
| TERM_VALUE | varchar(255)      | NO   | UNI |         |                |
+------------+-------------------+------+-----+---------+----------------+


+-------------+-------------------+------+-----+
| Field       | Type              | Null | Key |
+-------------+-------------------+------+-----+
| TERM_ID     | int(10) unsigned  | NO   | MUL |
| DOCUMENT_ID | int(10) unsigned  | NO   | PRI |
| OFFSET      | int(10) unsigned  | NO   | PRI |
+-------------+-------------------+------+-----+
```

The WROX_SEARCH_DOCUMENT table stores the address of each document indexed in the search engine and associates numeric keys to them. Also stored are the document's title and description, which will be displayed in the search results returned to the user. The words in each document are collected into WROX_SEARCH_TERM and are also assigned numeric keys. The terms are linked to the documents by the WROX_SEARCH_INDEX table, which references the keys to track which term is found where in each document.

Here is the complete SQL code for the five tables:

```
CREATE TABLE WROX_SEARCH_CRAWL (
    DOCUMENT_URL  VARCHAR(255)  NOT NULL
)
ENGINE=InnoDB DEFAULT CHARACTER SET latin1
    COLLATE latin1_general_cs;

CREATE TABLE WROX_SEARCH_STOP_WORD (
    TERM_VALUE  VARCHAR(255)  NOT NULL
)
ENGINE=InnoDB DEFAULT CHARACTER SET latin1
    COLLATE latin1_general_cs;

CREATE TABLE WROX_SEARCH_DOCUMENT (
```

```
    DOCUMENT_ID     INTEGER UNSIGNED  NOT NULL  AUTO_INCREMENT,
    DOCUMENT_URL    VARCHAR(255)      NOT NULL,
    DOCUMENT_TITLE  VARCHAR(255),
    DESCRIPTION     VARCHAR(255),

    PRIMARY KEY (DOCUMENT_ID),

    CONSTRAINT UNIQUE (DOCUMENT_URL)
)
ENGINE=InnoDB DEFAULT CHARACTER SET latin1
    COLLATE latin1_general_cs AUTO_INCREMENT=0;

CREATE TABLE WROX_SEARCH_TERM (
    TERM_ID     INTEGER UNSIGNED  NOT NULL  AUTO_INCREMENT,
    TERM_VALUE VARCHAR(255)       NOT NULL,

    PRIMARY KEY (TERM_ID),

    CONSTRAINT UNIQUE (TERM_VALUE)
)
ENGINE=InnoDB DEFAULT CHARACTER SET latin1
    COLLATE latin1_general_cs AUTO_INCREMENT=0;

CREATE TABLE WROX_SEARCH_INDEX (
    TERM_ID        INTEGER UNSIGNED  NOT NULL,
    DOCUMENT_ID    INTEGER UNSIGNED  NOT NULL,
    OFFSET         INTEGER UNSIGNED  NOT NULL,

    PRIMARY KEY (DOCUMENT_ID, OFFSET),

    FOREIGN KEY (TERM_ID)
        REFERENCES WROX_SEARCH_TERM(TERM_ID),

    FOREIGN KEY (DOCUMENT_ID)
        REFERENCES WROX_SEARCH_DOCUMENT(DOCUMENT_ID)
)
ENGINE=InnoDB DEFAULT CHARACTER SET latin1
    COLLATE latin1_general_cs;
```

Code and Code Explanation

Code for the search engine is contained in three files. The administrative interface is saved in the publicly accessible directory as `admin.php`. It should be protected from unauthorized use by including the `lib/401.php` include file. The front-end code is also saved in the `public_files` directory as `search.php`. The crawler/indexer functionality is saved outside the public area as `indexer.php`.

Administrative Interface

The administrative interface provides an area to enter addresses that will either be included or excluded from the index, and also maintains the list of stop words. The display consists of an HTML form with two `textarea`s. The processing of the input is done with PHP.

The first HTML textarea provides a place to enter the URLs of documents that will be included in the search engine's retrieval efforts. The second textarea provides a place for the list of stop words to be given. Each are pre-populated from appropriate database records with each item appearing on a separate line.

```php
<form method="post"
 action="<?php echo htmlspecialchars($_SERVER['PHP_SELF']); ?>">
 <table>
  <tr>
   <td style="vertical-align:top; text-align:right">
    <label for="addresses">Include Addresses</label></td>
   <td><small>Enter addresses to include in crawling, one address per
   line.</small><br/>
    <textarea name="addresses" id="addresses" rows="5" cols="60"><?php

$query = sprintf('SELECT DOCUMENT_URL FROM %sSEARCH_CRAWL ' .
    'ORDER BY DOCUMENT_URL ASC', DB_TBL_PREFIX);
$result = mysql_query($query, $GLOBALS['DB']);
while ($row = mysql_fetch_array($result))
{
    echo htmlspecialchars($row['DOCUMENT_URL']) . "\n";
}
mysql_free_result($result);

?></textarea>
   </td>
  </tr><tr>
   <td style="vertical-align:top; text-align:right">
    <label for="stop_words">Stop Words</label></td>
   <td><small>Enter words to omit from the index, one per line.</small><br/>
    <textarea name="stop_words" id="stop_words" rows="5" cols="60"><?php

$query = sprintf('SELECT TERM_VALUE FROM %sSEARCH_STOP_WORD ORDER BY ' .
    'TERM_VALUE ASC', DB_TBL_PREFIX);
$result = mysql_query($query, $GLOBALS['DB']);
while ($row = mysql_fetch_array($result))
{
    echo htmlspecialchars($row['TERM_VALUE']) . "\n";
}
mysql_free_result($result);

?></textarea>
   </td>
  </tr><tr>
   <td> </td>
   <td><input type="submit" value="Submit"/></td>
   <td><input type="hidden" name="submitted" value="1"/></td>
  </tr><tr>
 </table>
</form>
```

The addresses and stop words are updated each time the form is saved. Old records are discarded and the table is reinitialized using TRUNCATE TABLE on both the WROX_SEARCH_CRAWL and WROX_SEARCH_STOP_WORD tables. Alternatively, you can issue a query such as DELETE FROM WROX_SEARCH_CRAWL but TRUNCATE TABLE is oftentimes a more efficient approach than using DELETE if the entire table's data set is targeted. It also has the benefit of conveying more semantic meaning to someone else reading your code than DELETE.

```php
if (isset($_POST['submitted']))
{
    $query = sprintf('TRUNCATE TABLE %sSEARCH_CRAWL', DB_TBL_PREFIX);
    mysql_query($query, $GLOBALS['DB']);

    $addresses = explode_items($_POST['addresses'], "\n", false);
    if (count($addresses))
    {
        $values = array();
        foreach ($addresses as $address)
        {
            $values[] = mysql_real_escape_string($address, $GLOBALS['DB']);
        }
        $query = sprintf('INSERT INTO %sSEARCH_CRAWL (DOCUMENT_URL) ' .
            'VALUES ("%s")', DB_TBL_PREFIX,
            implode ('"), ("', $values));
        mysql_query($query, $GLOBALS['DB']);
    }

    $query = sprintf('TRUNCATE TABLE %sSEARCH_STOP_WORD', DB_TBL_PREFIX);
    mysql_query($query, $GLOBALS['DB']);

    $words = explode_items($_POST['stop_words'], "\n", false);
    if (count($words))
    {
        $values = array();
        foreach ($words as $word)
        {
            $values[] = mysql_real_escape_string($word, $GLOBALS['DB']);
        }
        $query = sprintf('INSERT INTO %sSEARCH_STOP_WORD (TERM_VALUE) ' .
            'VALUES ("%s")', DB_TBL_PREFIX, implode ('"), ("', $values));
        mysql_query($query, $GLOBALS['DB']);
    }
}
```

If you use PHP's explode() function to split the input text on newline characters (\n) into arrays, you may encounter blank lines or trailing carriage returns (\r) depending on what the user entered and his or her platform. Additional processing will be required to clean the list. explode_items() is a custom function that can be added to your growing lib/functions.php to augment explode() and accepts a block of text and an optional separator to parse into an array. As you do not want duplicate values, an optional argument can be provided that filters them out:

```php
// convert a list of items (separated by newlines by default) into an array
// omitting blank lines and optionally duplicates
function explode_items($text, $separator = "\n", $preserve = true)
{
    $items = array();
    foreach (explode($separator, $text) as $value)
    {
        $tmp = trim($value);
        if ($preserve)
        {
            $items[] = $tmp;
        }
        else
        {
            if (!empty($tmp))
            {
                $items[$tmp] = true;
            }
        }
    }

    if ($preserve)
    {
        return $items;
    }
    else
    {
        return array_keys($items);
    }
}
```

Each segment is run through `trim()` to remove any trailing whitespace and is collected. If duplicate entries are not required, the value is stored as an array key to ensure duplicates aren't allowed. The keys are then shifted to a usable array using `array_keys()` before they are returned. Alternatively, you could populate an array using the URLs and then call `array_unique()` to filter duplicates. I chose the key/ `array_keys()` approach, because it's more efficient with larger sets of data and it's known beforehand that only unique values should be returned.

Here is the complete code for `public_files/admin.php`:

```php
<?php
// include shared code
include '../lib/common.php';
include '../lib/db.php';
include '../lib/functions.php';

// must be logged in to access this page
include '401.php';

// processes incoming data if the form has been submitted
```

```php
if (isset($_POST['submitted']))
{
    // delete existing addresses
    $query = sprintf('TRUNCATE TABLE %sSEARCH_CRAWL', DB_TBL_PREFIX);
    mysql_query($query, $GLOBALS['DB']);

    // add addresses list to database
    $addresses = explode_items($_POST['addresses'], "\n", false);
    if (count($addresses))
    {
        $values = array();
        foreach ($addresses as $address)
        {
            $values[] = mysql_real_escape_string($address, $GLOBALS['DB']);
        }
        $query = sprintf('INSERT INTO %sSEARCH_CRAWL (DOCUMENT_URL) ' .
            'VALUES ("%s")', DB_TBL_PREFIX,
            implode ('"), ("', $values));
        mysql_query($query, $GLOBALS['DB']);
    }

    // delete existing stop words
    $query = sprintf('TRUNCATE TABLE %sSEARCH_STOP_WORD', DB_TBL_PREFIX);
    mysql_query($query, $GLOBALS['DB']);

    // add stop word list to database
    $words = explode_items($_POST['stop_words'], "\n", false);
    if (count($words))
    {
        $values = array();
        foreach ($words as $word)
        {
            $values[] = mysql_real_escape_string($word, $GLOBALS['DB']);
        }
        $query = sprintf('INSERT INTO %sSEARCH_STOP_WORD (TERM_VALUE) ' .
            'VALUES ("%s")', DB_TBL_PREFIX, implode ('"), ("', $values));
        mysql_query($query, $GLOBALS['DB']);
    }
}

// generate HTML form
ob_start();
?>
<form method="post"
 action="<?php echo htmlspecialchars($_SERVER['PHP_SELF']); ?>">
 <table>
  <tr>
   <td style="vertical-align:top; text-align:right">
    <label for="addresses">Include Addresses</label></td>
   <td><small>Enter addresses to include in crawling, one address per
    line.</small><br/>
    <textarea name="addresses" id="addresses" rows="5" cols="60"><?php
```

(continued)

(continued)

```php
//retrieve list of addresses
$query = sprintf('SELECT DOCUMENT_URL FROM %sSEARCH_CRAWL ' .
    'ORDER BY DOCUMENT_URL ASC', DB_TBL_PREFIX);
$result = mysql_query($query, $GLOBALS['DB']);
while ($row = mysql_fetch_array($result))
{
    echo htmlspecialchars($row['DOCUMENT_URL']) . "\n";
}
mysql_free_result($result);

  ?></textarea>
  </td>
 </tr><tr>
  <td style="vertical-align:top; text-align:right">
   <label for="stop_words">Stop Words</label></td>
  <td><small>Enter words to omit from the index, one per line.</small><br/>
   <textarea name="stop_words" id="stop_words" rows="5" cols="60"><?php

//retrieve list of stop words
$query = sprintf('SELECT TERM_VALUE FROM %sSEARCH_STOP_WORD ORDER BY ' .
    'TERM_VALUE ASC', DB_TBL_PREFIX);
$result = mysql_query($query, $GLOBALS['DB']);
while ($row = mysql_fetch_array($result))
{
    echo htmlspecialchars($row['TERM_VALUE']) . "\n";
}
mysql_free_result($result);

  ?></textarea>
  </td>
 </tr><tr>
  <td> </td>
  <td><input type="submit" value="Submit"/></td>
  <td><input type="hidden" name="submitted" value="1"/></td>
 </tr><tr>
 </table>
</form>
<?php
$GLOBALS['TEMPLATE']['content'] = ob_get_clean();

// display the page
include '../templates/template-page.php';
?>
```

Figure 4-1 shows the administration page viewed in a web browser with sample addresses and stop words populating the textarea fields.

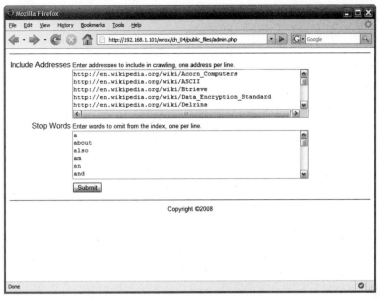

Figure 4-1

Also, here is a short list of English stop words to get you started. Mostly they are pronouns, prepositions and conjugations of the verb to be.

a	by	I	she	us
about	could	if	so	was
also	do	in	that	we
am	for	is	the	were
an	from	it	their	what
and	had	let	them	when
any	has	me	then	where
are	have	mine	there	which
as	he	my	these	while
at	her	of	they	why
be	him	on	this	with
been	his	or	through	you
being	hers	over	to	your
but	how	put	too	

Crawler/Indexer

Typically the crawler is the component of the search engine responsible for going out and retrieving content for the indexer to catalog. It reads the list of addresses from the database and downloads a copy of each document to queue locally to disk where the indexer can access them. Then the indexer component processes each file in the queue. This tag-team approach works well for large search sites with massive amounts of data continuously being indexed or if the crawler scans through the documents in search of links to other documents to retrieve (as is the case with recursive downloading/leeching). I have decided to combine the crawler and indexer components in this project. That is, the document is processed and added to the search index immediately after it is retrieved.

The script starts by deleting the stale index and retrieving the list of stop words. Again I choose to employ the technique of storing values as array keys to make checking against items in the list more efficient since every word in every document will be compared against it. One should write code for clarity, maintainability, and scalability first, and then optimize sections once performance bottlenecks are realized. However, it makes sense to make such optimizations beforehand if the situation is as obvious as this.

```
$query = sprintf('TRUNCATE TABLE %sSEARCH_INDEX', DB_TBL_PREFIX);
mysql_query($query, $GLOBALS['DB']);

$query = sprintf('TRUNCATE TABLE %sSEARCH_TERM', DB_TBL_PREFIX);
mysql_query($query, $GLOBALS['DB']);

$query = sprintf('TRUNCATE TABLE %sSEARCH_DOCUMENT', DB_TBL_PREFIX);
mysql_query($query, $GLOBALS['DB']);

$query = sprintf('SELECT TERM_VALUE FROM %sSEARCH_STOP_WORD', DB_TBL_PREFIX);
$result = mysql_query($query, $GLOBALS['DB']);
$stop_words = array();
while ($row = mysql_fetch_array($result))
{
    $stop_words[$row['TERM_VALUE']] = true;
}
mysql_free_result($result);
```

The script then retrieves the list of documents that need to be processed from the database and acts on each one. Retrieving files is done with assistance from the Client URL (CURL) library extension, a powerful library for transferring files over a wide variety of protocols. A CURL resource handle is obtained with curl_init() and several options are set with curl_setopt(). Close to 100 options can be set.

CURLOPT_FOLLOWLOCATION instructs CURL to follow HTTP 30x-style redirect responses. CURLOPT_HEADER disregards the response headers so they are not included with the returned content. CURLOPT_RETURNTRANSFER sets CURL to return content as a string instead of directing it to the output buffer. CURLOPT_URL specifies the URL address of a document to retrieve. Although most of the options are set outside the while loop because they only need to be set once, CURLOPT_URL is set for each document and is positioned inside the loop. (For a list of all available options, go to www.php.net/curl_setopt).

```
$ch = curl_init();

curl_setopt($ch, CURLOPT_FOLLOWLOCATION, true);
curl_setopt($ch, CURLOPT_HEADER, false);
curl_setopt($ch, CURLOPT_RETURNTRANSFER, true);
curl_setopt($ch, CURLOPT_USERAGENT, 'Search Engine Indexer');

$query = sprintf('SELECT DOCUMENT_URL FROM %sSEARCH_CRAWL', DB_TBL_PREFIX);
$result = mysql_query($query, $GLOBALS['DB']);
while ($row = mysql_fetch_array($result))
{
    echo 'Processing: ' . $row['DOCUMENT_URL'] . "...\n";

    curl_setopt($ch, CURLOPT_URL, $row['DOCUMENT_URL']);
    $file = curl_exec($ch);


    ...
}

curl_close($ch);
```

The document's title and description are extracted with the help of SimpleXML. Content is provided to `simplexml_load_string()`, which parses it as an XML document and returns an easily traversable object. The document's title, description, and address are stored in the WROX_SEARCH_DOCUMENT table where it is automatically assigned a unique index by MySQL. The index is retrieved with `mysql_insert_id()` so it can be used later to link words back to the document.

SimpleXML will generate warnings if the HTML code is not properly constructed. If the libtidy extension is installed, then you can use it to clean up the code prior to providing it to SimpleXML to parse. Otherwise you'll have to ignore the warnings or suppress them with the @ operator.

```
$file = tidy_repair_string($file);
$html = simplexml_load_string($file);

// or: $html = @simplexml_load_string($file);

if ($html->head->title)
{
    $title = $html->head->title;
}
else
{
    // use the filename if a title is not found
    $title = basename($row['DOCUMENT_URL']);
}

$description = 'No description provided.';
foreach($html->head->meta as $meta)
{
    if (isset($meta['name']) && $meta['name'] == 'description')
```

(continued)

(continued)

```
        {
            $description = $meta['content'];
            break;
        }
    }

    $query = sprintf('INSERT INTO %sSEARCH_DOCUMENT (DOCUMENT_URL, ' .
        'DOCUMENT_TITLE, DESCRIPTION) VALUES ("%s", "%s", "%s")',
        DB_TBL_PREFIX,
        mysql_real_escape_string($row['DOCUMENT_URL'], $GLOBALS['DB']),
        mysql_real_escape_string($title, $GLOBALS['DB']),
        mysql_real_escape_string($description, $GLOBALS['DB']));
    mysql_query($query, $GLOBALS['DB']);

    // retrieve the document's id
    $doc_id = mysql_insert_id($GLOBALS['DB']);
```

Only text rendered to the viewer should be included in the index. Because it doesn't make sense to include HTML tags in search results (and therefore the index), they are removed from the content with the strip_tags() function. Content can then be split into individual words with str_word_count(). Each word is checked against the stop words list, if it has already been added previously to the database and then added to the search index.

```
    $file = strip_tags($file);

    foreach (str_word_count($file, 1) as $index => $word)
    {
        // words should be stored as lowercase for comparisons
        $word = strtolower($word);

        if (isset($stop_words[$word])) continue;

        $query = sprintf('SELECT TERM_ID FROM %sSEARCH_TERM WHERE ' .
            'TERM_VALUE = "%s"',
            DB_TBL_PREFIX,
            mysql_real_escape_string($word, $GLOBALS['DB']));
        $result2 = mysql_query($query, $GLOBALS['DB']);
        if (mysql_num_rows($result2))
        {
            list($word_id) = mysql_fetch_row($result2);
        }
        else
        {
            $query = sprintf('INSERT INTO %sSEARCH_TERM (TERM_VALUE) ' .
                'VALUE ("%s")',
                DB_TBL_PREFIX,
                mysql_real_escape_string($word, $GLOBALS['DB']));
            mysql_query($query, $GLOBALS['DB']);

            $word_id = mysql_insert_id($GLOBALS['DB']);
        }
```

```
        mysql_free_result($result2);

        $query = sprintf('INSERT INTO %sSEARCH_INDEX (DOCUMENT_ID, ' .
            'TERM_ID, OFFSET) VALUE (%d, %d, %d)',
            DB_TBL_PREFIX,
            $doc_id,
            $word_id,
            $index);
        mysql_query($query, $GLOBALS['DB']);
}
```

Here is the complete code for `indexer.php`. As it is meant to be run as a shell script, the first line must point to the location of the PHP interpreter and the file's execute permissions must be set.

```
#! /usr/bin/php
<?php
// include shared code
include 'lib/common.php';
include 'lib/db.php';

// clear index tables
$query = sprintf('TRUNCATE TABLE %sSEARCH_INDEX', DB_TBL_PREFIX);
mysql_query($query, $GLOBALS['DB']);

$query = sprintf('TRUNCATE TABLE %sSEARCH_TERM', DB_TBL_PREFIX);
mysql_query($query, $GLOBALS['DB']);

$query = sprintf('TRUNCATE TABLE %sSEARCH_DOCUMENT', DB_TBL_PREFIX);
mysql_query($query, $GLOBALS['DB']);

// retrieve the list of stop words
$query = sprintf('SELECT TERM_VALUE FROM %sSEARCH_STOP_WORD', DB_TBL_PREFIX);
$result = mysql_query($query, $GLOBALS['DB']);
$stop_words = array();
while ($row = mysql_fetch_array($result))
{
    // since this list will be checked for each word, use term as the array
    // key-- isset($stop_words[<term>]) is more efficient than using
    // in_array(<term>, $stop_words)
    $stop_words[$row['TERM_VALUE']] = true;
}
mysql_free_result($result);

// open CURL handle for downloading
$ch = curl_init();

// set curl options
curl_setopt($ch, CURLOPT_FOLLOWLOCATION, true);
curl_setopt($ch, CURLOPT_HEADER, false);
curl_setopt($ch, CURLOPT_RETURNTRANSFER, true);
curl_setopt($ch, CURLOPT_USERAGENT, 'Search Engine Indexer');
```

(continued)

(continued)

```php
// fetch list of documents to index
$query = sprintf('SELECT DOCUMENT_URL FROM %sSEARCH_CRAWL', DB_TBL_PREFIX);
$result = mysql_query($query, $GLOBALS['DB']);
while ($row = mysql_fetch_array($result))
{
    echo 'Processing: ' . $row['DOCUMENT_URL'] . "...\n";

    // retrieve the document's content
    curl_setopt($ch, CURLOPT_URL, $row['DOCUMENT_URL']);
    $file = curl_exec($ch);

    $file = tidy_repair_string($file);
    $html = simplexml_load_string($file);

    // or: $html = @simplexml_load_string($file);

    // extact the title
    if ($html->head->title)
    {
        $title = $html->head->title;
    }
    else
    {
        // use the filename if a title is not found
        $title = basename($row['DOCUMENT_URL']);
    }

    // extract the description
    $description = 'No description provided.';
    foreach($html->head->meta as $meta)
    {
        if (isset($meta['name']) && $meta['name'] == 'description')
        {
            $description = $meta['content'];
            break;
        }
    }

    // add the document to the index
    $query = sprintf('INSERT INTO %sSEARCH_DOCUMENT (DOCUMENT_URL, ' .
        'DOCUMENT_TITLE, DESCRIPTION) VALUES ("%s", "%s", "%s")',
        DB_TBL_PREFIX,
        mysql_real_escape_string($row['DOCUMENT_URL'], $GLOBALS['DB']),
        mysql_real_escape_string($title, $GLOBALS['DB']),
        mysql_real_escape_string($description, $GLOBALS['DB']));
        mysql_query($query, $GLOBALS['DB']);

    // retrieve the document's id
    $doc_id = mysql_insert_id($GLOBALS['DB']);

    // strip HTML tags out from the content
```

```php
        $file = strip_tags($file);

        // break content into individual words
        foreach (str_word_count($file, 1) as $index => $word)
        {
            // words should be stored as lowercase for comparisons
            $word = strtolower($word);

            // skip word if it appears in the stop words list
            if (isset($stop_words[$word])) continue;

            // determine if the word already exists in the database
            $query = sprintf('SELECT TERM_ID FROM %sSEARCH_TERM WHERE ' .
                'TERM_VALUE = "%s"',
                DB_TBL_PREFIX,
                mysql_real_escape_string($word, $GLOBALS['DB']));
            $result2 = mysql_query($query, $GLOBALS['DB']);
            if (mysql_num_rows($result2))
            {
                // word exists so retrieve its id
                list($word_id) = mysql_fetch_row($result2);
            }
            else
            {
                // add word to the database
                $query = sprintf('INSERT INTO %sSEARCH_TERM (TERM_VALUE) ' .
                    'VALUE ("%s")',
                    DB_TBL_PREFIX,
                    mysql_real_escape_string($word, $GLOBALS['DB']));
                mysql_query($query, $GLOBALS['DB']);

                // determine the word's id
                $word_id = mysql_insert_id($GLOBALS['DB']);
            }
            mysql_free_result($result2);

            // add the index record
            $query = sprintf('INSERT INTO %sSEARCH_INDEX (DOCUMENT_ID, ' .
                'TERM_ID, OFFSET) VALUE (%d, %d, %d)',
                DB_TBL_PREFIX,
                $doc_id,
                $word_id,
                $index);
            mysql_query($query, $GLOBALS['DB']);
        }
    }

mysql_free_result($result);
curl_close($ch);
echo 'Indexing complete.' . "\n";
?>
```

You may choose to run the script manually from the command line, and then schedule it as a `cron` or scheduled tasks job to run periodically. Even if you decide to automate it, I recommend running `indexer.php` manually the first time to make sure everything indexes properly. It can be run from the command line like this, with output redirected to `indexlog.txt` for later analysis:

```
./indexer.php > indexlog.txt 2>&1 &
```

Front End

The front-end interface is what will be used by the site's users. It accepts the search terms from the user, queries the inverted index and return the matching results.

If a query has been submitted, the script uses the custom `explode_items()` function to break it down into an array of terms using a space as the separator. It then retrieves the list of stop words from the database and compares the search terms against it. Matching words are removed and will not be included in the eventual query of the index.

The number of `JOIN` clauses and conditions in the `WHERE` clause needed to query the index depends on the number of search words entered by the user so the query statement is built using three variables which are concatenated together. Afterwards, the query must be trimmed four spaces to remove the `WHERE` clauses' trailing `AND`.

Finally, the number of matching entries and the result set are returned to the user.

```php
$words = array();
if (isset($_GET['query']) && trim($_GET['query']))
{
    $words = explode_items($_GET['query'], ' ', false);

    $query = sprintf('SELECT TERM_VALUE FROM %sSEARCH_STOP_WORD',
        DB_TBL_PREFIX);
    $result = mysql_query($query, $GLOBALS['DB']);
    $stop_words = array();
    while ($row = mysql_fetch_assoc($result))
    {
        $stop_words[$row['TERM_VALUE']] = true;
    }
    mysql_free_result($result);

    $words_removed = array();
    foreach ($words as $index => $word)
    {
        if (isset($stop_words[strtolower($word)]))
        {
            $words_removed[] = $word;
            unset($words[$index]);
        }
    }
}
ob_start();
?>
<form method="get"
```

```
      action="<?php echo htmlspecialchars($_SERVER['PHP_SELF']); ?>">
     <div>
      <input type="text" name="query" id="query" value="<?php
       echo (count($words)) ? htmlspecialchars(join(' ', $words)) : '';?>"/>
      <input type="submit" value="Search"/>
     </div>
    </form>
    <?php

    if (count($words))
    {
        $join = '';
        $where = '';
        $query = 'SELECT DISTINCT D.DOCUMENT_URL, D.DOCUMENT_TITLE, ' .
            'D.DESCRIPTION FROM WROX_SEARCH_DOCUMENT D ';
        foreach ($words as $index => $word)
        {
            $join .= sprintf(
                'JOIN WROX_SEARCH_INDEX I%d ON D.DOCUMENT_ID = I%d.DOCUMENT_ID ' .
                'JOIN WROX_SEARCH_TERM T%d ON I%d.TERM_ID = T%d.TERM_ID ',
                $index, $index, $index, $index, $index);

            $where .= sprintf('T%d.TERM_VALUE = "%s" AND ', $index,
                mysql_real_escape_string(strtolower($word), $GLOBALS['DB']));
        }
        $query .= $join . 'WHERE ' . $where;

        // trimmed 4 characters to remove trailing ' AND'
        $query = substr($query, 0, strlen($query) - 4);

        $result = mysql_query($query, $GLOBALS['DB']);

        echo '<hr/>';
        $num_rows = mysql_num_rows($result);
        echo '<p>Search for <b>' . htmlspecialchars(join(' ', $words)) .
            '</b> yielded ' . $num_rows . ' result' .
            (($num_rows != 1) ? 's' : '') . ':</p>';

        echo '<ul>';
        while ($row = mysql_fetch_assoc($result))
        {
            echo '<li><b><a href="' .
                htmlspecialchars($row['DOCUMENT_URL']) . '">' .
                htmlspecialchars($row['DOCUMENT_TITLE']) . '</a></b>- ' .
                htmlspecialchars($row['DESCRIPTION']) . '<br/><i>' .
                htmlspecialchars($row['DOCUMENT_URL']) . '</i></li>';
        }
        echo '</ul>';
    }
    $GLOBALS['TEMPLATE']['content'] = ob_get_clean();
```

Each term may be checked for spelling using the Pspell extension and suggested spellings collected in a separate array. A resource handle to the spelling dictionary is obtained with `pspell_new()` which I have initialized with an English dictionary. You may provide the appropriate two-letter ISO 639 language code to specify an alternate language instead such as de for German, fr for French or eo for Esperanto.

The spelling of a word is checked with pspell_check() and an array of suggested alternates is retrieved with pspell_suggest(). Only the first spelling suggestion is used so not to overwhelm the user. The suggestion is also compared against the original word to ignore capitalization-related spelling "mistakes."

```php
// spell check the query words
$spell_error = false;
$suggest_words = array();
$ps = pspell_new('en');
foreach ($words as $index => $word)

    if (!pspell_check($ps, $word))
    {
        if ($s = pspell_suggest($ps, $word))
        {
            if (strtolower($s[0]) != strtolower($word))
            {
                // (ignore capitalization-related spelling errors)
                $spell_error = true;
                $suggest_words[$index] = $s[0];
            }
        }
    }
```

The $spelling_error variable is set any time a spelling error is encountered as a flag, so the script can decided whether a query showing the suggested corrections should be returned to the user alongside the results.

```php
if ($spell_error)
{
    foreach ($words as $index => $word)
    {
        if (isset($suggest_words[$index]))
        {
            $words[$index] = $suggest_words[$index];
        }
    }
    echo '<p>Possible misspelling. Did you mean <a href="' .
        htmlspecialchars($_SERVER['PHP_SELF']) .'?query=' .
        urlencode(htmlspecialchars(join(' ', $words))) . '">' .
        htmlspecialchars(join(' ', $words)) . '</a>?</p>';
}
```

Here is the complete code for public_files/search.php. Figure 4-2 shows the front end in action displaying search results and Figure 4-3 shows a suggested spelling correction.

```php
<?php
// include shared code
include '../lib/common.php';
include '../lib/db.php';
include '../lib/functions.php';

// accept incoming search terms if the form has been submitted
$words = array();
if (isset($_GET['query']) && trim($_GET['query']))
{
    $words = explode_items($_GET['query'], ' ', false);

    // remove stop words from query
    $query = sprintf('SELECT TERM_VALUE FROM %sSEARCH_STOP_WORD',
        DB_TBL_PREFIX);
    $result = mysql_query($query, $GLOBALS['DB']);
    $stop_words = array();
    while ($row = mysql_fetch_assoc($result))
    {
        $stop_words[$row['TERM_VALUE']] = true;
    }
    mysql_free_result($result);

    $words_removed = array();
    foreach ($words as $index => $word)
    {
        if (isset($stop_words[strtolower($word)]))
        {
            $words_removed[] = $word;
            unset($words[$index]);
        }
    }
}
// generate HTML form
ob_start();
?>
<form method="get"
 action="<?php echo htmlspecialchars($_SERVER['PHP_SELF']); ?>">
 <div>
  <input type="text" name="query" id="query" value="<?php
  echo (count($words)) ? htmlspecialchars(join(' ', $words)) : '';?>"/>
  <input type="submit" value="Search"/>
 </div>
</form>
<?php

// begin processing query
if (count($words))
{
    // spell check the query words
    $spell_error = false;
    $suggest_words = array();
```

(continued)

(continued)

```php
$ps = pspell_new('en');
foreach ($words as $index => $word)
{
    if (!pspell_check($ps, $word))
    {
        if ($s = pspell_suggest($ps, $word))
        {
            if (strtolower($s[0]) != strtolower($word))
            {
                // (ignore capitalization-related spelling errors)
                $spell_error = true;
                $suggest_words[$index] = $s[0];
            }
        }
    }
}

// formulate the search query using provided terms and submit it
$join = '';
$where = '';
$query = 'SELECT DISTINCT D.DOCUMENT_URL, D.DOCUMENT_TITLE, ' .
    'D.DESCRIPTION FROM WROX_SEARCH_DOCUMENT D ';
foreach ($words as $index => $word)
{
    $join .= sprintf(
        'JOIN WROX_SEARCH_INDEX I%d ON D.DOCUMENT_ID = I%d.DOCUMENT_ID ' .
        'JOIN WROX_SEARCH_TERM T%d ON I%d.TERM_ID = T%d.TERM_ID ',
        $index, $index, $index, $index, $index);

    $where .= sprintf('T%d.TERM_VALUE = "%s" AND ', $index,
        mysql_real_escape_string(strtolower($word), $GLOBALS['DB']));
}
$query .= $join . 'WHERE ' . $where;
// trimmed 4 characters o remove trailing ' AND'
$query = substr($query, 0, strlen($query) - 4);
$result = mysql_query($query, $GLOBALS['DB']);

// display results
echo '<hr/>';
$num_rows = mysql_num_rows($result);
echo '<p>Search for <b>' . htmlspecialchars(join(' ', $words)) .
    '</b> yielded ' . $num_rows . ' result' .
    (($num_rows != 1) ? 's' : '') . ':</p>';

// show suggested query if a possible misspelling was found
if ($spell_error)
{
    foreach ($words as $index => $word)
    {
        if (isset($suggest_words[$index]))
```

```
                {
                    $words[$index] = $suggest_words[$index];
                }
            }
        echo '<p>Possible misspelling. Did you mean <a href="' .
            htmlspecialchars($_SERVER['PHP_SELF']) .'?query=' .
            urlencode(htmlspecialchars(join(' ', $words))) . '">' .
            htmlspecialchars(join(' ', $words)) . '</a>?</p>';
    }

    echo '<ul>';
    while ($row = mysql_fetch_assoc($result))
    {
        echo '<li><b><a href="' .
            htmlspecialchars($row['DOCUMENT_URL']) . '">' .
            htmlspecialchars($row['DOCUMENT_TITLE']) . '</a></b>- ' .
            htmlspecialchars($row['DESCRIPTION']) . '<br/><i>' .
            htmlspecialchars($row['DOCUMENT_URL']) . '</i></li>';
    }
    echo '</ul>';
}
$GLOBALS['TEMPLATE']['content'] = ob_get_clean();

// display the page
include '../templates/template-page.php';
?>
```

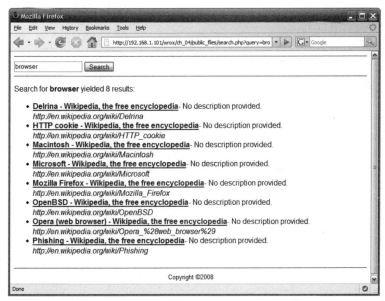

Figure 4-2

Figure 4-3

To integrate the search engine into your existing web site, place a form that submits its query to `search.php` to any page you see fit. Afterwards, log into `admin.php` and enter the address of any page you want to be searched as well as a list of stop words. After the addresses and stop words have been entered into the database, `indexer.php` can be run to build the inverted-index.

Summary

The search engine built in this project is rather basic. Although it does offer suggestions for perceived misspellings, it lacks other features that users have come to expect from search engines such as relevancy ranking and word-stemming.

The words' positions are also stored in the database, which shows where they were found within the documents. By comparing these values, you can identify which words appear closer to others or even sequentially. You may also want to consider the number of times a term appears in a document when sorting the results. Algorithms to rank items by relevancy are closely guarded secrets and there's no real right or wrong answer. Feel free to experiment.

Word-stemming is another area where there are many algorithms available with no one right way to do it. Stemming allows a user to enter *fish* in a query, for example, but receive results for *fishing*, *fishes*, and *fished* as well. The engine understands such words as just different forms of the same base word and retrieves them from the index as well.

Probably the easiest method of stemming to implement is to truncate common suffixes such as -s, -es, -ies, -ly, -ing, and -ed from the words before they are added to the database and then from the terms before they are used in the search query. This approach is naïve, however, as there are a large number of exceptions found in the English language. A search for *run* might include *runs* and *running*, but not *ran*. See `http://en.wikipedia.org/wiki/Stemming` for a brief overview of different stemming approaches and feel free to experiment.

In the following chapter you will design a web-based calendar application to help keep yourself organized.

5

Personal Calendar

Calendars are probably one of the greatest organizational inventions of all time. Although all of them serve the same function — to organize and present temporal information in a grid-like fashion — calendars can come in many different styles. The most common style displays the 28 to 31 days of a given month, but some special calendars show an entire year, a given week laid out by day, or even a day broken down by hour.

Calendars have found use on the Internet as well, often as a means of navigation. For example, blogs will often show a calendar listing the dates in a month when posts were made. By clicking a date you are redirected to a page where you can view events on that date.

Navigation aside, calendars are ultimately useful for keeping appointments, notes, meetings, and so on organized so people don't forget the events. Like most people, I use my calendar to help me remember important dates and appointments, sometimes many months in advance.

In this chapter, you'll design a web-based calendar application to help keep yourself organized.

Designing the Application

The application you will write in this chapter is a personal calendar to help you keep your day-to-day activities and appointments organized. It will make use of two different, styled calendars — a month view for quick navigation and a day view to list the events.

The most prominent calendar will display the day's events in quarter-hour increments starting at 9 in the morning and running until 5 in the evening (the classic 9-to-5 work day). However, the starting and ending times will be coded as constants so they can easily by changed later to suit your needs. It will have links to navigate to the previous or next day's event calendar.

Although the day-view calendar only shows events between 9:00 AM and 5:00 PM, some events may be scheduled beyond those hours. The events scheduled outside the viewed timeframe will be listed separately off to the side as a list.

The less prominent calendar will display the days in the currently viewed month and will be used to help navigate to previous or following months and jump to specific days.

A form will be used to allow the addition of new events to the calendar. It will accept a brief description or name of the event, the time it is scheduled for and if a reminder should be sent via e-mail an hour before the event is scheduled. There will also be a link to download the appointments as an `ics` file to make it easy to share the calendar with others.

You can see all these components laid out in Figure 5-1, which shows the personal calendar application in a web browser.

Figure 5-1

Designing the Database

The personal calendar application requires one database table to store the events and appointments. Each record consists of a unique ID, a brief event name or description, a timestamp, and a bit field to track whether an event will generate a reminder. One might conclude since the primary tracking field for the event is the timestamp, that this might serve as the primary key. Unfortunately, this is not the case, because more than one event can be scheduled for the same time period which is why the unique ID field is required.

```
+--------------+----------------------+------+-----+-------------------+
| Field        | Type                 | Null | Key | Default           |
+--------------+----------------------+------+-----+-------------------+
| EVENT_ID     | int(10) unsigned     | NO   | PRI | NULL              |
| EVENT_NAME   | varchar(100)         | NO   |     |                   |
| EVENT_TSTAMP | timestamp            | NO   |     | CURRENT_TIMESTAMP |
| NOTIFY       | tinyint(1) unsigned  | NO   |     | 0                 |
+--------------+----------------------+------+-----+-------------------+
```

Here is the complete SQL code to create the WROX_CALENDAR table.

```
CREATE TABLE WROX_CALENDAR (
    EVENT_ID       INTEGER UNSIGNED    NOT NULL  AUTO_INCREMENT,
    EVENT_NAME     VARCHAR(100)        NOT NULL,
    EVENT_TSTAMP   TIMESTAMP           NOT NULL,
    NOTIFY         TINYINT(1) UNSIGNED NOT NULL  DEFAULT 0,

    PRIMARY KEY (EVENT_ID)
)
ENGINE=MyISAM DEFAULT CHARACTER SET latin1
    COLLATE latin1_general_cs;
```

Code and Code Explanation

I will jump right into this application by first discussing how to generate a month-view calendar. Afterwards I will cover the personal calendar application as a whole and discuss the day-view calendar, form and events list. Then I will discuss the reminder and export convenience features.

Creating a Month-View Calendar

The code to generate a calendar that displays days within a month consists really of nothing more than a couple loops once information about the desired month has been established.

A unix timestamp is retrieved first either from a URL parameter or from the time() function, which returns the current timestamp. When the page is initially requested there is little likelihood that a timestamp will be sent in the URL so the current date will be the default. Afterwards a specific timestamp can be passed from links as other dates are navigated. The date() function can then use the timestamp value to identify important aspects of the date. It is a pretty powerful function that can do more than just format a timestamp for display; it can be used to determine the starting day of a month, the number of days in a month, whether the year is a leap year or not, and so on.

```
$timestamp = (isset($_GET['t'])) ? $_GET['t'] : time();

list($month, $day, $year) = explode('/', date('m/d/Y', $timestamp));
$first_day_of_month = date('w', mktime(0, 0, 0, $month, 1, $year));
$total_days = date('t', $timestamp);
```

Tables 5-1 and 5-2 show the available format specifiers the `date()` function accepts and their meaning.

Table 5-1: Date Format Specifiers for the `date()` Function

Specifier	Description	Example
D	Three-letter name of day	Sun
d	Day of month with leading 0	01
F	Full name of month	January
j	Day of month (no leading 0)	1
L	If the year is a leap year or not	0 (no), 1 (yes)
l	Full name of day	Sunday
M	Three-letter name of month	Jan
m	Month as number with leading 0	01
N	ISO-8601 day number	7 (Sunday)
n	Month as number (no leading 0)	1
o	ISO-8601 year number	2008
S	English ordinal suffix for day of month	Th
t	Number of days in a given month	31
W	ISO-8601 week number	42 (42nd week)
w	Numeric representation of the day of the week	0 (Sunday)
Y	Four-digit year	2008
y	Two-digit year	08
z	Day of the year (starts at 0)	42 (Feb 11th)

Table 5-2: Time Format Specifiers for the `date()` Function

Specifier	Description	Example
A	AM/PM designators (uppercase)	AM
a	AM/PM designators (lowercase)	am
B	Swatch Internet time	500
C	ISO-8601 date	2008-01-01T06:00:00-05:00
e	Time zone	America/New_York
G	24-hour hour (no leading 0)	13

Specifier	Description	Example
g	12-hour hour (no leading 0)	1
H	24-hour hour with leading 0	13
h	12-hour hour with leading 0	01
I	If daylight savings is in effect	0 (no), 1 (yes)
i	Minutes with leading 0	09
O	Offset from GMT	-0500
P	Offset from GMT with colon separator	-05:00
r	RFC-2822 date	Tue, 1 Jan 2008 06:00:00 - 0500
s	Seconds with leading 0	09
T	Abbreviated time zone	EST
U	Seconds since the unix epoch	1199185200
u	milliseconds	54321
Z	Timezone offset in seconds	-18000

A timestamp represents the date as an integer. More accurately, it represents the date in terms of the number of seconds since midnight UTC of January 1, 1970. To modify the timestamp for a future or previous date you can add/subtract the appropriate number of seconds or use the function strtotime(), which understands various string constructs.

```php
// link to preceding day. 60 x 60 x 24 = 86400 seconds in a day
echo '<a href="'. htmlspecialchars($_SERVER['PHP_SELF']) . '?t=' .
    ($timestamp - 86400) . '">&lt;</a>  ';

// link to preceding day using strtotime() function
echo '<a href="'. htmlspecialchars($_SERVER['PHP_SELF']) . '?t=' .
    strtotime('-1 day', $timestamp) . '">&lt;</a>  ';
```

A tracking variable is initialized to keep track of the current day's cell being generated by the loop. An outer while loop can use the variable to iterate until it has exceeded the allotted number of days for the month. Within the while loop, an inner for loop outputs a row of seven cells, one for each day of the week.

```php
<table>
<tr>
 <th>Sun</th><th>Mon</th><th>Tue</th><th>Wed</th><th>Thu</th>
 <th>Fri</th><th>Sat</th>
</tr>
<?php
$current = 1;
while ($current <= $total_days)
```

(continued)

(continued)

```php
{
    echo '<tr>';
    for ($i = 0; $i < 7; $i++)
    {
        if (($current == 1 && $i < $first_day_of_month) ||
            ($current > $total_days))
        {
            echo '<td> </td>';
            continue;
        }

        echo '<td>' . $current . '</td>';
        $current++;
    }
    echo '</tr>';
}
?>
</table>
```

The following code demonstrates how by pulling all these pieces together — accepting an incoming timestamp, determining information about the represented month, adjusting the timestamp to formulate new links and using loops to display a grid — you are able to generate a month-view calendar. public_files/month.php serves as an example of a basic calendar which you can later modify to suit your own needs. The output is shown in Figure 5-2.

```php
<?php
include '../lib/common.php';

// accept incoming URL parameter
$timestamp = (isset($_GET['t'])) ? $_GET['t'] : time();

// determine useful aspects of the requested month
list($month, $day, $year) = explode('/', date('m/d/Y', $timestamp));
$first_day_of_month = date('w', mktime(0, 0, 0, $month, 1, $year));
$total_days = date('t', $timestamp);

// output table header
ob_start();
echo '<table id="calendar">';
echo '<tr id="calendar_header"><th colspan="7">';
echo '<a href="' . htmlspecialchars($_SERVER['PHP_SELF']) . '?t=' .
    strtotime('-1 month', $timestamp) . '">&lt;</a>  ';
echo date('F', $timestamp) . ' ' . $year;
echo '  <a href="' . htmlspecialchars($_SERVER['PHP_SELF']) . '?t=' .
    strtotime('+1 month', $timestamp) . '">&lt;</a>';
echo '</th></tr>';
echo '<tr><th>Sun</th><th>Mon</th><th>Tue</th><th>Wed</th><th>Thu</th>' .
    '<th>Fri</th><th>Sat</th></tr>';

// output date cells
$current = 1;
while ($current <= $total_days)
```

```php
    {
        echo '<tr class="calendar_dates">';
        for ($i = 0; $i < 7; $i++)
        {
            if (($current == 1 && $i < $first_day_of_month) ||
                ($current > $total_days))
            {
                echo '<td class="empty"> </td>';
                continue;
            }

            echo '<td>' . $current . '</td>';
            $current++;
        }
        echo '</tr>';
    }
    echo '</table>';
    $GLOBALS['TEMPLATE']['content'] = ob_get_clean();

    // assign styles for calendar
    $GLOBALS['TEMPLATE']['extra_head'] = '<link rel="stylesheet" type="text/css" ' .
        'href="css/monthly_calendar.css"/>';

    // display page
    include '../templates/template-page.php';
?>
```

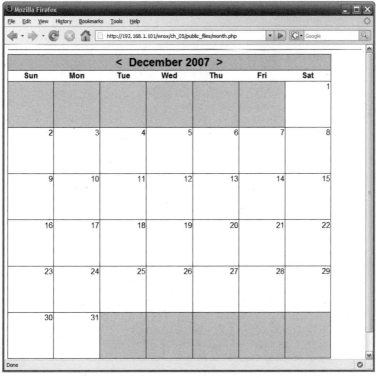

Figure 5-2

Creating a Day-View Calendar

The overall logic of generating a day-view calendar is similar to that of the month-view calendar. However, instead of outputting a cell for each day, the calendar shows a single day broken up into quarter-hour increments. An outer `for` loop iterates from a starting hour to an ending hour whereas an inner `for` loop increments through intervals of 15 (60 minutes in an hour divided into quarter segments is 15 minutes) and outputs the table's cells.

When working with time values it is often easier to work with a 24-hour clock or *military time*. If you're not familiar with the concept, the 24-hour clock is a convention of identifying hours sequentially from 0 (midnight) to 23 (11:00 PM) instead of repeating 1 to 12 and using AM to denote morning hours and PM for evening hours. Most parts of the world use a 24-hour clock as well as a lot of computer software (MySQL denotes time using the 24-hour format), whereas the United States, Canada, and Mexico use a 12-hour format. Even though the `for` loop iterates through the day using a 24-hour clock, the code converts the time and displays it using AM and PM designators. Table 5-3 compares the two time formats.

```php
define('DAY_HR_START', 9);
define('DAY_HR_END', 17);

echo '<table>';

for ($i = DAY_HR_START; $i <= DAY_HR_END; $i++)
{
    for ($j = 0; $j < 60; $j += 15)
    {
        $hour = $i;
        $minutes = $j;
        $meridian = 'AM';

        if ($hour > 12)
        {
            $meridian = 'PM';
            $hour -= 12;
        }
        else if ($hour == 12)
        {
            $meridian = 'PM';
        }

        echo '<tr>';
        printf('<td>%02d:%02d %s</td>', $hour, $minutes, $meridian);
        echo '<td> </td>';
        echo '</tr>';
    }
}
echo '</table>';
```

Table 5-3: Comparison of the 12-hr and 24-hr Clocks

Morning Hours				Evening Hours			
12-hr	24-hr	12-hr	24-hr	12-hr	24-hr	12-hr	24-hr
12 AM (midnight)	00	6 AM	06	12 PM (noon)	12	6 PM	18
1 AM	01	7 AM	07	1 PM	13	7 PM	19
2 AM	02	8 AM	08	2 PM	14	8 PM	20
3 AM	03	9 AM	19	3 PM	15	9 PM	21
4 AM	04	10 AM	10	4 PM	16	10 PM	22
5 AM	05	11 AM	11	5 PM	17	11 PM	23

Adding and Showing Events

An HTML form is needed to collect information about the event from the user. The date will be determined automatically based on the page viewed, so the form posts back to the page with the timestamp in the `action` URL. The form will gather the name of the event, the starting time and whether or not a reminder should be sent via e-mail.

```
<h2>Add Event</h2>
<form action="<?php echo htmlspecialchars($_SERVER['PHP_SELF']) . '?t=' .
 $timestamp; ?>"method="post">
 <table>
  <tr>
   <td class="label"><label for="evt_name">Event:</label></td>
   <td><input type="text" id="evt_name" name="evt_name"></td>
  </tr><tr>
   <td class="label"><label for="evt_hour">Time:</label></td>
   <td>
    <select name="evt_hour" id="evt_hour">
     <option value="12">12</option>
<?php

     for ($i = 1; $i < 12; $i++)
     {
         printf('<option value="%d">%02d</option>', $i, $i);
     }
?>
    </select> : <select name="evt_min">
<?php
     for ($i = 0; $i < 59; $i += 15)
     {
         printf('<option value="%d">%02d</option>', $i, $i);
     }
?>
    </select>
    <select name="evt_pm">
     <option value="no">AM</option>
     <option value="yes">PM</option>
```

(continued)

(continued)

```
        </select>
      </td>
    </tr><tr>
     <td class="label">Notify</td>
     <td>
      <input type="radio" name="evt_notify" id="evt_notify_yes" value="yes"
       checked="checked"/>
      <label for="evt_notify_yes">Yes</label>
      <input type="radio" name="evt_notify" id="evt_notify_no" value="no"/>
      <label for="evt_notify_no">No</label>
     </td>
    </tr><tr>
     <td></td>
     <td>
      <input type="hidden" name="submitted" value="true"/>
      <input type="submit" value="Add Event"/></td>
    </tr>
   </table>
  </form>
```

Code can be positioned at the beginning of the script immediately after a timestamp has been gleaned and the needed aspects of the month have been determined with `date()` to validate the incoming values and add the event to the database.

```
if (isset($_POST['submitted']))
{
    // validate incoming values
    $evt_name = (isset($_POST['evt_name'])) ? $_POST['evt_name'] : '';
    $evt_name = trim($evt_name);
    if (!$evt_name)
    {
        $evt_name = 'Unknown';
    }
    $evt_pm = (isset($_POST['evt_pm']) && $_POST['evt_pm'] == 'yes');
    $evt_hour = (isset($_POST['evt_hour'])) ? (int)$_POST['evt_hour'] : 0;
    if ($evt_pm)
    {
        $evt_hour += 12;
    }
    if ($evt_hour == 24)
    {
        $evt_hour = 12;
    }
    else if ($evt_hour == 12)
    {
        $evt_hour = 0;
    }
    $evt_min = (isset($_POST['evt_min'])) ? (int)$_POST['evt_min'] : 0;
    $evt_notify = (isset($_POST['evt_notify']) &&
        $_POST['evt_notify'] == 'yes');

    // add to database
    $query = sprintf('INSERT INTO %sCALENDAR (EVENT_NAME, EVENT_TSTAMP, ' .
        'NOTIFY) VALUES ("%s", "%04d-%02d-%02d %02d:%02d:00", %d)',
        DB_TBL_PREFIX,
```

```
            mysql_real_escape_string($evt_name, $GLOBALS['DB']),
            $year, $month, $day,
            $evt_hour, $evt_min,
            $evt_notify);
        mysql_query($query, $GLOBALS['DB']);
}
```

The logic to display the events can be incorporated into the loop that generates the day-view calendar. Within the inner `for` loop a query is sent to the database to retrieve any events for the current timeslot. Personally, I prefer to use MySQL's `UNIX_TIMESTAMP()` function when retrieving dates from a database table. It returns the date and time as a unix timestamp as opposed to MySQL's *Y-m-d h:m:s* format, which is easier to manipulate in PHP using the `date()` function.

```
for ($hour = DAY_HR_START; $hour <= DAY_HR_END; $hour++)
{
    for ($minute = 0; $minute < 60; $minute += 15)
    {
        echo '<tr>';
$d_meridian = 'AM';

$d_hour = $hour;
        if ($hour >= 12)
        {

$d_meridian = 'PM';

$d_hour = ($hour > 12)?$hour - 12:$hour;
        }
printf('<td>%d: %02d %s</td>', $d_hour, $minutes, $d_meridian);
        echo '<td>';

        $query = sprintf('SELECT EVENT_NAME FROM %sCALENDAR WHERE ' .
            'EVENT_TSTAMP = "%04d-%02d-%02d %02d:%02d:00"',
            DB_TBL_PREFIX,
            $year, $month, $day,
            $i, $j);
        $result = mysql_query($query, $GLOBALS['DB']);

        if (mysql_num_rows($result))
        {
            while ($row = mysql_fetch_assoc($result))
            {
                echo '<div>' . htmlspecialchars($row['EVENT_NAME']) .
                    '</div>';
            }
        }
        else
        {
            echo ' ';
        }
        mysql_free_result($result);
        echo '</td>';
        echo '</tr>';
    }
}
echo '</table>';
```

It is possible for some events to be scheduled outside the timeframe displayed by the daily-view calendar, but it is just as important that they be displayed as well. It is possible to submit a query to select the events for the given day that are outside the time period and displayed in a bulleted list.

```php
<h2>Also Scheduled</h2>
<?php
// retrieve and display events that fall outside the daily-view hours
$query = sprintf('SELECT EVENT_NAME, UNIX_TIMESTAMP(EVENT_TSTAMP) AS ' .
    'EVENT_TSTAMP FROM %sCALENDAR WHERE EVENT_TSTAMP NOT BETWEEN ' .
    '"%4d-%02d-%02d %02d:00:00" AND "%4d-%02d-%02d %02d:59:59" ORDER BY ' .
    'EVENT_TSTAMP ASC, EVENT_NAME ASC',
    DB_TBL_PREFIX,
    $year, $month, $day, DAY_HR_START,
    $year, $month, $day, DAY_HR_END);
$result = mysql_query($query, $GLOBALS['DB']);

echo '<ul>';
if (mysql_num_rows($result))
{
    while ($row = mysql_fetch_assoc($result))
    {
        echo '<li>' . date('h:i A - ', $row['EVENT_TSTAMP']) .
        htmlspecialchars($row['EVENT_NAME']) . '</li>';
    }
}
else
{
    echo '<p><i>No other events scheduled</i></p>';
}
mysql_free_result($result);
echo '</ul>';
```

The following code listing for `public_files/calendar.php` incorporates all of the previously discussed concepts to create the main functionality of the personal calendar application. One line not discussed yet adds a link to `export.php` so the user can download the calendar information. Figure 5-1 (shown earlier) shows the interface in a web browser.

```php
<?php
include '../lib/common.php';
include '../lib/db.php';

print_r($_GET);
print_r($_POST);
// view definitions
define('DAY_HR_START', 9);
define('DAY_HR_END', 17);

// accept incoming URL parameter
$timestamp = (isset($_GET['t'])) ? $_GET['t'] : time();

// determine useful aspects of the requested month
list($month, $day, $year) = explode('/', date('m/d/Y', $timestamp));
$first_day_of_month = date('w', mktime(0, 0, 0, $month, 1, $year));
```

```php
$total_days = date('t', $timestamp);

// add new event
if (isset($_POST['submitted']))
{
    // validate incoming values
    $evt_name = (isset($_POST['evt_name'])) ? $_POST['evt_name'] : '';
    $evt_name = trim($evt_name);
    if (!$evt_name)
    {
        $evt_name = 'Unknown';
    }
    $evt_pm = (isset($_POST['evt_pm']) && $_POST['evt_pm'] == 'yes');
    $evt_hour = (isset($_POST['evt_hour'])) ? (int)$_POST['evt_hour'] : 0;
    if ($evt_pm)
    {
        $evt_hour += 12;
    }
    if ($evt_hour == 24)
    {
        $evt_hour = 12;
    }
    else if ($evt_hour == 12)
    {
        $evt_hour = 0;
    }
    $evt_min = (isset($_POST['evt_min'])) ? (int)$_POST['evt_min'] : 0;
    $evt_notify = (isset($_POST['evt_notify']) &&
        $_POST['evt_notify'] == 'yes');
    // add to database
    $query = sprintf('INSERT INTO %sCALENDAR (EVENT_NAME, EVENT_TSTAMP, ' .
        'NOTIFY) VALUES ("%s", "%04d-%02d-%02d %02d:%02d:00", %d)',
        DB_TBL_PREFIX,
        mysql_real_escape_string($evt_name, $GLOBALS['DB']),
        $year, $month, $day,
        $evt_hour, $evt_min,
        $evt_notify);
    mysql_query($query, $GLOBALS['DB']);
}

// output table header
ob_start();
echo '<table id="day_calendar">';
echo '<tr id="day_calendar_header"><th colspan="2">';
echo '<a href="'. htmlspecialchars($_SERVER['PHP_SELF']) . '?t=' .
    strtotime('-1 day', $timestamp) . '">&lt;</a>  ';
echo date('l F d, Y', $timestamp);
echo '  <a href="'. htmlspecialchars($_SERVER['PHP_SELF']) . '?t=' .
    strtotime('+1 day', $timestamp) . '">&gt;</a>';
echo '</th></tr>';

// output cells
```

(continued)

(continued)

```php
for ($i = DAY_HR_START; $i <= DAY_HR_END; $i++)
{
    for ($j = 0; $j < 60; $j += 15)
    {
        echo '<tr>';

        if ($i < 12)
        {
            printf('<td class="time">%d:%02d %s</td>', $i, $j, 'AM');
        }
        else if ($i > 12)
        {
            printf('<td class="time">%d:%02d %s</td>', $i - 12,
                $j, 'PM');
        }
        else
        {
            printf('<td class="time">%d:%02d %s</td>', $i, $j, 'PM');
        }
        echo '<td class="event">';

        $query = sprintf('SELECT EVENT_NAME FROM %sCALENDAR WHERE ' .
            'EVENT_TSTAMP = "%04d-%02d-%02d %02d:%02d:00"',
            DB_TBL_PREFIX,
            $year, $month, $day,
            $i, $j);
        $result = mysql_query($query, $GLOBALS['DB']);

        if (mysql_num_rows($result))
        {
            while ($row = mysql_fetch_assoc($result))
            {
                echo '<div>' . htmlspecialchars($row['EVENT_NAME']) .
                    '</div>';
            }
        }
        else
        {
            echo ' ';
        }
        mysql_free_result($result);
        echo '</td>';
        echo '</tr>';
    }
}
echo '</table>';

// display month calendar
echo '<table id="calendar">';
echo '<tr id="calendar_header"><th colspan="7">';
echo '<a href="' . htmlspecialchars($_SERVER['PHP_SELF']) . '?t=' .
    strtotime('-1 month', $timestamp) . '">&lt;</a>  ';
echo date('F', $timestamp) . ' ' . $year;
```

```php
echo '  <a href="' . htmlspecialchars($_SERVER['PHP_SELF']) . '?t=' .
    strtotime('+1 month', $timestamp) . '">&gt;</a>';
echo '</th></tr>';
echo '<tr><th>Sun</th><th>Mon</th><th>Tue</th><th>Wed</th><th>Thu</th>' .
    '<th>Fri</th><th>Sat</th></tr>';
$current = 1;
while ($current <= $total_days)
{
    echo '<tr class="calendar_dates">';
    for ($i = 0; $i < 7; $i++)
    {
        if (($current == 1 && $i < $first_day_of_month) ||
            ($current > $total_days))
        {
            echo '<td class="empty"> </td>';
            continue;
        }
        echo '<td><a href="' . htmlspecialchars($_SERVER['PHP_SELF']) .
            '?t=' . mktime(0, 0, 0, $month, $current, $year) . '">' .
            $current . '</a></td>';
        $current++;
    }
    echo '</tr>';
}
echo '</table>';

// Form to add event
?>
<h2>Add Event</h2>
<form action="<?php echo htmlspecialchars($_SERVER['PHP_SELF']) . '?t=' .
 $timestamp; ?>" method="post">
 <table>
  <tr>
   <td class="label"><label for="evt_name">Event:</label></td>
   <td><input type="text" id="evt_name" name="evt_name"></td>
  </tr><tr>
   <td class="label"><label for="evt_hour">Time:</label></td>
   <td>
    <select name="evt_hour" id="evt_hour">
     <option value="12">12</option>
<?php

    for ($i = 1; $i < 12; $i++)
    {
        printf('<option value="%d">%02d</option>', $i, $i);
    }
?>
    </select> : <select name="evt_min">
<?php
    for ($i = 0; $i < 59; $i += 15)
    {
            printf('<option value="%d">%02d</option>', $i, $i);
    }
?>
```

(continued)

(continued)

```
      </select>
      <select name="evt_pm">
       <option value="no">AM</option>
       <option value="yes">PM</option>
      </select>
     </td>
    </tr><tr>
     <td class="label">Notify</td>
     <td>
      <input type="radio" name="evt_notify" id="evt_notify_yes" value="yes"
       checked="checked"/>
      <label for="evt_notify_yes">Yes</label>
      <input type="radio" name="evt_notify" id="evt_notify_no" value="no"/>
      <label for="evt_notify_no">No</label>
     </td>
    </tr><tr>
     <td></td>
     <td>
      <input type="hidden" name="submitted" value="true"/>
      <input type="submit" value="Add Event"/></td>
    </tr>
   </table>
  </form>

  <h2>Also Scheduled</h2>
  <?php
  // retrieve and display events that fall outside the daily-view hours
  $query = sprintf('SELECT EVENT_NAME, UNIX_TIMESTAMP(EVENT_TSTAMP) AS ' .
      'EVENT_TSTAMP FROM %sCALENDAR WHERE EVENT_TSTAMP NOT BETWEEN ' .
      '"%4d-%02d-%02d %02d:00:00" AND "%4d-%02d-%02d %02d:59:59" ORDER BY ' .
      'EVENT_TSTAMP ASC, EVENT_NAME ASC',
      DB_TBL_PREFIX,
      $year, $month, $day, DAY_HR_START,
      $year, $month, $day, DAY_HR_END);
  $result = mysql_query($query, $GLOBALS['DB']);

  echo '<ul>';
  if (mysql_num_rows($result))
  {
      while ($row = mysql_fetch_assoc($result))
      {
          echo '<li>' . date('h:i A - ', $row['EVENT_TSTAMP']) .
          htmlspecialchars($row['EVENT_NAME']) . '</li>';
      }
  }
  else
  {
      echo '<p><i>No other events scheduled</i></p>';
  }
  mysql_free_result($result);
  echo '</ul>';

  // link to download iCal file
```

```
echo '<p><a href="export.php">Export as iCalendar file</a></p>';


$GLOBALS['TEMPLATE']['content'] = ob_get_clean();

$GLOBALS['TEMPLATE']['extra_head'] = '<link rel="stylesheet"' .
    'type="text/css" href="css/daily.css"/>';

include '../templates/template-page.php';
?>
```

Sending Reminders

The project requirements also call for the ability for reminders to be sent when an event approaches. The first part of this is already in place with the form — selecting the option to be reminded or not. The preference is stored in the database for later examination. A separate script must be written to run periodically to check the database for upcoming events with the preference set. The script can then be scheduled the same way the mailing list scripts in chapter 3 were.

The script must know where to send the reminders so the e-mail address is provided as a constant. It must also determine the current date and time values to be able to construct the desired WHERE clause in the query. The query retrieves any events from the database that are scheduled to take place in the next hour from the current 15-minute timeframe, constructs an e-mail message, and mails it out.

Here is the complete code listing for public_files/notify.php. Because it will be run as a shell script instead of in response to a user request, the first line must be #! /usr/bin/php (or whichever path your installation's PHP interpreter resides at) and the file's execute permissions must be set correctly.

```
#! /usr/bin/php
<?php
include '../lib/common.php';
include '../lib/db.php';

// the e-mail address that will receive reminders
define('E-mail_ADDR', 'tboronczyk@example.com');

// determine the current date and time values
list($month, $day, $year, $hour, $minute, $am) = explode('/',
    date('m/d/Y/G/i/A'));

// retrieve upcoming events
$query = sprintf('SELECT EVENT_NAME, UNIX_TIMESTAMP(EVENT_TSTAMP) AS ' .
    'EVENT_TSTAMP FROM %sCALENDAR WHERE NOTIFY = 1 AND EVENT_TSTAMP BETWEEN ' .
    '"%4d-%02d-%02d %02d:%02d:00" AND "%4d-%02d-%02d %02d:%02d:00" ORDER BY ' .
    'EVENT_TSTAMP ASC, EVENT_NAME ASC',
    DB_TBL_PREFIX,
    $year, $month, $day, $hour, $minute,
    $year, $month, $day, $hour, $minute + 15);

$result = mysql_query($query, $GLOBALS['DB']);
if (mysql_num_rows($result))
{
    // construct the reminder message
```

(continued)

(continued)

```
    $msg = 'Don\'t forget!  You have the following events scheduled:' . "\n\n";
    while ($row = mysql_fetch_assoc($result))
    {
        $msg .= '  * ' . date('h:i A - ', $row['EVENT_TSTAMP']) .
            $row['EVENT_NAME'] . "\n";
    }

    // send the message
    mail(E-mail_ADDR, "Reminders for $month/$day/$year $hour:$minute $am", $mgs);
}
mysql_free_result($result);
mysql_close($GLOBALS['DB']);
?>
```

The script is written to look at events scheduled in the next hour from the current 15-minute timeframe, so it should be scheduled to run once every 15 minutes. You may refer back to chapter 3 if you need to review scheduling a script with `cron` or the Windows Scheduled Tasks applet.

Exporting the Calendar

The final feature of the personal calendar application is the ability to export the saved entries as an `iCalendar` file so they can easily be shared with others. `iCalendar` is a text-based format to exchange calendar information and is standardized as RFC 2445 (available online at `http://rfc.net/rfc2445 .txt`). The `iCalendar` format defines various components such as a calendar, an event, an alarm, busy times, and to-do lists. However, the only ones used in this application are the calendar, event, and alarm.

Some components may nest within other components and each component follows the schema `BEGIN:`*component*, *properties*, or other components then `END:`*component*. Each property is listed as an identifier and its value separated by a colon, one on each line. Each line terminates with a carriage return and a new line character (`\r\n`).

The `iCalendar` file begins with `BEGIN:VCALENDAR` and ends with `END:VCALENDAR`. Between the two delimiters are contained a few properties necessary to indicate which version of `iCalendar` is being adhered to and the collection of other components which populates the calendar.

```
BEGIN:VCALENDAR
VERSION:2.0
PRODID:-//Wrox//PHP Reuse//EN
...
END:VCALENDAR
```

The component that collects several properties to define an event is `VEVENT`. In particular, the properties I'm interested in are `DTSTART` and `DTEND`, which define the starting and ending time of an event and `SUMMARY`, which provides a brief textual description. Here's an example of an event listing:

```
BEGIN:VEVENT
DTSTART:20071228T103000
DTEND:20071228T110000
SUMMARY:Dentist Appointment
END:VEVENT
```

The alarm component VALARM may be nested within a VEVENT and contains information an iCalendar application uses to trigger reminders. The properties I'm interested in are ACTION and TRIGGER. The TRIGGER property defines when to trigger the alert and the ACTION property defines how the alarm is issued. The application can be instructed to display the alert (DISPLAY), e-mail it (E-mail), play a sound (AUDIO), or trigger some other program (PROCEDURE). Here's the sample event again, but this time with a defined alert component to issue an on-screen reminder an hour beforehand.

```
BEGIN:VEVENT
DTSTART:20071228T103000
DTEND:20071228T110000
SUMMARY:Dentist Appointment
BEGIN:VALARM
TRIGGER:-PT60M
SUMMARY:You have a dentist appointment in 1 hour
ACTION:DISPLAY
END:VALARM
END:VEVENT
```

Here is the complete code for public_files/export.php, which queries the database and constructs an iCalendar file. A listing of all the properties for the calendar, event, and alarm components is provided in Table 5-4.

```php
<?php
include '../lib/common.php';
include '../lib/db.php';

define('CRLF', "\r\n");

// retrieve all events
$query = sprintf('SELECT EVENT_NAME, UNIX_TIMESTAMP(EVENT_TSTAMP) AS ' .
    'EVENT_TSTAMP, NOTIFY FROM %sCALENDAR ORDER BY EVENT_TSTAMP ASC, ' .
    'EVENT_NAME ASC',
    DB_TBL_PREFIX);
$result = mysql_query($query, $GLOBALS['DB']);

// generate iCalendar
ob_start();
echo 'BEGIN:VCALENDAR' . CRLF;
echo 'PRODID:-//Wrox//PHP Reuse//EN' . CRLF;
echo 'VERSION:2.0' . CRLF;

while ($row = mysql_fetch_assoc($result))
{
    echo 'BEGIN:VEVENT' . CRLF;
    echo 'DTSTART:' . date('Ymd\THis', $row['EVENT_TSTAMP']) . CRLF;
    echo 'DTEND:' . date('Ymd\THis', strtotime('+30 minutes',
        $row['EVENT_TSTAMP'])) . CRLF;
    echo 'SUMMARY:' . htmlspecialchars($row['EVENT_NAME']) . CRLF;
    if ($row['NOTIFY'])
    {
        echo 'BEGIN:VALARM' . CRLF;
        echo 'ACTION:DISPLAY' . CRLF;
```

(continued)

(continued)

```
            echo 'SUMMARY:' . date('m/d/Y H:i A - ', $row['EVENT_TSTAMP']) .
                htmlspecialchars($row['EVENT_NAME']) . CRLF;
            echo 'TRIGGER:-PT60M' . CRLF;
            echo 'END:VALARM' . CRLF;
        }
        echo 'END:VEVENT' . CRLF;
    }
    mysql_free_result($result);

    echo 'END:VCALENDAR' . CRLF;
    $ics = ob_get_clean();
    // send iCalendar file to browser
    header('Content-Type: text/calendar');
    header('Content-Disposition: attachment; filename="export.ics";');
    header('Content-Transfer-Encoding: binary');
    header('Content-Length: ' . strlen($ics));
    echo $ics;

    mysql_close($GLOBALS['DB']);
    ?>
```

Table 5-4: Properties for the iCalendar Calendar, Event, and Alarm Components

Component/Property	Description
VCALENDAR	Core object that contains all other properties and components that define the calendar
CALSCALE	Sets the calendar scale, default is GREGORIAN
METHOD	Defines the method associated with the calendar (used by the iCalendar Transport-Independent Interoperability Protocol)
PRODID	(Required) The product identifier of the application used to generate the iCalendar file
VERSION	(Required) iCalendar version
VEVENT	Component that groups properties to describe an event
ATTACH	Associates an external document with the event
ATTENDEE	Specifies an event participant
CATEGORIES	Associates the component with a particular category for organizational purposes
CLASS	Sets the access scope for the event, default is PUBLIC
COMMENT	Associates a short comment with the event
CONTACT	Associates contact information with the event
CREATED	Specifies the date and time the event was created

Component/Property	Description
DESCRIPTION	Provides long description of an event
DTEND	Specifies the date and time the event ends
DTSTAMP	Specifies the date and time the event was created
DTSTART	(Required) Specifies the date and time the event begins
DURATION	Specifies the duration of the event (reoccurring events)
EXDATE	Specifies an exception date/time for the event (reoccurring events)
EXRULE	Defines a repeating pattern rule (reoccurring events)
GEO	Specifies the geographical coordinates (latitude and longitude) where the event will take place
LAST-MOD	Specifies the date and time the information associated with the event was last modified
LOCATION	Specifies the location where the event will take place
ORGANIZER	Specifies the organizer of an event (group calendars)
PRIORITY	Specifies the relative priority of the event
RDATE	Specifies the dates and times for a reoccurrence set (reoccurring events)
RECURRENCE-ID	Used with SEQ and UID to identify a specific instance of a reoccurring event (reoccurring events)
RELATED	Specifies the relationship between an alarm trigger and the beginning or end of the event, default is START
RESOURCES	Specifies equipment or resources needed at the event
RRULE	Specifies a repeating pattern rule (reoccurring events)
SEQ	Specifies the revision number in a sequence of revisions to the event
STATUS	Specifies the completion or confirmation status for an event (group calendars)
SUMMARY	Provides a short summary of the event
TRANSP	Specifies whether the time occupied by an event is marked "busy" or not
UID	Specifies a globally unique identifier
URL	Associates a URL with the event
VALARM	Component that groups properties to define an alarm
ACTION	(Required) Specifies which action to invoke when triggering an alarm (may be AUDIO, DISPLAY, EMAIL or PROCEDURE)
ATTACH	Associates an external document with the alarm

Table continued on following page

Component/Property	Description
DESCRIPTION	(Required if ACTION is DISPLAY or EMAIL) Provides a more complete description of an event than the SUMMARY property
DURATION	Specifies the duration of the alarm
SUMMARY	(Required if ACTION is EMAIL) Provides a short summary for the alarm
TRIGGER	(Required) Specifies when an alarm will be triggered

After the calendar information has been exported as an iCalendar file, it can be shared with others. Figures 5-3 and 5-4 show the information after it has been imported into a couple different desktop calendar programs. Figure 5-3 shows it in Microsoft Windows Calendar, which ships with its new Vista operating system; Figure 5-4 shows it in the Mozilla Thunderbird program running the Lightning integrated calendar extension.

Figure 5-3

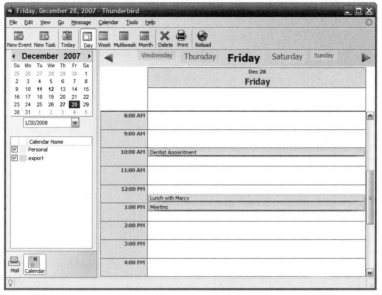

Figure 5-4

Summary

Calendars primarily help people organize when and where they need to be. However, they can also be used as a form of navigation. In this chapter, you created a personal calendar application, which records events and displays them in a day-view calendar and also uses a month-view calendar to aid in navigating to different dates. The web-based calendar also allows you to export the event information in the iCalendar format so you can easily share it with others.

In the following chapter, you'll build an online file manager utility. Not only will it allow you to more easily manage files on a remote server; it also provides an opportunity to learn about Ajax and how it affects a user's experience with an interface.

6

Ajax File Manager

A file manager allows a user to do exactly what its name implies — manage files. All graphical desktop systems come with some type of file manager. In fact, you're probably familiar with some of the well-known managers such as Microsoft Explorer on the Windows platform, Finder on Mac OS X, and the open-source Konqueror and Nautilus on Linux. These may not be very flashy and exciting programs, but they do help people perform essential file-related tasks nevertheless. Users quickly grow accustomed to their system's file manager and using it quickly becomes second nature.

However, the same user who feels comfortable managing local files on his or her machine might feel uneasy downloading a new program to do the same tasks on a remote server. I doubt photo-sharing web sites like Flickr would be as popular as they are if the only way members could upload photos was by using an FTP client. Instead, sites often offer a variety of ways to transfer and manage files — one of which is a web-based file manager.

In this chapter, you will build a web-based file manager that will allow users to transfer files between the server and their computers. Users will also be able to rename and delete files and create, rename, and delete directories. The utility can be integrated into your web site to offer people more flexibility in how they manage their remote files.

Design of the Ajax File Manager

In this chapter, you'll build your own file manager to allow users to manage files and directories on a remote web server. The core requirements are pretty straightforward; users will be able to:

❏ Upload files from a local computer to the remote server

❏ Download files from the server to their computer

❏ Rename or delete a remote file

❏ Create a new remote directory

❑   Rename or delete a remote directory

❑   Navigate the directory structure in an intuitive manner

The utility presents a scrollable table listing the remote directories and files. Each entry shows a small mime-type icon based on the file's extension, the name, the size, and the date it was uploaded. Below the listing is a series of action icons forming a menu to perform various tasks (see Figure 6-1).

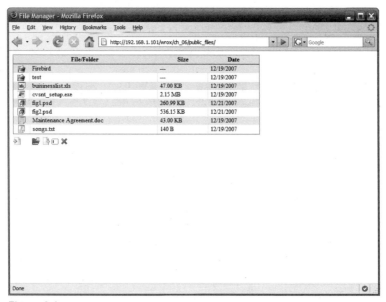

Figure 6-1

JavaScript is used heavily on the client-side to make the file manager more user-friendly. The user will be able to see changes to the remote file system in real time without having to reload the entire web page. He or she will perform actions by selecting the target file or directory from the listing and then clicking the appropriate action icon. If more information is needed to complete a task (such as the new file name for a rename) a form will be displayed with JavaScript alongside the action icons. Figure 6-2 shows the detail of a file upload.

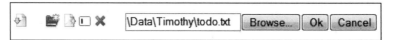

Figure 6-2

JavaScript and Ajax

Hiding and displaying the forms alongside the action icons is something that can be accomplished with basic JavaScript and will certainly be discussed later in this chapter. However, more complex scripting is needed for the file listing to reflect the state of the remote directory without requiring a full page reload. For this you must have a basic understanding of Ajax.

Not too many years ago a developer used to be able to get by with just knowing HTML. Then forms and CGI came about, followed by JavaScript and CSS. The simple days are long gone; now web sites are offering the same functionality that used to be the exclusive domain of desktop applications. You need to know a whole slew of different technologies and languages just to be even a moderately capable web developer.

A new buzzword, Ajax (which stands for *Asynchronous JavaScript And XML*), has surfaced in the past few years referring to the use of JavaScript to dynamically update a page's contents. Many web applications use JavaScript in this manner to improve functionality and add special eye-candy effects. It's not really a new concept, however; in fact developers who have been around a while may know it by another name — DHTML (Dynamic HTML).

The basic underpinning of the Ajax paradigm is the ability to make an HTTP request behind the scenes while a visitor is viewing a page. The web server responds with a message that JavaScript then parses and uses to update the page by replacing content, changing styles, and so on. Oftentimes the response message is sent as XML, but it can also be an HTML fragment, plain text, or even JavaScript code. You may find it easier to send responses as one of the latter three and use XML only when it's really necessary.

Please keep in mind that this is a PHP book, not a JavaScript book. JavaScript is a programming language in its own right and I can't delve into all of its intricacies. I'll cover just what you're sure to need. I will offer this advice, though: be critical. A lot of resources are available to help you learn JavaScript. However, for some reason many of them are filled with meaningless hype or present bad code. Perhaps this is because of the language's checkered past. My rule of thumb is to run away screaming in the opposite direction if you see browser detection performed by checking the user agent string or if the author says JavaScript is a lighter version of Java (which is utterly wrong). I recommend ppk on JavaScript written by Peter-Paul Koch and published by New Riders for solid, practical and sound information.

The XMLHttpRequest Object

The JavaScript implementation in most modern browsers uses the XMLHttpRequest object to transact the HTTP request, but some older versions of Internet Explorer do this through some version of the Microsoft.XmlHttp ActiveX object. They're all used pretty much the same way but getting the initial reference to the correct object is the tricky part. As such, this is a prime candidate for reusable code.

Save the following JavaScript function as public_file/js/ajax.js to encapsulate the logic of identifying which object is available and to return an instance reference:

```
function createXMLHTTPObject()
{
    if (typeof XMLHttpRequest != 'undefined')
    {
        return new XMLHttpRequest();
    }
    else if (window.ActiveXObject)
    {
        var axo = [
            'Microsoft.XmlHttp',
```

(continued)

(continued)

```
            'MSXML2.XmlHttp',
            'MSXML2.XmlHttp.3.0',
            'MSXML2.XmlHttp.4.0',
            'MSXML2.XmlHttp.5.0'
        ];

        for (var i = axo.length - 1; i > -1; i--)
        {
            try
            {
                httpObj = new ActiveXObject(axo[i]);
                return httpObj;
            }
            catch(e) {}
        }
    }

    throw new Error('XMLHTTP not supported');
}
```

The function checks first whether the more widely used XMLHttpRequest is available. If so, it returns an instance of it to the calling code. Otherwise the code checks for one of the various versions of the Microsoft.XmlHttp ActiveX objects. An exception will be thrown if no suitable objects are available to the client.

Communicating with the server from the client is easy once the correct reference is obtained. Table 6-1 shows the object's methods and Table 6-2 shows its properties.

Table 6-1: XMLHttpRequest **Methods**

Method	Description
abort()	Cancel the request
getAllResponseHeaders()	Retrieve all the HTTP response headers
getResponseHeader(name)	Retrieve the value of a particular header
open(method, url, async[, username [, password]])	Establish a connection between the client and server
	method specifies which HTTP method will be used (that is, GET, POST, and so on).
	url is the URL of the requested resource.
	async is a Boolean value indicating whether the request will be made asynchronously or not.
	username and password are optional arguments when authentication is required to access the resource.
send(data)	Send the request
setRequestHeader(name, value)	Set a header's value

Table 6-2: `XMLHttpRequest` **Properties**

Property	Description
onreadystatechange	Event handler assigned to fire each time `readyState` changes
readyState	The current request of the state: 0 Uninitialized — the object has been created but `open()` hasn't been called 1 Loaded — `open()` has been called but `send()` has not 2 Loaded — `send()` has been called and the request's headers have been received 3 Interactive — the response is being received 4 Completed
responseText	The response as text
responseXML	The response as XML
status	The HTTP response code (that is, `200`, `404`, and so on)
statusText	The text accompanying the request's HTTP response code (that is, `OK`, `File not found`, and so on)

To perform an Ajax request, the `onreadystatechange` property is assigned a function as an event handler, which contains the code to parse the response coming back from the server. The handler must check to make sure the value of `readyState` is 4, which means the request has completed. Other `readyState` values indicate different stages in the request process as identified previously in Table 6-2.

The connection itself is initiated by calling the object's `open()` method which accepts the request method, the URL and whether or not the connection should be asynchronous (`true`) or synchronous/blocking (`false`). You will almost always use `true` for this argument or otherwise the user will be blocked from anything on the page until the request has completed. Keep in mind as well that the URL *must* be in same domain from which the original page was requested. This is by design and was done as a security precaution. The `send()` method then sends the request to the server.

Here is some code to illustrate this process:

```
<script type="text/javascript" src="js/ajax.js"></script>
<script type="text/javascript">
window.onload = function()
{
    window.httpObj = createXMLHTTPObject();
}

function doRequest()
```

(continued)

141

(continued)

```
{
    window.httpObj.onreadystatechange = function()
    {
        if (window.httpObj.readyState == 4 && window.httpObj.responseText)
        {
            // code to parse the response and update the page's content
            // goes here
        }
    }

    var url = 'process.php?param1=value+1&param2=value+2&nocache=' +
        (new Date()).getTime();
    window.httpObj.open('GET', url , true);
    window.httpObj.send(null);
}
</script>
```

I passed `null` as an argument to `send()` in the example, because I used the GET method. The data was provided as parameters in the URL string. To use POST instead, set the appropriate HTTP headers with `setRequestHandler()` and provide the encoded data to `send()`. Here is an example using POST:

```
function doRequest()
{
    ...
    var data = 'param1=value+1&param2=value+2';
    var url = 'process.php?cache=' + (new Date()).getTime();

    window.httpObj.open('POST', url, true);
    window.httpObj.setRequestHeader('Content-type',
        'application/x-www-form-urlencoded');
    window.httpObj.setRequestHeader('Content-length', data.length);
    window.httpObj.setRequestHeader('Connection', 'close');

    window.httpObj.send(data);
}
```

I recommend appending a timestamp to the URL regardless if you're sending the information via GET or POST. This ensures the URL is unique and prevents the request from being cached by the browser or any intermediate proxies.

Code and Code Explanation

Now that you have a basic understanding of how JavaScript can make a behind-the-scenes request, I will continue with the file manager's code. As I progress you will see how all this integrates into the project so the entire page does not need to be reloaded after each action.

Main Interface

The main interface must present the user with a listing of files and directories on the server and a way to manage them. HTML provides the structure while PHP and JavaScript will work hand-in-hand to add the functionality.

The initial HTML code doesn't display any file listing content. Instead, a `div` element can be assigned the id `file_datagrid` and act as a placeholder. The JavaScript `XMLHttpRequest` object will send a request to PHP and retrieve an HTML snippet showing the information. The snippet will then be assigned to the `div`'s `innerHTML` property to be displayed. A new snippet will be requested each time something changes, saving the user from needless page reloads.

```
<div class="datagrid" id="file_datagrid"></div>
```

`img` tags will display the action icons on the page which users will be able to click to download the selected file or open a directory, create a new directory, upload a file, and rename and delete entries. They aren't surrounded by a tags as I will be assigning `onclick` handlers to turn them into clickable elements. Instead, they will be assigned appropriate `id`s.

```
<img src="img/open.gif" id="btn_open" title="Download/Open" alt="Download/Open"/>
<img src="img/new.gif" id="btn_new_folder" title="New" alt="New"/>
<img src="img/upload.gif" id="btn_upload" title="Upload" alt="Upload"/>
<img src="img/rename.gif" id="btn_rename" title="Rename" alt="Rename"/>
<img src="img/delete.gif" id="btn_delete" title="Delete" alt="Delete"/>
```

Certain actions require more information to be collected from the user to be processed successfully. Specifically, the `new` action needs a form to accept a name for the new directory, the `upload` action needs a form to accept the file and the `rename` action needs a form to accept the new name for a file or directory. Each form associated with an action should have its `display` property set to `none` so it is hidden. JavaScript will change the style to make the form visible when it's needed.

```
<form action="process.php?new" id="form_new" method="post"
 style="display:none;">
 <div>
  <input type="text" name="name" id="form_new_name"/>
  <input type="submit" id="form_new_submit" value="Ok"/>
  <input type="reset" id="form_new_reset" value="Cancel"/>
 </div>
</form>
<form action="process.php?rename" id="form_rename" method="post"
 style="display:none;">
 <div>
  <input type="text" name="name" id="form_rename_name"/>
  <input type="submit" id="form_rename_submit" value="Ok"/>
  <input type="reset" id="form_rename_reset" value="Cancel"/>
 </div>
</form>
<form action="upload.php" id="form_upload" method="post"
 enctype="multipart/form-data" style="display:none;">
 <div>
```

(continued)

143

(continued)

```
      <input type="file" name="file" id="form_upload_name" />
      <input type="hidden" name="directory" id="form_upload_directory" value=""/>
      <input type="submit" id="form_upload_submit" value="Ok"/>
      <input type="reset" id="form_upload_reset" value="Cancel"/>
    </div>
  </form>
```

A hidden `iframe` element should exist as well which will be used when uploading a new file. The idea is that the `form_upload` form will target the `iframe` when it submits, which in turn will load the response. The response will contain JavaScript code which will be executed by the browser and alert the user when the upload is complete. This gives the illusion of uploading the file in the background.

```
<iframe id="my_iframe" name="my_iframe" style="display:none;"></iframe>
```

Here is the entire code listing for the main interface which I have saved as `public_files/index.html`:

```
<!DOCTYPE html PUBLIC "-//W3C//DTD XHTML 1.0 Transitional//EN"
  "http://www.w3.org/TR/xhtml1/DTD/xhtml1-transitional.dtd">
<html xmlns="http://www.w3.org/1999/xhtml" xml:lang="en" lang="en">
  <head>
    <title>File Manager</title>
    <script type="text/javascript" src="js/ajax.js"></script>
    <script type="text/javascript" src="js/filemanager.js"></script>
    <link rel="stylesheet" href="css/styles.css"/>
  </head>
  <body>
    <div class="datagrid" id="file_datagrid"></div>
    <div id="toolbar">
      <img src="img/open.gif" id="btn_open" title="Download/Open"
        alt="Download/Open"/>
      <img src="img/new.gif" id="btn_new_folder" title="New" alt="New"/>
      <img src="img/upload.gif" id="btn_upload" title="Upload" alt="Upload"/>
      <img src="img/rename.gif" id="btn_rename" title="Rename" alt="Rename"/>
      <img src="img/delete.gif" id="btn_delete" title="Delete" alt="Delete"/>
      <form action="process.php?new" id="form_new" method="post"
        style="display:none;">
        <div>
          <input type="text" name="name" id="form_new_name"/>
          <input type="submit" id="form_new_submit" value="Ok"/>
          <input type="reset" id="form_new_reset" value="Cancel"/>
        </div>
      </form>
      <form action="process.php?rename" id="form_rename" method="post"
        style="display:none;">
        <div>
          <input type="text" name="name" id="form_rename_name"/>
          <input type="submit" id="form_rename_submit" value="Ok"/>
          <input type="reset" id="form_rename_reset" value="Cancel"/>
        </div>
      </form>
      <form action="upload.php" id="form_upload" method="post"
        enctype="multipart/form-data" style="display:none;">
```

```
    <div>
      <input type="file" name="file" id="form_upload_name" />
      <input type="hidden" name="directory" id="form_upload_directory" value=""/>
      <input type="submit" id="form_upload_submit" value="Ok"/>
      <input type="reset" id="form_upload_reset" value="Cancel"/>
    </div>
    </form>
    <iframe id="my_iframe" name="my_iframe" style="display:none;"></iframe>
  </div>
 </body>
</html>
```

The `js/helper.js` code is referenced within the head section of the HTML file, which makes the function to obtain an `XMLHttpRequest` object available. Other JavaScript will be stored in `js/filemanager.js`; this file is referenced as well. The style directives formatting the file listing table and toolbar are stored in the `css/styles.css` file. Here are the contents:

```
a
{
    color: #06C;
}


a img
{
    border: none;
}

td
{
    vertical-align: top;
}

div.datagrid
{
    border: 1px solid #999;
    height: 250px;
    overflow: auto;
    width: 530px;
}

div.datagrid table
{
    border-collapse: collapse;
    font-size: 80%;
    width: 100%;
}
```

(continued)

(continued)

```
div.datagrid thead
{
    background: #EEE;
}

div.datagrid thead th
{
    border-bottom: 1px solid #000;
}

div.datagrid tbody tr
{
    cursor: pointer;
}

div.datagrid tbody td
{
    padding:1px 5px;
}

div.datagrid a
{
  display: block;
  text-decoration: none;
}

tr.oddrow
{
    background-color: #EFEFFF;
}

tr.evenrow td
{
    border-left: 1px solid #EFEFFF;
}

tr.selectedRow
{
  background-color: #C3C3FE;
}

#toolbar
{
    margin-top: 5px;
}

#toolbar img
{
    cursor: pointer;
}
```

```
#toolbar *
{
    float: left;
    padding-right: 3px;
}

#btn_open,
#btn_delete
{
    margin-right: 20px;
}
```

Client-Side Functionality

With the structure and basic presentation complete, I will now review the client-side logic and PHP code that provides the file manager's functionality.

JavaScript Events

Knowing which JavaScript events to hook into and assigning appropriate code to the event handlers is the key to making the page dynamic. The first event triggered when the page has finished loading in the user's browser is the `window` object's `onload` *event*. As such, this is typically a good place to initialize global variables and linking other callback functions to events. Wiring the majority of your events like this instead of mixing `onevents` in the elements allows you to keep JavaScript logic separate from your HTML code, which in turn makes everything easier to maintain.

```
window.onload = function()
{
    window.directory = '/';  // current directory viewed
    window.filename = '';    // currently selected file

    document.getElementById('btn_open').onclick = openSelected;

    document.getElementById('btn_new_folder').onclick = showNewFolder;
    document.getElementById('form_new_submit').onclick = doNewFolder;
    document.getElementById('form_new_reset').onclick = hideForms;

    document.getElementById('btn_upload').onclick = showUploadFile;
document.getElementById('form_upload').target = 'my_iframe';
    document.getElementById('form_upload_submit').onclick = doUploadFile;
document.getElementById('form_upload_reset').onclick = hideForms;

    document.getElementById('btn_rename').onclick = showRename;
    document.getElementById('form_rename_submit').onclick = doRename;
    document.getElementById('form_rename_reset').onclick = hideForms;

    document.getElementById('btn_delete').onclick = doDelete;

    refreshFilesList();
}
```

The global variables `directory` and `filename` appear at the start of the callback function; `directory` will track the current directory viewed by the user and `filename` will store the name of a selected entry so the user can perform an action on the file or directory. Then the functions that handle the click events for the action icons and forms buttons are assigned. A call to `refreshFilesList()` is made which loads the file listing.

Retrieving the File Listing

The `refreshFilesList()` function is responsible for initiating the Ajax request to fill the `file_datagrid` div element. The listing is generated by PHP and sent as an HTML fragment, which will then be placed within the div using its `innerHTML` property. You've already seen how to transact an Ajax request previously in this chapter, so the code should be easy to follow.

```
function refreshFilesList()
{
    hideForms();

    var url = 'process.php?action=list&dir=' + window.directory + '&nocache=' +
        (new Date()).getTime();

    window.httpObj = createXMLHTTPObject();
    window.httpObj.open('GET', url , true);

    window.httpObj.onreadystatechange = function()
    {
        if (window.httpObj.readyState == 4 && window.httpObj.responseText)
        {
            // populate the fields
            document.getElementById('file_datagrid').innerHTML =
                window.httpObj.responseText;

            window.filename = '';  // selected file
        }
    }

    window.httpObj.send(null);
}
```

Note that the currently viewed directory is sent as a parameter to the PHP script so it knows what to include in the listing. Also remember you need to track the entry in the file listing when the user selects a file or directory to perform an operation to formulate other Ajax calls. Each time the listing is loaded you should clear this so `window.filename` is set to an empty string.

Some actions need to make the forms visible (such as renaming an entry or uploading a new file). Since the file listing will be refreshed each time one of these actions is performed, it makes sense to call some code that ensures all the forms are hidden again from within the `refreshFilesList()` function. I've placed this code in `hideForms()`.

```
function hideForms()
{
    document.getElementById('form_new').style.display = 'none';
    document.getElementById('form_rename').style.display = 'none';
    document.getElementById('form_upload').style.display = 'none';
}
```

Helper Functions

There are a few additional helper functions you need to add to your JavaScript code and now seems just as good a time as any. The following couple of functions don't effect the functioning of the core actions, but provide the user the ability to select a file or directory from the file listing and have visual feedback when they hover over a listing item.

When an item is selected, its name is placed in `filename` and its class name should be set to `selectedRow` so that it can take on styling provided in the CSS file. This is what the `selectTableRow()` function accomplishes. The `unselectTableRow()` function clears the `filename` property and removes any element associations with the `selectedRow` class.

```
function selectTableRow(data, e)
{
    unselectTableRow();
    e.type = e.className;
    e.className = 'selectedRow';
    window.filename = data;
}

function unselectTableRow()
{
    for (i = 0, s = getElementsByClass('selectedRow'); i < s.length; i++)
    {
        s[i].className = s[i].type;
    }

    hideForms();
}
```

JavaScript doesn't have a method to retrieve elements by class name as it does for ids, so a custom function is needed to do this. The `getElementsByClass()` function accepts a class name to search for and returns an array containing references to all the elements within it.

```
function getElementsByClass(search)
{
    var classElements = new Array();
    var els = document.getElementsByTagName('*');
    var pattern = new RegExp('(^|\\s)' + search + '(\\s|$)');

    for (var i = 0, j = 0; i < els.length; i++)
    {
        if (pattern.test(els[i].className))
        {
            classElements[j] = els[i];
            j++;
        }
    }

    return classElements;
}
```

`highlightTableRow()` and `unhighlightTableRow()` add visual feedback when the mouse moves over entries in the table by changing the background color. The color is specified when the cursor is placed over the entry and cleared when it's moved off.

149

```
function highlightTableRow(e)
{
    if (e.className != 'selectedRow')
    {
        e.style.backgroundColor = '#C3C3FE';
    }
}

function unhighlightTableRow(e)
{
    e.style.backgroundColor - '',
}
```

Uploading New Files

Remember that the file upload form is submitted normally but targets the hidden iframe. This enables the user to upload a file without the entire page refreshing and the upload appears to take place behind the scenes. Even though the iframe is hidden, the document it loads will still be parsed by the browser so it's possible to notify the user to the success or failure of the upload by returning JavaScript.

If the upload is successful, the JavaScript loaded in to the iframe needs to be parent.refreshFilesList(). refreshFilesList() will update the file and directory listing and hide the upload form. It isn't visible from within the iframe initially so we need to instruct JavaScript to look outside the frame by using parent.

If for some reason the upload fails, then the iframe JavaScript calls parent.uploadFailed().

```
function uploadFailed()
{
    alert('Failed to upload file.');
    hideForms();
}
```

showRenameForm() makes the form_upload form visible so you are able to collect more information from the user. The actual upload is performed when the user submits the form so the code associated with doUpload() just needs to set the hidden field with the current directory value prior to the form's submission.

```
function showUploadFile()
{
    hideForms();
    document.getElementById('form_upload').reset();
    document.getElementById('form_upload').style.display = '';
}

function doUpload()
{
    document.getElementById('form_upload_directory').value = window.directory;
}
```

Creating New Directories

Two JavaScript functions provide the client-side functionality necessary to create a new directory. The first, showNewFolder(), initiates the process by making the form_new form visible so the user can enter the new directory's name:

```
function showNewFolder()
{
    hideForms();
    document.getElementById('form_new_name').value = '';
    document.getElementById('form_new').style.display = '';
}
```

The doNewFolder() function is called when the user clicks the form's submit button. It transacts the Ajax request and refreshes the file listing if the directory was created successfully (it knows this because the processing script will return OK). If there is a problem, a message is shown. Because this function takes over the responsibility of handling the form submission, it should return false to prevent the browser from submitting the form and reloading the page.

```
function doNewFolder()
{
    var url = 'process.php?action=new&dir=' + window.directory + '&name=' +
        document.getElementById('form_new_name').value + '&nocache=' +
        (new Date()).getTime();

    window.httpObj = createXMLHTTPObject();
    window.httpObj.open('GET', url , true);

    window.httpObj.onreadystatechange = function()
    {
        if (window.httpObj.readyState == 4 && window.httpObj.responseText)
        {
            if (window.httpObj.responseText == 'OK')
            {
                refreshFilesList();
            }
            else
            {
                alert('Unable to create directory.');
            }
        }
    }

    window.httpObj.send(null);
    return false;
}
```

Renaming a File or Directory

The code to rename an entry is very similar to that responsible for creating new directories. showRenameForm() makes the form_rename form visible, so you are able to collect more information from the user.

However, you don't want the form to show if the user has not selected an entry or if the entry is the parent directory (indicated by ..) so the function should return in either case. And whereas just `window.directory` is passed when creating a new folder, you must also pass `window.filename` and the new name for the target in the request's parameters.

```
function showRename()
{
    // don't rename a parent directory or if no file is selected
    if (window.filename == '..' || window.filename == '')
    {
        return;
    }

    hideForms();
    document.getElementById('form_rename_name').value = window.filename;
    document.getElementById('form_rename').style.display = '';
}

function doRename()
{
    var url = 'process.php?action=rename&dir=' + window.directory +
        '&oldfile=' + window.filename + '&newfile=' +
        document.getElementById('form_rename_name').value + '&nocache=' +
        (new Date()).getTime();

    window.httpObj = createXMLHTTPObject();
    window.httpObj.open('GET', url , true);

    window.httpObj.onreadystatechange = function()
    {
        if (window.httpObj.readyState == 4 && window.httpObj.responseText)
        {
            if (window.httpObj.responseText == 'OK')
            {
                refreshFilesList();
            }
            else
            {
                alert('Unable to rename entry.');
            }
        }
    }

    window.httpObj.send(null);
    return false;
}
```

Deleting a File or Directory

There is no form to show when deleting an entry so there is only one JavaScript function for this piece of functionality. `doDelete()` first checks to make sure a file or directory has been selected and that it is not the parent directory. It then confirms the user actually intends to delete the entry before sending the request to the server. The file listing is refreshed if the deletion is successful or an alert message is shown.

```
function doDelete()
{
    // don't delete a parent directory or if no file is selected
    if (window.filename == '..' || window.filename == '')
    {
        return;
    }

    if (!confirm('Are you sure you wish to delete?'))
    {
        return;
    }

    var url = 'process.php?action=delete&dir=' + window.directory + '&file=' +
        window.filename + '&nocache=' + (new Date()).getTime();

    window.httpObj = createXMLHTTPObject();
    window.httpObj.open('GET', url , true);

    window.httpObj.onreadystatechange = function()
    {
        if (window.httpObj.readyState == 4 && window.httpObj.responseText)
        {
            if (window.httpObj.responseText == 'OK')
            {
                refreshFilesList();
            }
            else
            {
                alert('Unable to delete entry.');
            }
        }
    }

    httpObj.send(null);
}
```

Downloading a File and Opening a Directory

What happens when the user clicks on the btn_open icon depends on what type of entry he or she selected in the file listing. In the case of a directory, the new working directory needs to be validated and assigned to window.directory. The entry is validated and the window.location property is set to the download URL when retrieving a file.

The openSelected() function passes the information to the server and receives back an encoded JavaScript object which can be evaluated (with eval). The object's properties can be inspected to determine the entry type and what the appropriate course of action is — either refresh or download. It's much easier to ask the server if the requested entry is a directory or file at this point (and probably more secure) than having to track it in JavaScript from the beginning. The response object's retType property will be set to directory to indicate the entry is a directory or file to indicate a file.

If the user is opening a folder other than the new working directory, the name is set in window.directory and the file list is refreshed. Otherwise the window's location property is set to the download script, causing the browser to download the file.

```
function openSelected()
{
    var url = 'process.php?action=open&dir=' + window.directory + '&file=' +
        window.filename + '&nocache=' + (new Date()).getTime();

    window.httpObj = createXMLHTTPObject();
    window.httpObj.open('GET', url , true);

    window.httpObj.onreadystatechange = function()
    {
        if (window.httpObj.readyState == 4 && window.httpObj.responseText)
        {
            var result = eval('(' + window.httpObj.responseText + ')');
            if (result.retType == 'directory')
            {
                window.directory = result.directory;
                refreshFilesList();
            }
            else if (result.retType == 'file')
            {
                window.location = 'download.php?&dir=' + window.directory +
                    '&file=' + window.filename + '&nocache=' +
                    (new Date()).getTime();
            }
            else
            {
                alert('Unknown error.');
            }
        }
    }

    window.httpObj.send(null);
    return false;
}
```

Here is the complete code listing for js/filemanager.js:

```
// retrieve all elements of a given class
function getElementsByClass(search)
{
    var classElements = new Array();
    var els = document.getElementsByTagName('*');
    var pattern = new RegExp('(^|\\s)' + search + '(\\s|$)');

    for (var i = 0, j = 0; i < els.length; i++)
    {
        if (pattern.test(els[i].className))
        {
            classElements[j] = els[i];
```

```
                j++;
            }
        }

        return classElements;
    }

    // mark a row as selected
    function selectTableRow(data, e)
    {
        unselectTableRow();
        e.type = e.className;
        e.className = 'selectedRow';
        window.filename = data;
    }

    // unselect row
    function unselectTableRow()
    {
        for (i = 0, s = getElementsByClass('selectedRow'); i < s.length; i++)
        {
            s[i].className = s[i].type;
        }

        hideForms();
    }

    // highlight a table row on mouseover
    function highlightTableRow(e)
    {
        if (e.className != 'selectedRow')
        {
            e.style.backgroundColor = '#C3C3FE';
        }
    }

    // remove the highlighting on mouseout
    function unhighlightTableRow(e)
    {
        e.style.backgroundColor = '';
    }

    // register event handlers and set initial view
    window.onload = function()
    {
        window.directory = '/';  // current directory viewed
        window.filename = '';    // currently selected file

        // event handlers
        document.getElementById('btn_open').onclick = openSelected;

        document.getElementById('btn_new_folder').onclick = showNewFolder;
        document.getElementById('form_new_submit').onclick = doNewFolder;
        document.getElementById('form_new_reset').onclick = hideForms;
```

(continued)

(continued)

```javascript
    document.getElementById('btn_upload').onclick = showUploadFile;
    document.getElementById('form_upload').target = 'my_iframe';
    document.getElementById('form_upload_submit').onclick = doUploadFile;
    document.getElementById('form_upload_reset').onclick = hideForms;

    document.getElementById('btn_rename').onclick = showRename;
    document.getElementById('form_rename_submit').onclick = doRename;
    document.getElementById('form_rename_reset').onclick = hideForms;

    document.getElementById('btn_delete').onclick = doDelete;

    // load the file listing
    refreshFilesList();
}

// retrieve display of files and directories
function refreshFilesList()
{
    hideForms();

    var url = 'process.php?action=list&dir=' + window.directory + '&nocache=' +
        (new Date()).getTime();

    window.httpObj = createXMLHTTPObject();
    window.httpObj.open('GET', url , true);

    window.httpObj.onreadystatechange = function()
    {
        if (window.httpObj.readyState == 4 && window.httpObj.responseText)
        {
            // populate the fields
            document.getElementById('file_datagrid').innerHTML =
                window.httpObj.responseText;

            window.filename = '';   // selected file
        }
    }

    window.httpObj.send(null);
}

// hide all input forms
function hideForms()
{
    document.getElementById('form_new').style.display = 'none';
    document.getElementById('form_rename').style.display = 'none';
    document.getElementById('form_upload').style.display = 'none';
}

// alert user the upload failed
function uploadFailed()
{
    alert('Failed to upload file.');
```

```
        hideForms();
    }

    // show form to upload a new file
    function showUploadFile()
    {
        hideForms();
        document.getElementById('form_upload').reset();
        document.getElementById('form_upload').style.display = '';
    }

    // set form_upload_directory (allow browser to handle form
    // submission)
    function doUploadFile()
    {
        document.getElementById('form_upload_directory').value = window.directory;
    }

    // show form to create new folder
    function showNewFolder()
    {
        hideForms();
        document.getElementById('form_new_name').value = '';
        document.getElementById('form_new').style.display = '';
    }

    // create a new folder
    function doNewFolder()
    {
        var url = 'process.php?action=new&dir=' + window.directory + '&name=' +
            document.getElementById('form_new_name').value + '&nocache=' +
            (new Date()).getTime();

        window.httpObj = createXMLHTTPObject();
        window.httpObj.open('GET', url , true);

        window.httpObj.onreadystatechange = function()
        {
            if (window.httpObj.readyState == 4 && window.httpObj.responseText)
            {
                if (window.httpObj.responseText == 'OK')
                {
                    refreshFilesList();
                }
                else
                {
                    alert('Unable to create directory.');
                }
            }
        }

        window.httpObj.send(null);
```

(continued)

(continued)

```
        return false;
    }

    // show form to rename a file or directory
    function showRename()
    {
        // don't rename a parent directory or if no file is selected
        if (window.filename == '..' || window.filename == '')
        {
            return;
        }

        hideForms();
        document.getElementById('form_rename_name').value = window.filename;
        document.getElementById('form_rename').style.display = '';
    }

    // rename the file or directory
    function doRename()
    {
        var url = 'process.php?action=rename&dir=' + window.directory +
            '&oldfile=' + window.filename + '&newfile=' +
            document.getElementById('form_rename_name').value + '&nocache=' +
            (new Date()).getTime();

        window.httpObj = createXMLHTTPObject();
        window.httpObj.open('GET', url , true);

        window.httpObj.onreadystatechange = function()
        {
            if (window.httpObj.readyState == 4 && window.httpObj.responseText)
            {
                if (window.httpObj.responseText == 'OK')
                {
                    refreshFilesList();
                }
                else
                {
                    alert('Unable to rename entry.');
                }
            }
        }

        window.httpObj.send(null);
        return false;
    }

    // delete a directory or file
    function doDelete()
    {
        // don't delete a parent directory or if no file is selected
        if (window.filename == '..' || window.filename == '')
```

```
            {
                return;
            }

            if (!confirm('Are you sure you wish to delete?'))
            {
                return;
            }

            var url = 'process.php?action=delete&dir=' + window.directory + '&file=' +
                window.filename + '&nocache=' + (new Date()).getTime();

            window.httpObj = createXMLHTTPObject();
            window.httpObj.open('GET', url , true);

            window.httpObj.onreadystatechange = function()
            {
                if (window.httpObj.readyState == 4 && window.httpObj.responseText)
                {
                    if (window.httpObj.responseText == 'OK')
                    {
                        refreshFilesList();
                    }
                    else
                    {
                        alert('Unable to delete entry.');
                    }
                }
            }

        httpObj.send(null);
}

// download the selected file or traverse into the selected directory
function openSelected()
{
    var url = 'process.php?action=open&dir=' + window.directory + '&file=' +
        window.filename + '&nocache=' + (new Date()).getTime();

    window.httpObj = createXMLHTTPObject();
    window.httpObj.open('GET', url , true);

    window.httpObj.onreadystatechange = function()
    {
        if (window.httpObj.readyState == 4 && window.httpObj.responseText)
        {
            var result = eval('(' + window.httpObj.responseText + ')');
            if (result.retType == 'directory')
            {
                window.directory = result.directory;
                refreshFilesList();
            }
            else if (result.retType == 'file')
```

(continued)

(continued)

```
                    {
                        window.location = 'download.php?&dir=' + window.directory +
                            '&file=' + window.filename + '&nocache=' +
                            (new Date()).getTime();
                    }
                    else
                    {
                        alert('Unknown error.');
                    }
                }
            }

        window.httpObj.send(null);
        return false;
    }
```

Server-Side Functionality

I've discussed all the JavaScript needed for the project and now I'm sure you're anxious to get back to PHP. Hopefully you've noticed all the Ajax requests reference three PHP files: `process.php`, `upload.php`, and `download.php`. I'll look at the simpler `download.php` and `upload.php` files first and save the lengthier `process.php` for last.

Downloading Files or Opening Directories

Let's take a look at `download.php`. There's a good chance it would open in the same browser window taking the user away from the file manager as if the user were following a direct link to a file on the server. This certainly isn't the desired behavior. By filtering the request through a PHP file you can easily send additional headers to instruct the browser to prompt the user with a download dialog box instead.

The files themselves don't have to be stored in a web-accessible directory, which is handy in the case of more sensitive content or to prevent leaching of large files. However, ensure that users cannot request files outside of a specially designated base directory. You don't want someone to gain access to sensitive system files or another user's personal data.

Here's is the code for `public_files/download.php`:

```php
<?php
include '../lib/common.php';
include '../lib/config.php';

// prevent users from traversing outside the base directory
$dir = BASEDIR . $_POST['dir'];
$target = realpath($dir . '/' . $_GET['file']);
if (strpos($target, BASEDIR) !== 0)
{
    die();
}

// send the file if it exists
if (file_exists($target) && is_file($target))
```

```
    {
        header('Content-Type: application/force-download');
        header('Content-Disposition: attachment; filename="' .
            $_GET['file'] . '";');
        header('Content-Transfer-Encoding: binary');
        header('Content-Length: ' . filesize($target));
        readfile($target);
    }
?>
```

There are several benefits to filtering requests through PHP like this. It wouldn't take much time to add code designed to count the number of times a particular file is downloaded to track its popularity. Or you can throttle the download speed if bandwidth is at a premium.

Uploading Files

Using the $_FILES superglobal array in PHP to upload files was first discussed in Chapter 2. You'll recall the array is multidimensional with the name assigned to the HTML form's input element serving as the first index and the following for the second: name, tmp_name, size, type, and error.

The uploaded file is temporarily stored and will be deleted once the script is done running, so it is necessary to copy the file to its permanent location using move_uploaded_file(). When that is done, the script outputs the appropriate JavaScript to call refreshFilesList() or uploadFailed(). Remember that this page will be loaded in the hidden iframe so the function must be prefixed with parent or else JavaScript won't be able to find the functions.

Here is the code for public_files/upload.php:

```
<?php
include '../lib/common.php';
include '../lib/config.php';

// make sure we have all expected parameters
if (!isset($_POST['directory'])) return;

// the file uploaded successfully
if (!$_FILES['file']['error'])
{
    // prevent users from traversing outside the base directory
    $dir = realpath(BASEDIR . $_POST['dir']);
    $target = BASEDIR . $dir . '/' . $_FILES['file']['name'];
    if (strpos($target, BASEDIR) !== 0)
    {
        echo '<script type="text/javascript">parent.uploadFailed();</script>';
        die();
    }

    // must move the file to a permanent location
    if (move_uploaded_file($_FILES['file']['tmp_name'], $target))
```

(continued)

161

(continued)

```
        {
            echo '<script type="text/javascript">parent.refreshFilesList();' .
                '</script>';
        }
        else
        {
            // there was a problem moving the file
            echo '<script type="text/javascript">parent.uploadFailed();</script>';
        }
    }
    // there was a problem uploading the file
    else
    {
        echo '<script type="text/javascript">parent.uploadFailed();</script>';
    }
?>
```

The process.php Script

The `process.php` script is the workhorse of the backend support scripts and handles most of the requests. The file starts with two helper functions, `size_human_read()` and `directory_row()`, and then continues with a `switch` structure to handle the different request actions.

When you read the size of a file using `stat()`, the value comes back in bytes. It would be nice to display the size in a more human readable format and this is exactly what the `size_human_read()` function does. I've borrowed code found in the php.net manual that accomplishes this.

```
// see http://us2.php.net/manual/en/function.filesize.php#77518
function size_human_read ($size)
{
    $sizes = array('B', 'KB', 'MB', 'GB');

    $prev_s = end($sizes);
    foreach ($sizes as $s)
    {
        if ($size < 1024)
        {
            break;
        }
        if ($s != $prev_s)
        {
            $size /= 1024;
        }
    }
    if ($s == $sizes[0])
    {
        return sprintf('%01d %s', $size, $s);
    }
    else
    {
        return sprintf('%01.2f %s', $size, $s);
    }
}
```

`directory_row()` generates an HTML table row to display the file listing entry. The function accepts the filename and whether or not it should include its size and timestamp in the output. The HTML generated also includes an `img` element representing the file type based on the file extension. JavaScript is attached directly to the `tr` to handle visual feedback for mouseover events and to call `selectTableRow()` when the user selects an entry.

```php
function directory_row($file, $show_stats = true)
{
    // get information for $file
    $is_dir = is_dir($file);
    $info = stat($file);

    // keep track of row count to alternating odd/even styles
    static $row_count;
    if (!isset($row_count))
    {
        $row_count = 1;
    }
    else
    {
        $row_count++;
    }

    ob_start();
    echo '<tr class="' . (($row_count % 2 == 0) ? 'even' : 'odd' ). 'row"';

    echo 'onmouseover="highlightTableRow(this)"';
    echo 'onmouseout="unhighlightTableRow(this)"';
    echo 'onclick="selectTableRow(\'' . basename($file) . '\', this);"';
    echo '">';

    echo '<td style="width:25px; text-align: center;">';
    echo '<img style="height: 16px; width: 16px;" src="img/';
    if ($is_dir && basename($file) == '..')
    {
        echo 'up';
    }
    else if ($is_dir)
    {
        echo 'dir';
    }
    else
    {
        $ext = substr($file, strrpos($file, '.') + 1);
        if (file_exists('img/' . $ext . '.gif'))
        {
            echo $ext;
        }
        else
        {
            echo 'unknown';
        }
    }
    echo '.gif"/></td>';
```

(continued)

(continued)

```
echo '<td>' . basename($file) . '</td>';
if ($show_stats)
{
    echo '<td>';
    if ($is_dir)
    {
        echo '---';
    }
    else
    {
        echo size_human_read($info['size']);
    }
    echo '</td>';
    echo '<td>' . date('m/d/Y', $info['mtime']) . '</td>';
}
else
{
    echo '<td> </td><td> </td>';
}
echo '</tr>';
$r = ob_get_contents();
ob_end_clean();

return $r;
}
```

The rest of process.php is organized as a switch constructed with each action as a separate branch. The incoming action parameter is examined to determine which branch should be executed. The first case handles list and is responsible for returning the HTML table listing the contents of the directory. Directory and file names are gathered into two separate arrays and later fed to the directory_row() helper function.

It is very important for the security of your system that users are not allowed to traverse the entire directory hierarchy. Checks must be in place that restrict them to the contents of some base directory.

```
if (!isset($_GET['action'])) return;
switch ($_GET['action'])
{
    case 'list':

        if (!isset($_GET['dir'])) return;

        $directory = realpath(BASEDIR . $_GET['dir']);
        if (strpos($directory, BASEDIR) !== 0) return;

        $ds = array();  // directories
        $fs = array();  // files

        if($dir = opendir($directory))
        {
            while($file = basename(readdir($dir)))
            {
                if($file == '.' || $file == '..')
```

```php
                {
                        continue;
                }

                if (is_dir($directory . '/' . $file))
                {
                        $ds[] = $file;
                }
                else if(is_file($directory . '/' . $file))
                {
                        $fs[] = $file;
                }
        }
        closedir($dir);
    }
    natcasesort($ds);  // natural case-insensitive sort
    natcasesort($fs);
?>
 <table>
  <thead>
   <tr><th colspan="2">File/Folder</th><th>Size</th><th>Date</th></tr>
  </thead>
  <tbody>
<?php
        // don't show .. for root directory
        if (BASEDIR == $directory)
        {
            if (count($ds))
            {
                echo directory_row($directory . '/' . array_shift($ds),
                    TYPE_DIRECTORY, true);
            }
            else if (count($fs))
            {
                echo directory_row($directory . '/' . array_shift($fs),
                    TYPE_FILE, true);
            }
        }
        else
        {
            echo directory_row('..', TYPE_DIRECTORY, false);
        }

        foreach ($ds as $d)
        {
            echo directory_row($directory . '/' . $d, TYPE_DIRECTORY);
        }
        foreach ($fs as $file)
        {
            echo directory_row($directory . '/' . $file, TYPE_FILE);
        }
?>
    </tbody>
    </table>
<?php
        break;
```

The second case handles `delete` and deletes a selected file or a directory. Users will not be able to delete directories that are not empty — that is, we will not recursively delete entries. Either OK or ERROR is returned depending if the deletion was successful.

```php
case 'delete':

    if (!isset($_GET['dir']) || !isset($_GET['file']))
    {
        return;
    }

    $directory = realpath(BASEDIR . $_GET['dir']);
    if (strpos($directory, BASEDIR) !== 0)
    {
        return;
    }

    $target = $directory . '/' . $_GET['file'];

    if (file_exists($target))
    {
        if (is_dir($target) && @rmdir($target))
        {
            echo 'OK';
        }
        else if (is_file($target) && @unlink($target))
        {
            echo 'OK';
        }
        else
        {
            echo 'ERROR';
        }
    }
    else
    {
        echo 'ERROR';
    }
    break;
```

Renaming an entry and creating a new directory are handled by the switch's `rename` and `new` branch respectively. They return OK if the operation was successful or ERROR if a problem was encountered.

```php
case 'rename':

    if (!isset($_GET['dir']) || !isset($_GET['oldfile']) ||
        !isset($_GET['newfile']))
    {
        return;
    }

    $directory = realpath(BASEDIR . $_GET['dir']);
    if (strpos($directory, BASEDIR) !== 0)
```

```
    {
        return;
    }

    $old = $directory . '/' . $_GET['oldfile'];
    $new = $directory . '/' . $_GET['newfile'];

    if (file_exists($old) && @rename($old, $new))
    {
        echo 'OK';
    }
    else
    {
        echo 'ERROR';
    }
    break;

case 'new':

    if (!isset($_GET['dir']) || !isset($_GET['name']))
    {
        return;
    }

    $directory = realpath(BASEDIR . $_GET['dir']);
    if (strpos($directory, BASEDIR) !== 0)
    {
        return;
    }

    $target = $directory . '/' . $_GET['name'];

    if (!file_exists($target) && @mkdir($target))
    {
        echo 'OK';
    }
    else
    {
        echo 'ERROR';
    }
    break;
```

The responsibilities of the open branch may not be as intuitive as the switch's other branches. Remember, the logic for opening a directory was written in the JavaScript code and that for opening a file is in a separate script. The client needs to know first if it is trying to open a directory or a file so it can call the correct code. The open branch therefore determines the file type of the requested entry.

Besides the HTML snippet, previous code showed responding plain text back to the client; this is useful for receiving status notifications. This branch may send back multiple pieces of information, so instead I send a JSON (JavaScript Object Notation) encoded object. JavaScript can pass the string to its eval() function and work the results as it does with any other object. I find this method much easier than sending the response in XML and having to parse it.

```php
case 'open':

    if (!isset($_GET['dir']) || !isset($_GET['file']))
    {
        return;
    }

    $directory = realpath(BASEDIR . $_GET['dir']);
    if (strpos($directory, BASEDIR) !== 0)
    {
        return;
    }

    $target = $directory . '/' . $_GET['file'];

    if (file_exists($target))
    {
        if (is_file($target))
        {
            echo json_encode(array(
                'retType' => 'file'));
        }
        else if (is_dir($target))
        {
            echo json_encode(array(
                'retType' => 'directory',
                'directory' => substr($target, strlen(BASEDIR))));
        }
    }
    break;
```

Here is the complete code listing for public_files/process.php:

```php
<?php
include '../lib/common.php';
include '../lib/config.php';

// see http://us2.php.net/manual/en/function.filesize.php#77518
function size_human_read ($size)
{
    // Only format B through GB. If someone can afford the bandwidth to
    // transfer files >= TB then he can afford to pay me to patch this
    // code if beyond that is required! :)
    $sizes = array('B', 'KB', 'MB', 'GB');

    $prev_s = end($sizes);
    foreach ($sizes as $s)
    {
        if ($size < 1024)
        {
            break;
        }
        if ($s != $prev_s)
```

```php
        {
            $size /= 1024;
        }
    }
    if ($s == $sizes[0])
    {
        return sprintf('%01d %s', $size, $s);
    }
    else
    {
        return sprintf('%01.2f %s', $size, $s);
    }
}

// return HTML row for file display
function directory_row($file, $show_stats = true)
{
    // get information for $file
    $is_dir = is_dir($file);
    $info = stat($file);

    // keep track of row count to alternating odd/even styles
    static $row_count;
    if (!isset($row_count))
    {
        $row_count = 1;
    }
    else
    {
        $row_count++;
    }

    ob_start();
    echo '<tr class="' . (($row_count % 2 == 0) ? 'even' : 'odd' ). 'row"';

    // attach JavaScript handlers
    echo 'onmouseover="highlightTableRow(this)"';
    echo 'onmouseout="unhighlightTableRow(this)"';
    echo 'onclick="selectTableRow(\'' . basename($file) . '\', this);"';
    echo '">';

    // identify appropriate MIME icon to display
    echo '<td style="width:25px; text-align: center;">';
    echo '<img style="height: 16px; width: 16px;"src="img/';
    if ($is_dir && basename($file) == '..')
    {
        echo 'up';
    }
    else if ($is_dir)
    {
        echo 'dir';
    }
    else
```

(continued)

(continued)

```php
        {
            $ext = substr($file, strrpos($file, '.') + 1);
            if (file_exists('img/' . $ext . '.gif'))
            {
                echo $ext;
            }
            else
            {
                echo 'unknown';
            }
        }
        echo '.gif"/></td>';

        // display file information
        echo '<td>' . basename($file) . '</td>';
        if ($show_stats)
        {
            echo '<td>';
            if ($is_dir)
            {
                echo '---';
            }
            else
            {
                echo size_human_read($info['size']);
            }
            echo '</td>';
            echo '<td>' . date('m/d/Y', $info['mtime']) . '</td>';
        }
        else
        {
            echo '<td> </td><td> </td>';
        }
        echo '</tr>';
        $r = ob_get_contents();
        ob_end_clean();

        return $r;
    }

if (!isset($_GET['action'])) return;
switch ($_GET['action'])
{
    // return HTML table with directory contents
    case 'list':

        // ensure all necessary parameters are available
        if (!isset($_GET['dir'])) return;

        // prevent users from traversing outside the base directory
        $directory = realpath(BASEDIR . $_GET['dir']);
        if (strpos($directory, BASEDIR) !== 0) return;

        $ds = array();  // directories
```

```php
        $fs = array();  // files

        if($dir = opendir($directory))
        {
            while($file = basename(readdir($dir)))
            {
                if($file == '.' || $file == '..')
                {
                    continue;
                }

                if (is_dir($directory . '/' . $file))
                {
                    $ds[] = $file;
                }
                else if(is_file($directory . '/' . $file))
                {
                    $fs[] = $file;
                }
            }
            closedir($dir);
        }
        natcasesort($ds);  // natural case-insensitive sort
        natcasesort($fs);
?>
 <table>
  <thead>
   <tr><th colspan="2">File/Folder</th><th>Size</th><th>Date</th></tr>
  </thead>
  <tbody>
<?php
        // don't show .. for root directory
        if (BASEDIR == $directory)
        {
            if (count($ds))
            {
                echo directory_row($directory . '/' . array_shift($ds),
                    TYPE_DIRECTORY, true);
            }
            else if (count($fs))
            {
                echo directory_row($directory . '/' . array_shift($fs),
                    TYPE_FILE, true);
            }
        }
        else
        {
            echo directory_row('..', TYPE_DIRECTORY, false);
        }

        foreach ($ds as $d)
```

(continued)

171

(continued)

```php
        {
            echo directory_row($directory . '/' . $d, TYPE_DIRECTORY);
        }
        foreach ($fs as $file)
        {
            echo directory_row($directory . '/' . $file, TYPE_FILE);
        }
?>
    </tbody>
    </table>
<?php
        break;

    // delete a directory or file
    case 'delete':

        // ensure all necessary parameters are available
        if (!isset($_GET['dir']) || !isset($_GET['file']))
        {
            return;
        }

        // prevent users from traversing outside the base directory
        $directory = realpath(BASEDIR . $_GET['dir']);
        if (strpos($directory, BASEDIR) !== 0)
        {
            return;
        }

        $target = $directory . '/' . $_GET['file'];

        if (file_exists($target))
        {
            if (is_dir($target) && @rmdir($target))
            {
                    echo 'OK';
            }
            else if (is_file($target) && @unlink($target))
            {
                echo 'OK';
            }
            else
            {
                echo 'ERROR';
            }
        }
        else
        {
            echo 'ERROR';
        }
        break;
```

```php
    // rename a directory or file
case 'rename':

    // ensure all necessary parameters are available
    if (!isset($_GET['dir']) || !isset($_GET['oldfile']) ||
        !isset($_GET['newfile']))
    {
        return;
    }

    // prevent users from traversing outside the base directory
    $directory = realpath(BASEDIR . $_GET['dir']);
    if (strpos($directory, BASEDIR) !== 0)
    {
        return;
    }

    $old = $directory . '/' . $_GET['oldfile'];
    $new = $directory . '/' . $_GET['newfile'];

    if (file_exists($old) && @rename($old, $new))
    {
        echo 'OK';
    }
    else
    {
        echo 'ERROR';
    }
    break;

// create a new directory
case 'new':

    // ensure all necessary parameters are available
    if (!isset($_GET['dir']) || !isset($_GET['name']))
    {
        return;
    }

    // prevent users from traversing outside the base directory
    $directory = realpath(BASEDIR . $_GET['dir']);
    if (strpos($directory, BASEDIR) !== 0)
    {
        return;
    }

    $target = $directory . '/' . $_GET['name'];

    if (!file_exists($target) && @mkdir($target))
    {
        echo 'OK';
    }
```

(continued)

173

(continued)

```
            else
            {
                echo 'ERROR';
            }
            break;

        // return information needed to open a folder or file
        case 'open':

            // ensure all necessary parameters are available
            if (!isset($_GET['dir']) || !isset($_GET['file']))
            {
                return;
            }

            // prevent users from traversing outside the base directory
            $directory = realpath(BASEDIR . $_GET['dir']);
            if (strpos($directory, BASEDIR) !== 0)
            {
                return;
            }

            $target = $directory . '/' . $_GET['file'];

            if (file_exists($target))
            {
                if (is_file($target))
                {
                    echo json_encode(array(
                        'retType' => 'file'));
                }
                else if (is_dir($target))
                {
                    echo json_encode(array(
                        'retType' => 'directory',
                        'directory' => substr($target, strlen(BASEDIR))));
                }
            }
            break;
    }
?>
```

The Configuration File

Besides saving all the code files in the appropriate places in the directory structure, you will also need to create a directory that will act as the root of the file system. You certainly don't want to expose your entire system. Looking at upload.php and download.php you see a constant used named BASEDIR. Create the file lib/config.php and define it to point a directory that will serve as the base directory. Then, create the directory itself and make sure it is writeable by the web server processes.

```
<?php
define('BASEDIR', '/srv/apache/wrox/ch_06/files');
?>
```

Summary

In this chapter, you got a taste of building a rich Internet application with PHP and JavaScript by building a web-based file manager application. By integrating such a utility, you can offer people more flexibility in how they manage their remote files. Users are able to transfer files, rename and delete files, and create, rename, and delete directories. The nice thing is the user is able to see changes to the remote file system in real time without having to reload the entire page after each action.

Some other features you might like to add if you are considering building up from the code presented here are support for multiple users by logging in and providing each their own directory and incorporating a feedback icon while the AJAX transaction is being processed.

Regardless, the file manager you've just completed will be put to good use as a back-end for the file-based photo album you'll build in the next chapter.

7

Online Photo Album

Digital photography has become commonplace today. Many people snap pictures and upload them from the camera to their home computers. Some cameras even capture short movie clips saved in the Apple QuickTime file format (MOV). These pictures and videos are then shared with friends and family. In this chapter you will build the front end to a basic online photo album to collect and share these memories.

Design of the Online Photo Album

The photo album site could have a database-driven backend; each album would be assigned a unique ID and saved in some table. Perhaps another table would correlate images to the appropriate album. However, the file system is a natural choice to keep things organized so a database solution complicates the project more than it really needs to be. Each directory will represent a photo album and the files stored within it the associated pictures. Creating an album is now as simple as creating a directory and uploading files — something you did in the previous chapter!

The File Upload utility you created in the previous chapter can serve as an excellent back end to create and manage albums. The base directory holding all albums can be stored either outside or within a web accessible directory; it's a matter of preference if you want the original images to be accessible only through the album application or not. I've chosen to store mine outside the web root.

Some may argue this isn't a good idea as files stored outside the publically accessible directory must be filtered through PHP and causes additional overhead or is a pain when image sizes become too large. By moving these files to a public location this additional overhead is eliminated. However, with the images outside the public area you are able to implement filtering the requests to allow bandwidth throttling, referrer checking as a leeching deterrent, and so on. So it really does just boil down to a matter of preference.

With half the project already completed then, you need to focus on developing the front end and supporting code files. The front end will be able to present three views to the user:

❏ Listing of all available albums

❏ Display preview thumbnails of all the images and movies in the selected album

❏ Show the image or movie file itself

The front end should be able to present three views to the visitor. The first is a listing of all available albums. Selecting an album should then present the album description and thumbnail images of the album's pictures and videos. The user will be able to click a thumbnail and be presented with the final view — the image itself.

The support code will provide the ability to examine files in the album directories and create the thumbnails for the files on the fly. Each album directory may also have a text file to store a description about the collection as well.

Code and Code Explanation

I'll start first by explaining the front-end code. Afterwards I'll walk you through writing the code to generate the movie file thumbnails and other helper code.

Views

The requirement to handle three views can be met by analyzing the incoming parameters and acting accordingly. The album list will be presented if no parameters are passed (or if the passed parameters are invalid). If both an album and file parameter are passed, then the image or video may be displayed. If just an album is provided, then thumbnails will be shown. If the requested image, video, or file doesn't exist or is outside the allowed base directory, the visitor will be redirected to the initial album listing.

```
$album = (isset($_GET['album'])) ? $_GET['album'] : '';
$album_p = BASEDIR . '/' . $album;

$file = (isset($_GET['file'])) ? $_GET['file'] : '';
$file_p = $album_p . '/' . $file;

if ($album && $file)
{    // generate image view
}
else if ($album)
{
    // generate album view
}
else
{
    // list all albums
}
```

The first branch of the if-structure is executed when both the album and image references are passed in the URL and is responsible for displaying the image or movie itself. First you must check that the incoming values really do reference a file in BASEDIR (as we used in the previous chapter to define the base file directory). If not, then the view redirects to show the entire album listing.

```
if (strpos(realpath($album_p), BASEDIR) !== 0 ||
    strpos(realpath($file_p), BASEDIR) !== 0 || !file_exists($file_p))
{
    header('Location: ' . htmlspecialchars($_SERVER['PHP_SELF']));
    exit();
}
ob_start();
```

You must be aware of what type of file you are displaying, whether it is an image file or a QuickTime video, simply because the two file types are embedded into the resulting HTML document differently. An image file is included using the img element while the movie is done with the object or the non-standard embed elements.

```
switch (substr($file, strrpos($file, '.') + 1))
{
    case 'jpg':
    case 'jpeg':
        echo '<img src="view.php?file=' . urlencode($album . '/' .
            $file) . '"alt="' . htmlspecialchars($file) . '"/>';
        break;

    case 'mov':
        echo '<object type="video/quicktime"data="view.php?file=' .
            urlencode($album . '/' . $file) . '">';
        echo '<param name="movie"value="view.php?file=' .
            urlencode($album . '/' . $file) . '"/>';
        echo '<embed type="video/quicktime"src="view.php?file=' .
            urlencode($album . '/' . $file) . '"/>';
        echo '</object>';
        break;

    default:
        header('Location: ' . htmlspecialchars($_SERVER['PHP_SELF']));
        exit();
}

$GLOBALS['TEMPLATE']['content'] = ob_get_contents();
ob_end_clean();
```

The second branch in the if statement is responsible for generating a grid displaying thumbnail images of all the images and movie clips in the viewed album. It too should verify the provided album name doesn't lead to a directory-traversal attack by pointing to something outside the defined area. It then opens the album's directory and reads in a list of all the files.

```
$dir = opendir($album_p);
$images = array();
while ($f = basename(readdir($dir)))
{
    if ($f == '.' || $f == '..')
    {
        continue;
    }
    if (!is_dir($f))
    {
        $ext = (substr($f, strpos($f, '.') + 1));
        if ($ext == 'jpg' || $ext == 'jpeg' || $ext == 'mov')
        {
            $images[] = $f;
        }
    }
}
closedir($dir);
```

The list of files can be sorted once it is retrieved.

```
natcasesort($images);
```

A table showing the thumbnails is generated by iterating through the array that stores the image and movie file references. A counter variable keeps track of the current column being processed in the loop, and in my case I provide three columns. The total number of thumbnails required may not be equally divisible by the number of columns you choose, so it is wise to supply a `while` loop to output blank cells if so required in the last row before closing the `table` element.

```
$counter = 0;
$columns = 3;
echo '<table border="1">';
foreach ($images as $image)
{
    if (0 == ($counter % $columns))
    {
        echo '<tr>';
    }
    echo '<td style="width: '. (100 / $columns) . '%; ';
    echo 'vertical-align: top; padding: 10px; text-align: center;">';
    printf ('<a href="%s?album=%s&file=%s"><img src="thumbnail.php?' .
        'file=%s"alt="%s"/></a> ',
        htmlspecialchars($_SERVER['PHP_SELF']),
        urlencode($album),
        urlencode($image),
        urlencode($album . '/' . $image),
        htmlspecialchars($image));
    echo '</td>';
    if (0 == (++$counter % $columns))
```

```
        {
            echo '</tr>';
        }
    }
    while ($counter++ % $columns)
    {
        echo '<td> </td>';
    }
    if (substr(ob_get_contents(), -5) == '</td>')
    {
        echo '</tr>';
    }
    echo '</table>';
```

The final clause of the if-statement generates the listing of all available albums. It reads in the list of album directory, sorts them and then outputs them however you choose. In this case I present them marked up as an unordered list using the ul element.

```
$albums = array();
$dir = opendir(BASEDIR);
while($f = basename(readdir($dir)))
{
    if($f == '.' || $f == '..') continue;

    if (is_dir(BASEDIR . '/' . $f))
    {
        $albums[] = $f;
    }
}
closedir($dir);

natcasesort($albums);

echo '<p>Albums</p>';
echo '<ul>';
foreach ($albums as $album)
{
    printf('<li><a href="%s?album=%s">%s</a></li>',
        htmlspecialchars($_SERVER['PHP_SELF']),
        urlencode($album),
        htmlspecialchars($album));
}
echo '</ul>';
```

Differentiating between image files and video files are done by looking at the file's extension; this could prove problematic if a file is saved with the wrong extension. It may be better to examine the file's contents or mime type as well. The Fileinfo extension offers a function useful in guessing a file's type by looking for certain "magic" byte sequences at specific positions within it.

The extension is not part of the core PHP installation (although it is expected to be in PHP6) so you may need to install it from PECL (the PHP Extension Code Library). When using `Fileinfo`, a reference to the mime-type database file must first be established. Then the file name is passed to `finfo_file()` to retrieve the file's type as shown in this example:

```php
<?php
// gain access to the mime database file
$finfo = finfo_open(FILEINFO_MIME);

// determine the file's extension and mime-type
$ext = substr($file, strrpos($file, '.') + 1);
$mime = finfo_file($finfo, $file_p);

// close mime file resource
finfo_close($finfo);

// act accordingly based on file type
if ($mime == 'image/jpeg' && ($ext == 'jpg' || $ext == 'jpeg'))
{
    ...
}
else if ($mime == 'video/quicktime' && $ext == 'mov')
{
    ...
}
else
{
    ...
}
?>
```

However, if `Fileinfo` is not readily at your disposal and you must detect by extension, then you might want to consider creating a helper function and save a copy of it in your ever-growing `lib/functions.php` file. Here is such a sample, courtesy of Graham Christensen, the technical editor of this book:

```php
function get_image_type($filename)
{
    if (substr($filename, -3) == 'mov'))
    {
        return 'mov';
    }
    $image_data = getimagesize($filename);
    if (isset($image_data['mime']) &&
        substr($image_data['mime'], 0, 5) == 'image')
    {
        return substr($image_data['mime'], 4);
    }
    return false;
}
```

Here is the complete code listing, which I've saved as `public_files/album.php` and uses the `get_image_type()` function:

```php
<?php
// include shared code
include '../lib/config.php';
include '../lib/functions.php';

// accept incoming parameters
$album = (isset($_GET['album'])) ? $_GET['album'] : '';
$album_p = BASEDIR . '/' . $album;

$file = (isset($_GET['file'])) ? $_GET['file'] : '';
$file_p = $album_p . '/' . $file;

// generate image view
if ($album && $file)
{
    // redirect to album list if album or file is outside allowed base
    // directory or does not exist
    if (strpos(realpath($album_p), BASEDIR) !== 0 ||
        strpos(realpath($file_p), BASEDIR) !== 0 || !file_exists($file_p))
    {
        header('Location: ' . htmlspecialchars($_SERVER['PHP_SELF']));
        exit();
    }
    ob_start();

    // provide link for album view
    echo '<p><a href="' . htmlspecialchars($_SERVER['PHP_SELF']) . '?album='.
        urlencode($album) . '">&lti; Back to ' . htmlspecialchars($album) .
        '</a></p>';

    switch (get_image_type(BASEDIR.'/'.$album.'/'.$file))
    {
        case false:
            header('Location: ' . htmlspecialchars($_SERVER['PHP_SELF']));

        // QuickTime files are included using the object/embed elements
        case 'mov':
            echo '<object type="video/quicktime"data="view.php?file=' .
                urlencode($album . '/' . $file) . '">';
            echo '<param name="movie"value="view.php?file=' .
                urlencode($album . '/' . $file) . '"/>';
            echo '<embed type="video/quicktime"src="view.php?file=' .
                urlencode($album . '/' . $file) . '"/>';
            echo '</object>';
            break;

        default:
            echo '<img src="view.php?file=' . urlencode($album . '/' . $file) .
                '"alt="' . htmlspecialchars($file) . '"/>';
    }

    $GLOBALS['TEMPLATE']['content'] = ob_get_contents();
    ob_end_clean();
}
```

(continued)

(continued)

```php
    // generate album view
    else if ($album)
    {
        // redirect to album list if album does not exist or is outside the
        // allowed base directory
        if (strpos(realpath($album_p), BASEDIR) !== 0 || !file_exists($album_p))
        {
            header('Location: ' . htmlspecialchars($_SERVER['PHP_SELF']));
            exit();
        }
        ob_start();

        // provide link for album index
        echo '<p><a href="' . htmlspecialchars($_SERVER['PHP_SELF']) . '">' .
            '&lti; Back to album index</a></p>';

        // retrieve album description if available
        if (file_exists($album_p . '/desc.txt'))
        {
            echo '<p>' . nl2br(file_get_contents($album_p . '/desc.txt')) . '</p>';
        }

        // read in list of image and QuickTime files
        $dir = opendir($album_p);
        $images = array();
        while($f = basename(readdir($dir)))
        {
            if (get_image_type($album_p.'/'.$f))
            {
                $images[] = $f;
            }
        }
        closedir($dir);

        // sort images
        natcasesort($images);

        //display thumbnails in a table
        $counter = 0;
        $columns = 3;
        echo '<table border="1">';
        foreach ($images as $image)
        {
            if (0 == ($counter % $columns))
            {
                echo '<tr>';
            }
            echo '<td style="width: ' . (100 / $columns) . '%; ';
            echo 'vertical-align: top; padding: 10px; text-align: center;">';

            printf ('<a href="%s?album=%s&file=%s"><img src="thumbnail.php?' .
                'file=%s"alt="%s"/></a> ',
                htmlspecialchars($_SERVER['PHP_SELF']),
```

```
            urlencode($album),
            urlencode($image),
            urlencode($album . '/' . $image),
            htmlspecialchars($image));

        echo '</td>';
        if (0 == (++$counter % $columns))
        {
            echo '</tr>';
        }
    }
    // finish table's row with blank cells if necessary
    while ($counter++ % $columns)
    {
        echo '<td> </td>';
    }
    if (substr(ob_get_contents(), -5) == '</td>')
    {
        echo '</tr>';
    }
    echo '</table>';

    $GLOBALS['TEMPLATE']['content'] = ob_get_contents();
    ob_end_clean();
}

// generate default view showing list of available albums
else
{
    ob_start();

    // retrieve list of albums
    $albums = array();
    $dir = opendir(BASEDIR);
    while($f = basename(readdir($dir)))
    {
        if($f == '.' || $f == '..') continue;

        if (is_dir(BASEDIR . '/' . $f))
        {
            $albums[] = $f;
        }
    }
    closedir($dir);

    // sort albums
    natcasesort($albums);

    // display album list
    echo '<p>Albums</p>';
    echo '<ul>';
    foreach ($albums as $album)
```

(continued)

```
        {
            printf('<li><a href="%s?album=%s">%s</a></li>',
            htmlspecialchars($_SERVER['PHP_SELF']),
            urlencode($album),
            htmlspecialchars($album));
        }
        echo '</ul>';

        $GLOBALS['TEMPLATE']['content'] = ob_get_contents();
        ob_end_clean();
}

// display the page
include '../templates/template-page.php';
?>
```

Figure 7-1 shows the first view a user would see a list of all available album directories. Figure 7-2 shows the thumbnail previews and Figure 7-3 shows the viewing of an image.

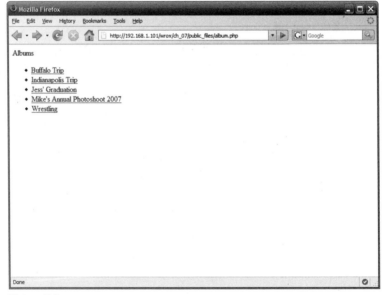

Figure 7-1

Figure 7-2

Figure 7-3

Helper Files

The main album file is responsible only for generating the three views. Other files are called from the HTML output to generate the thumbnail images (thumbnail.php) or to view the file (view.php). The code for view.php should determine the type of file that will be output so the appropriate Content-Type header can be set and then dump the file using readfile():

```php
<?php
// include shared code
include '../lib/config.php';

// make sure users only access files in the albums
$file = (isset($_GET['file'])) ? (BASEDIR . '/' . $_GET['file']) : '';
if ($file && strpos(realpath($file), BASEDIR) === 0 && file_exists($file))
{
    // dump file content to browser
    switch(substr($file, strrpos($file, '.') + 1))
    {
        // file is jpeg image
        case 'jpg':
        case 'jpeg':
            header('Content-Type: image/jpeg');
            readfile($file);
            break;

        // file is QuickTime movie
        case 'mov':
            header('Content-Type: movie/quicktime');
            readfile($file);
    }
}
?>
```

The logic of thumbnail.php is similar — first identify the type of file that will be made into a thumbnail and then output the thumbnail. The reasoning for identifying the file type is different from view.php, although, since Content-Type for a thumbnail will always be image/jpeg. The type is needed because it will dictate how the thumbnail is generated.

You've seen how to generate a jpeg thumbnail and encapsulated that logic in Chapter 2 with the JpegThumbnail class. A similar class will be written for creating the thumbnail for the QuickTime video.

```php
<?php
// include shared code
include '../lib/config.php';

// make sure users only access files in the albums
$file = (isset($_GET['file'])) ? (BASEDIR . '/' . $_GET['file']) : '';
if ($file && strpos(realpath($file), BASEDIR) === 0 && file_exists($file))
{
    // output thumbnail
    switch (substr($file, strrpos($file, '.') + 1))
```

```
        {
            // thumbnail is for jpeg image
            case 'jpg':
            case 'jpeg':
                include '../lib/JpegThumbnail.php';
                $thumbnail = new JpegThumbnail(100, 100);
                header('Content-Type: image/jpeg');
                imagejpeg($thumb = $thumbnail->generate($file), '', 100);
                imagedestroy($thumb);
                break;

            // thumbnail is for QuickTime video
            case 'mov':
                include '../lib/MovThumbnail.php';
                $thumbnail = new MovThumbnail();
                header('Content-Type: movie/quicktime');
                imagejpeg($thumb = $thumbnail->generate($file), '', 100);
                imagedestroy($thumb);
                break;
        }
    }
?>
```

To distinguish between thumbnails for still pictures and videos and to give the album's visitors an extra visual cue to what they're clicking on, you may also want to overlay a small indicator over the QuickTime thumbnails. Visitors can then have advance notice they will be viewing a movie should they click the video's thumbnail. The indicator doesn't have to be anything too fancy; a small QuickTime logo or video symbol is suitable.

```
<?php
$icon = imagecreatefromjpeg('overlay.jpg');

// determine dimensions of thumbnail image
$width = imagesx($img);
$height = imagesy($img);

// determine indicator dimensions
$icon_width = imagesx($icon);
$icon_height = imagesy($icon);

// copy indicator to lower right-hand corner of thumbnail
imagecopymerge($img, $icon, $width - $icon_width, $height - $icon_height,
    $icon_width, $icon_height, 100);

imagedestroy($icon);
?>
```

Figure 7-4 shows an enlarged thumbnail image for a QuickTime movie with an overlaid indicator icon.

Figure 7-4

QuickTime Thumbnails

Resizing an image is discussed in Chapter 2, when you took in the uploaded image and resized it for use as an avatar icon. The logic is encapsulated as `JpegThumbnail` so the code could be reused. The class handles generating thumbnails from images but doesn't meet our requirement to handle QuickTime files, however, and an additional class is needed. Table 7-1 shows the publically available methods for `MovThumbnail`.

Table 7-1: MovThumbnail Properties and Methods

Property	Description
height	The specified height of the thumbnail image
width	The specified width of the thumbnail image
Method	
__construct(width, height)	Initialize a new `MovThumbnail` object with the specified `width` and `height`
generate(movie, [filename])	Create a thumbnail image of `movie` and either send it to the browser or save to a file if `filename` is provided

Documentation on the QuickTime video format is available online at `http://developer.apple.com/documentation/QuickTime/QTFF/qtff.pdf`. The format is essentially a container format holding video, audio, and text. This makes your attempt to extract a preview image easier because the media streams aren't combined and the video stream is often stored as a sequence of JPEG images.

You're welcome to read through the format's documentation if you want to properly parse the file's contents. However, it would be much faster (in both development and script execution time) to take advantage of the sequentially stored images. You can open the video file and seek for the special byte marker that indicates the beginning of a JPEG file. Then you can buffer the contents from that point onward until you encounter the marker for the end of the image.

This method won't work for other popular file formats such as AVI (most often encoded with DivX), MPEG, or WMV. You will need to seek out the appropriate documentation on the desired file format and study it to support those.

```php
<?php
define('SOI', pack('n', 0xFFD8));  // jpeg start marker
define('EOI', pack('n', 0xFFD9));  // jpeg end marker

class MovThumbnail
{
    public $width;  // maximum thumbnail width
    public $height; // maximum thumbnail height

    // initialize a new MovThumbnail object
    public function __construct($width = 100, $height = 100)
    {
        $this->width = $width;
        $this->height = $height;
    }

    // accept a source file location and return an open image handle or
    // save to disk if destination provided
    public function generate($src, $dest = '')
    {
        // locate the first SOI marker
        for (
          $fp = fopen($src, 'rb'), $bytes = null;
          $bytes != SOI && !feof($fp);
          $bytes = fread($fp, 2)
        );

        // extract jepg image
        for (
          $buffer = $bytes;
          $bytes != EOI && !feof($fp);
          $bytes = fread($fp, 2), $buffer .= $bytes
        );

        // construct image from buffer
        $img = imagecreatefromstring($buffer);

        // retrieve image dimensions
        $width = imagesx($img);
        $height = imagesy($img);

        // determine if resize is necessary
        if(($lowest = min($this->width / $width, $this->height / $height)) < 1)
        {
            // resize
            $sm_width = floor($lowest * $width);
```

(continued)

(continued)

```
            $sm_height = floor($lowest * $height);
            $buffer = imagecreatetruecolor($sm_width, $sm_height);
            imagecopyresized($buffer, $img, 0,0, 0,0, $sm_width, $sm_height,
                $width, $height);
            imagedestroy($img);
            $img = $buffer;
        }

        // save to disk or return the open image handle
        return ($dest) ? imagejpeg($img, $dest, 100) : $img;
    }
}
?>
```

Thumbnail Caching

Dynamically generating thumbnails on the fly is certainly convenient, but you may find the album's performance somewhat lacking depending on the original size of an image, how many images are in an album and the load on the server. You may therefore want to put some form of caching in place. To keep everything simple and easy to update, I recommend making the modifications thumbnail.php.

Since all cached thumbnail images will be stored in one central cache directory, the inherent protection that comes from the album and image names being a unique combination is lost. The received file parameter may be run through sha1() to make sure valid thumbnail caches aren't overwritten.

The script should check to see if the thumbnail already exists within the cache directory and then its timestamp can be compared with that of the original image. If the thumbnail is newer than the original image then the thumbnail is still fresh and can be sent to the viewer instead of having to generate a new one for each request. However, if the thumbnail is older than the original image then it means someone updated the album and the thumbnail must be regenerated.

```
<?php
// include shared code
include '../lib/config.php';

// assumes CACHEDIR is defined alongside BASEDIR in config.php

// make sure users only access files in the albums
$file = (isset($_GET['file'])) ? (BASEDIR . '/' . $_GET['file']) : '';
if ($file && strpos(realpath($file), BASEDIR) === 0 && file_exists($file))
{
    // file name hashed to ensure unique names for cache files
    $cache_file = sha1(realpath($file));

    // retrieve timestamps to determine cached file's "freshness"
    $f_time = filemtime($file);
    $c_time = (file_exists(CACHEDIR . '/' . $cache_file)) ?
        filemtime(CACHEDIR . '/' . $cache_file) : 0;
    // output thumbnail
    switch (substr($file, strrpos($file, '.') + 1))
```

```
    {
        // thumbnail is for jpeg image
        case 'jpg':
        case 'jpeg':
            header('Content-Type: image/jpeg');

            // cache still valid
            if ($f_time <= $c_time)
            {
                readfile(CACHEDIR . '/' . $cache_file);
            }
            // regenerate cache file
            else
            {
                include '../lib/JpegThumbnail.php';
                $thumbnail = new JpegThumbnail(100, 100);
                imagejpeg($thumb = $thumbnail->generate($file), '', 100);
                imagejpeg($thumb, CACHEDIR . '/' . $cache_file, 100);
                imagedestroy($thumb);
            }
        break;

        // thumbnail is for quicktime video
        case 'mov':
            header('Content-Type: movie/quicktime');
            if ($f_time <= $c_time)
            {
                readfile(CACHEDIR . '/' . $cache_file);
            }
            else
            {
                include '../lib/MovThumbnail.php';
                $thumbnail = new MovThumbnail();
                imagejpeg($thumb = $thumbnail->generate($file), '', 100);
                imagejpeg($thumb, CACHEDIR . '/' . $cache_file, 100);
                imagedestroy($thumb);
            }
        break;
    }
}
?>
```

Summary

In this chapter you built a basic online photo album to share pictures and QuickTime videos with family and friends. The project was simple to complete because we were able to take advantage of code from other projects highlighting the importance of writing code with reusability in mind.

In the next chapter you will write an online shopping cart utility to enable your site for e-commerce.

8

Shopping Cart

The Internet started out in the late 1960s as a government research project to link computers together in a robust network. As it evolved from this packet-switching experiment to a functional network capable of transferring information between computer systems, it became an important tool in academia. Mosaic, one of the first web browsers that was released in 1993, changed the face of the Internet forever by making the World Wide Web accessible to the ordinary person. Forward-thinking businessmen saw great potential in this new and growing medium and started advertising and selling their wares online.

The term *e-commerce* was coined to denote such electronic commerce that takes place over the Internet. E-commerce still flourishes even though the face of the Internet has changed many times over since its early days as new technologies and applications emerge. Over the past decade or so, consumer confidence has continued to rise and more and more people are making purchases online.

The shopping cart has come to be the ubiquitous e-commerce application, so in this chapter you'll write your own shopping cart around which you can build up an e-commerce website.

Designing the Shopping Cart

In its most basic form, a shopping cart is nothing more than code that maintains a list of selected items a shopper selects until he or she is ready for purchase. Remember that HTTP is a stateless protocol. Each page request takes place without knowledge of previous requests or expectations for future requests, so the list of items is generally saved using some session or cookie-based mechanism. This cart will use PHP's built-in session handling functionality.

A shopping cart class will keep track of the selected items and offer methods to add and remove items. A pair of front-end scripts will act as a virtual storefront and integrate the class to allow users to:

❑ View various product categories, a list of products within each category and details of each product

❑ Add and remove items in a virtual shopping cart

❑ Change an item's quantity in the cart

An administrative interface will also be built to allow you to easily manage the available categories and products. The interface will offer the following functionality:

❑ Add, delete, and modify categories

❑ Add, delete, and modify products within the categories

You've seen in previous projects how the Ajax paradigm allows for a more intuitive interaction between users and forms and so the administration interface will make use of JavaScript in this manner.

Designing the Database

Two tables provide the storage requirements for this project. The first table, WROX_SHOP_INVENTORY will store the ids and names of the various product categories.

```
+---------------+-------------------+------+-----+---------+----------------+
| Field         | Type              | Null | Key | Default | Extra          |
+---------------+-------------------+------+-----+---------+----------------+
| CATEGORY_ID   | int(10) unsigned  | NO   | PRI | NULL    | auto_increment |
| CATEGORY_NAME | varchar(100)      | NO   |     |         |                |
+---------------+-------------------+------+-----+---------+----------------+
```

Here is the SQL code for WROX_SHOP_INVENTORY:

```
CREATE TABLE WROX_SHOP_CATEGORY (
    CATEGORY_ID    INTEGER UNSIGNED  NOT NULL  AUTO_INCREMENT,
    CATEGORY_NAME  VARCHAR(100)      NOT NULL,

    PRIMARY KEY (CATEGORY_ID)
)
ENGINE=InnoDB DEFAULT CHARACTER SET latin1
    COLLATE latin1_general_cs;
```

The product information will be stored in WROX_SHOP_INVENTORY. Besides an integer primary key and name, a description, price, and the URL for an image of the product will be collected as well. A foreign key refers back to WROX_SHOP_CATEGORY to maintain the product's association within a category.

```
+------------------+------------------+------+-----+--------------+----------------+
| Field            | Type             | Null | Key | Default      | Extra          |
+------------------+------------------+------+-----+--------------+----------------+
| ITEM_ID          | int(10) unsigned | NO   | PRI | NULL         | auto_increment |
| ITEM_NAME        | varchar(100)     | NO   |     |              |                |
| ITEM_DESCRIPTION | text             | YES  |     | NULL         |                |
| PRICE            | double(5,2)      | NO   |     |              |                |
| ITEM_IMAGE       | varchar(255)     | YES  |     | img/none.gif |                |
| CATEGORY_ID      | int(10) unsigned | NO   | MUL |              |                |
+------------------+------------------+------+-----+--------------+----------------+
```

Here is the SQL code for WROX_SHOP_INVENTORY:

```
CREATE TABLE WROX_SHOP_INVENTORY (
    ITEM_ID            INTEGER UNSIGNED  NOT NULL  AUTO_INCREMENT,
    ITEM_NAME          VARCHAR(100)      NOT NULL,
    ITEM_DESCRIPTION   TEXT              DEFAULT '',
    PRICE              DOUBLE(5,2)       NOT NULL,
    ITEM_IMAGE         VARCHAR(255)      DEFAULT 'img/none.gif',
    CATEGORY_ID        INTEGER UNSIGNED  NOT NULL,

    PRIMARY KEY (ITEM_ID),

    FOREIGN KEY (CATEGORY_ID)
        REFERENCES WROX_SHOP_CATEGORY(CATEGORY_ID)
        ON DELETE CASCADE
)
ENGINE=InnoDB DEFAULT CHARACTER SET latin1
    COLLATE latin1_general_cs AUTO_INCREMENT=0;
```

Note that I specified the InnoDB storage engine for both tables and applied an ON DELETE CASCADE constraint to the foreign key in WROX_SHOP_INVENTORY. This is critical to allow MySQL to enforce the product/category relationship and automatically remove any product records when the category they are organized under is deleted.

Code and Code Explanation

I will first discuss writing the ShoppingCart class as it is used by the storefront files. Then I will discuss the two front-end files, shop.php and cart.php. Finally, I will cover the administrative files, which you will use to populate the inventory database with entries.

The ShoppingCart Class

The first component I will present is the ShoppingCart class. The class will be responsible for maintaining the list of items shoppers have selected until they are ready to check out. Essentially this list is an array, but various methods and properties will be made available to make working with the list easier. Table 8-1 shows the properties ShoppingCart will expose and Table 8-2 shows the methods.

Table 8-1: ShoppingCart Properties

Property	Description
contents	Returns the entire contents of the cart as an array
isEmpty	Returns Boolean whether or not the cart is empty
totalItems	Returns the total number of distinct items in the cart
totalQty	Returns the total quantity of items in the cart

Table 8-2: ShoppingCart Methods

Method	Description
construct()	Initializes a new ShoppingCart object
addItem(item[, qty])	Adds an item to the shopping cart
qtyItem(item)	Returns the quantity of an item in the cart
removeItem(item)	Removes an item from the shopping cart
removeAll()	Empties the contents of the shopping cart

The class will need one private property to store the list of products which will be initialized to a blank array in the constructor. The array will later store the quantity of each item keyed by the product id when items are added to the cart.

```php
class ShoppingCart
{
    private $items;

    public function __construct()
    {
        $this->items = array();
    }
...
}
```

The public properties offered by ShoppingCart should be read-only and offer a view of the current state of the cart. Thus, I have decided to expose them through __get(). They don't exist as variables within the class but rather they are calculated whenever their values are needed. A switch is used to determine which property was called and return the correct information.

```php
public function __get($value)
{
    switch ($value)
    {
        case 'contents':
```

```
            return $this->items;
            brake;

        case 'isEmpty':
            return (count($this->items) == 0);
            break;

        case 'totalItems':
            return count($this->items);
            break;

        case 'totalQty':
            return array_sum($this->items);
            break;
    }
}
```

To add a product to the shopping cart, addItem() accepts the item's id and then assigns the item to the internal items property. By default, the quantity will be 1 unless an optional value is also passed.

```
public function addItem($item, $qty = 1)
{
    $this->items[$item] = $qty;
}
```

The quantity of a product in the cart can be verified with the qtyItem(). It accepts the item id and checks the internal list. If the requested item isn't found then qtyItem() returns 0.

```
public function qtyItem($item)
{
    if (!isset($this->items[$item]))
    {
        return 0;
    }
    else
    {
        return $this->items[$item];
    }
}
```

Removing items from the cart may be done with the removeItem() and removeAll() methods. removeItem() removes a particular product indicated by the item's id while removeAll() will purge all items from the cart by reassigning an empty array to the internal list.

```
public function removeItem($item)
{
    unset($this->items[$item]);
}

public function removeAll()
{
    $this->items = array();
}
```

Here is the entire code listing for `lib/ShoppingCart.php`:

```php
<?php
class ShoppingCart
{
    // collection of items placed in the shopping cart
    private $items;

    // initialize a ShoppingCart object
    public function __construct()
    {
        $this->items = array();
    }

    // expose read-only convenience properties
    public function __get($value)
    {
        switch ($value)
        {
            // contents - returns the entire contents of the cart
            case 'contents':
                return $this->items;
                brake;

            // isEmpty - returns whether or not the cart is empty
            case 'isEmpty':
                return (count($this->items) == 0);
                break;

            // totalItems - returns the total number of distinct items
            // in the cart
            case 'totalItems':
                return count($this->items);
                break;

            // totalQty - returns the total quantity of items in the cart
            case 'totalQty':

                return array_sum($this->total);
                break;
        }
    }

    // add an item to the shopping cart
    public function addItem($item, $qty = 1)
    {
        if (!$qty)
        {
            $this->removeItem($item);
        }
```

```
        else
        {
            $this->items[$item] = $qty;
        }
    }

    // returns an item's quantity in the cart
    public function qtyItem($item)
    {
        if (!isset($this->items[$item]))
        {
            return 0;
        }
        else
        {
            return $this->items[$item];
        }
    }

    // empty the contents of the shopping cart
    public function removeAll()
    {
        $this->items = array();
    }

    // remove an item from the shopping cart
    public function removeItem($item)
    {
        unset($this->items[$item]);
    }
}
?>
```

Working with the Shopping Cart

Most of the work done with the shopping cart will be in cart.php. Calls from shop.php to add and remove items from the cart will be made to cart.php, which will take the appropriate action and redirect to the storefront. For example, cart.php?add&item=xxx will add the indicated item to the cart and cart.php?remove&item=xxx will remove it. A call to cart.php?empty will completely empty the cart. Therefore the first part of cart.php will need to create or resume the session and obtain an instance of the ShoppingCart class. Then any incoming parameters will be analyzed, validated and acted upon.

Before the script redirects the visitor to another page, the shopping cart must be serialized and stored back to the $_SESSION array. The serialize() function converts data structures such as arrays and objects into a representation that can safely be stored. The representation is passed to unserialize() which recreates the data structure and its state.

```
include '../lib/ShoppingCart.php';

session_start();
if (isset($_SESSION['cart']))
{
    $cart = unserialize($_SESSION['cart']);
}
else
{
    $cart = new ShoppingCart();
}

if (isset($_GET['empty']))
{
    $cart->removeAll();
    $_SESSION['cart'] = serialize($cart);
    header('Location: shop.php');
    end();
}
```

In the case of objects, in order to successfully unserialize the data structure the class definition must be available. Just the object's properties and state are stored — not the method definitions. This is important to remember because lib/ShoppingCart.php must be included in both shop.php and cart.php as the ShoppingCart object will be passed between the two in the user's session. You cannot simply serialize an object in one script and unserialize it in another without the class's definition available or PHP will generate an error such as the following:

```
Notice: main() [function.main]: The script tried to execute a method or
access a property of an incomplete object. Please ensure that the class
definition "ShoppingCart" of the object you are trying to operate on was loaded
before unserialize() gets called or provide an __autoload() function to load
the class definition.
```

Both calls to add and remove an item from the cart must include an item parameter so this commonality should be checked first and validated. If it is valid, then the appropriate action is performed on the cart depending on whether add or remove was detected.

```
if (isset($_GET['item']))
{
    $query = sprintf('SELECT ITEM_ID FROM %sSHOP_INVENTORY WHERE ' .
        'ITEM_ID = %d',
        DB_TBL_PREFIX,
        $_GET['item']);
    $result = mysql_query($query, $GLOBALS['DB']);

    if (mysql_num_rows($result))
    {
        $row = mysql_fetch_assoc($result);
        $item = $row['ITEM_ID'];

        // add item to cart
        if (isset($_GET['add']))
```

```
        {
            $cart->addItem($item);
        }

        // remove item from cart
        else if (isset($_GET['remove']))
        {
            $cart->removeItem($item);
        }
    }
    mysql_free_result($result);

    $_SESSION['cart'] = serialize($cart);
    header('Location: ' . htmlspecialchars($_SERVER['HTTP_REFERER']));
    exit();
}
```

A `for` loop can be used to iterate through the contents of the cart to present an order summary. Only the item's id and quantity are stored in the cart so a query is made to retrieve the item's description and pricing information.

```
if ($cart->isEmpty)
{
    echo '<p><b>Your cart is empty.</b></p>';
}
else
{
    $total = 0;
    echo '<table>';
    echo '<tr><th>Item</th><th>Qty</th><th>Price</th><th>Total</th></tr>';
    foreach ($cart->contents as $id => $qty)
    {
        $query = sprintf('SELECT ITEM_NAME, PRICE FROM %sSHOP_INVENTORY ' .
            'WHERE ITEM_ID = %d',
            DB_TBL_PREFIX,
            $id);
        $result = mysql_query($query, $GLOBALS['DB']);

        $row = mysql_fetch_assoc($result);
        echo '<tr>';
        echo '<td>' . $row['ITEM_NAME'] . '</td>';
        echo '<td>' . $qty . '</td>';
        echo '<td>$' . number_format($row['PRICE'], 2) . '</td>';
        echo '<td>$' . number_format($row['PRICE'] * $qty, 2) . '</td></tr>';

        $total += $row['PRICE'] * $qty;
        mysql_free_result($result);
    }
    echo '</table>';

    echo '<p>Total Items: ' . $cart->totalItems . '<br/>';
    echo 'Total Quantity: ' . $cart->totalQty . '</p>';
    echo '<p><b>Total Price: $' . number_format($total, 2) . '</b></p>';
}
```

This summary doesn't allow the user to adjust the quantity of an item in his cart though which presents a minor problem. This can be easily resolved by augmenting the display with HTML `form` tags and replacing the quantity value with `select` elements. The select lists will be preset with the item's current quantity but the shopper will be able to change them to adjust the number of an item in the cart as desired. (A `select` list limits the number of items a customer may purchase. Depending on your checkout procedure, you may provide them more flexibility with their quantities by providing a text `input` field.)

```php
echo '<form method="post" action="cart.php?update">';
...
echo '<select name="qty[' . $id . ']">';
for ($i=0; $i < 11; $i++)
{
    echo '<option ';
    echo ($i == $qty) ? 'selected="selected" ' : '';
    echo 'value="' . $i . '">' . $i . '</option>';
}
echo '</select>';
...
echo '<input type="submit" value="Update"/>';
```

The form should submit itself back to `cart.php` and append an `update` parameter to the URL. Prior to displaying the summary table the parameter can be identified and the contents of the cart updated accordingly.

```php
if (isset($_GET['update']))
{
    foreach ($_POST['qty'] as $item => $qty)
    {
        $cart->addItem($item, $qty);
    }
}
```

Links to navigate back and forth within the shopping system should also be made available to the shopper. For example, a link to view the category lists should appear at the top of a page. If the shopper came from viewing the list of items in a particular category, then a link to return there should be made available as well. A `category` parameter can be passed to `cart.php` so the script knows which category to link back to. For now note that this script will be named `shop.php`; I discuss it in the next section.

```php
echo '<p><a href="shop.php">Back to all categories</a>';

if (isset($_GET['category']))
{
    $query = sprintf('SELECT CATEGORY_ID, CATEGORY_NAME FROM ' .
        '%sSHOP_CATEGORY WHERE CATEGORY_ID = %d',
    DB_TBL_PREFIX,
    $_GET['category']);
    $result = mysql_query($query, $GLOBALS['DB']);

    if (mysql_num_rows($result))
```

```
    {
        $row = mysql_fetch_assoc($result);
        echo ' / <a href="shop.php?category=' . $row['CATEGORY_ID'] .
            '">Back to ' . $row['CATEGORY_NAME'] . '</a>';
    }
    mysql_free_result($result);
}
echo '</p>';
```

The address given in the `form` element's `action` property must be modified to include the `category` value if it exists so that shoppers won't lose the link to the previous category when they update the quantities in their cart.

```
echo '<form method="post" action="cart.php?update';
if  (isset($row['CATEGORY_ID']))
{
    echo '&category=' . $row['CATEGORY_ID'];
}
echo '">';
```

The item name in the listing can also be made into a link to lead the shopper back to the product's description page.

```
echo '<a href="shop.php?item=' . $id . '">' . $row['ITEM_NAME'] . '</a>';
```

Figure 8-1 shows cart.php in action by displaying the contents of a user's shopping cart.

Figure 8-1

Here is the complete code listing for `public_files/cart.php`:

```php
<?php
include '../lib/common.php';
include '../lib/db.php';
include '../lib/ShoppingCart.php';

// create or resume session and retrieve shopping cart
session_start();
if (isset($_SESSION['cart']))
{
    $cart = unserialize($_SESSION['cart']);
}
else
{
    $cart = new ShoppingCart();
}

// empty the shopping cart and redirect user to list of categories
if (isset($_GET['empty']))
{
    $cart->removeAll();
    $_SESSION['cart'] = serialize($cart);
    header('Location: shop.php');
    end();
}

// item parameter indicates an attempt to add or remove items
if (isset($_GET['item']))
{
    // verify item is valid
    $query = sprintf('SELECT ITEM_ID FROM %sSHOP_INVENTORY WHERE ' .
        'ITEM_ID = %d',
        DB_TBL_PREFIX,
        $_GET['item']);
    $result = mysql_query($query, $GLOBALS['DB']);

    if (mysql_num_rows($result))
    {
        $row = mysql_fetch_assoc($result);
        $item = $row['ITEM_ID'];

        // add item to cart
        if (isset($_GET['add']))
        {
            $cart->addItem($item);
        }

        // remove item from cart
        else if (isset($_GET['remove']))
        {
            $cart->removeItem($item);
        }
    }
```

```php
    mysql_free_result($result);

    // save cart to session and redirect to the previously viewed page
    $_SESSION['cart'] = serialize($cart);
    header('Location: ' . htmlspecialchars($_SERVER['HTTP_REFERER']));
    exit();
}

// view shopping cart's contents
else
{
    // update item quantities in shopping cart
    if (isset($_GET['update']))
    {
        foreach ($_POST['qty'] as $item => $qty)
        {
            $cart->addItem($item, $qty);
        }
    }

    ob_start();

    echo '<h1>Your Cart</h1>';
    echo '<p><a href="shop.php">Back to all categories</a>';

    // verify category parameter and construct suitable back link if passed
    if (isset($_GET['category']))
    {
        $query = sprintf('SELECT CATEGORY_ID, CATEGORY_NAME FROM ' .
            '%sSHOP_CATEGORY WHERE CATEGORY_ID = %d',
            DB_TBL_PREFIX,
            $_GET['category']);
        $result = mysql_query($query, $GLOBALS['DB']);

        if (mysql_num_rows($result))
        {
            $row = mysql_fetch_assoc($result);
            echo ' / <a href="shop.php?category=' . $row['CATEGORY_ID'] .
                '">Back to ' . $row['CATEGORY_NAME'] . '</a>';
        }
        mysql_free_result($result);
    }
    echo '</p>';

    if ($cart->isEmpty)
    {
        echo '<p><b>Your cart is empty.</b></p>';
    }
    else
```

(continued)

(continued)

```php
{
    // display empty cart link
    echo '<p><a href="cart.php?empty">';
    echo '<img src="img/cartempty.gif" alt="Empty Cart"/></a></p>';

    // encapsulate list in form so quantities may be changed
    echo '<form method="post" action="cart.php?update';
    // if a category was passed and was validated successfully earlier
    // then append it to the action url so the back link remains available
    if (isset($row['CATEGORY_ID']))
    {
        echo '&category=' . $row['CATEGORY_ID'];
    }
    echo '">';

    // list each item in the cart, keeping track of total price
    $total = 0;
    echo '<table>';
    echo '<tr><th>Item</th><th>Qty</th><th>Price</th><th>Total</th></tr>';
    foreach ($cart->contents as $id => $qty)
    {
        $query = sprintf('SELECT ITEM_NAME, PRICE FROM %sSHOP_INVENTORY ' .
            'WHERE ITEM_ID = %d',
            DB_TBL_PREFIX,
            $id);
        $result = mysql_query($query, $GLOBALS['DB']);

        $row = mysql_fetch_assoc($result);
        echo '<tr>';
        echo '<td><a href="shop.php?item=' . $id . '">' . $row['ITEM_NAME'] .
            '</a></td>';
        echo '<td><select name="qty[' . $id . ']">';
        for ($i=0; $i < 11; $i++)
        {
            echo '<option ';
            if ($i == $qty)
            {
                echo 'selected="selected" ';
            }
            echo 'value="' . $i . '">' . $i . '</option>';

        }
        echo '</td>';
        echo '<td>$' . number_format($row['PRICE'], 2) . '</td>';
        echo '<td>$' . number_format($row['PRICE'] * $qty, 2) . '</td>';
        echo '</tr>';

        $total += $row['PRICE'] * $qty;
        mysql_free_result($result);
    }
    echo '</table>';
    echo '<input type="submit" value="Update"/>';
```

```
            echo '<p>Total Items: ' . $cart->totalItems . '<br/>';
            echo 'Total Quantity: ' . $cart->totalQty . '</p>';
            echo '<p><b>Total Price: $' . number_format($total, 2) . '</b></p>';

            // display link to checkout
            echo '<p><a href="checkout.php">';
            echo '<img src="img/checkout.gif" alt="Proceed to Checkout"/></a></p>';
        }

        // save cart to session and display the page
        $_SESSION['cart'] = serialize($cart);

        $GLOBALS['TEMPLATE']['content'] = ob_get_clean();    include '../templates/
template-page.php';
    }
?>
```

Building the Storefront

The next file to be presented is shop.php. You've seen it referenced in cart.php and it is used to display categories, product lists, and individual product descriptions.

Like cart.php, shop.php begins with creating or resuming an existing session and obtaining a reference to a ShoppingCart object. It doesn't modify the contents of the cart but still needs to have the cart available when showing the individual product page to determine whether to show an Add to cart or Remove from cart link.

```
include '../lib/ShoppingCart.php';

session_start();
if (isset($_SESSION['cart']))
{
    $cart = unserialize($_SESSION['cart']);
}
else
{
    $cart = new ShoppingCart();
}
```

Depending on which parameters are passed to the script, its display behavior will be different. For example, if item=xxx is passed in the URL, then the script will display a product page. category=xxx will cause shop.php to generate a listing of all of the products within the requested category. No parameters will default to a list of all available categories. Invalid parameters will also redirect the shopper to the list of product categories.

```
if (isset($_GET['item']))
{
    // display sales page for a particular item
    ...
}
else if (isset($_GET['category']))
```

(continued)

(continued)

```
{
    // display list of items in category
    ...
}
else
{
    // display main list of categories
    ...
}
```

You will need to verify the parameter's value is valid by querying the database. If no records are returned from the query then it is safe to presume the value is invalid and you should redirect the user to shop.php (providing no parameters) so they can see the list of categories. Here is a sample showing the item parameter's validation; the process is the same to validate category albeit with a different query.

```
$query = sprintf('
    SELECT
        ITEM_ID, ITEM_NAME, ITEM_DESCRIPTION, PRICE, ITEM_IMAGE,
        C.CATEGORY_ID, CATEGORY_NAME
    FROM
        %sSHOP_INVENTORY I
            JOIN %sSHOP_CATEGORY C ON I.CATEGORY_ID = C.CATEGORY_ID
    WHERE
        ITEM_ID = %d',
    DB_TBL_PREFIX,
    DB_TBL_PREFIX,
    $_GET['item']);
$result = mysql_query($query, $GLOBALS['DB']);

if (!mysql_num_rows($result))
{
    mysql_free_result($result);
    header('Location: shop.php');
    exit();
}

$row = mysql_fetch_assoc($result);
```

Here is a query to validate category:

```
$query = sprintf('SELECT CATEGORY_ID, CATEGORY_NAME FROM ' .
    '%sSHOP_CATEGORY WHERE CATEGORY_ID = %d',
    DB_TBL_PREFIX,
    $_GET['category']);
```

Allow me to present the code responsible for generating the list of categories first. I realize that the logic appears in the last block of the shop.php page's main if structure. However, I would like to present the screens in the order in which users will see them.

A query is sent to the database to retrieve the list of product categories. By joining the WROX_SHOP_ CATEGORY table against WROX_SHOP_INVENTORY and grouping the results by the category id, you are able to retrieve the number of items under each category at the same time. Use JOIN (instead of LEFT JOIN), so the categories without any items will not be returned in the result set.

You can display the results anyway you want, but I've chosen here to display them as a simple unordered list. This is shown in Figure 8-2.

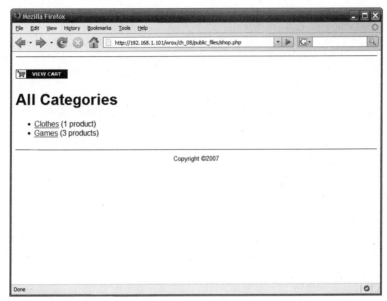

Figure 8-2

```
$query = sprintf('
    SELECT
        C.CATEGORY_ID, CATEGORY_NAME, COUNT(ITEM_ID) AS ITEM_COUNT
    FROM
        %sSHOP_CATEGORY C
            JOIN %sSHOP_INVENTORY I ON C.CATEGORY_ID = I.CATEGORY_ID
    GROUP BY
        C.CATEGORY_ID
    ORDER BY
        CATEGORY_NAME ASC',
    DB_TBL_PREFIX,
    DB_TBL_PREFIX);
$result = mysql_query($query, $GLOBALS['DB']);

echo '<ul>';
while ($row = mysql_fetch_assoc($result))
{
    printf('<li><a href="shop.php?category=%d">%s</a> (%d %s)</li>',
        $row['CATEGORY_ID'],
```

(continued)

211

(continued)

```
            $row['CATEGORY_NAME'],
            $row['ITEM_COUNT'],
            (($row['ITEM_COUNT'] == 1) ? 'product' : 'products'));
    }
    mysql_free_result($result);
    echo '</ul>';
```

Moving forward in what the customer should see but backwards in the script's organization, you now address generating the list of items within the selected category. When the script detects the `category` parameter it retrieves the items' ids, names, and image URLs from the database and displays the information with a `while` loop. Figure 8-3 shows the category's contents displayed.

Figure 8-3

```
// retrieve items
$query = sprintf('SELECT ITEM_ID, ITEM_NAME, ITEM_IMAGE ' .
    'FROM %sSHOP_INVENTORY WHERE CATEGORY_ID = %d ORDER BY ITEM_NAME ASC',
    DB_TBL_PREFIX,
    $id);
$result = mysql_query($query, $GLOBALS['DB']);

while ($row = mysql_fetch_assoc($result))
{
    echo '<table>';
    echo '<tr><td><img src="' . $row['ITEM_IMAGE'] .
        '" style="width:50px;height:50px;"/></td>';
    echo '<td><a href="shop.php?item=' . $row['ITEM_ID'] . '">' .
        $row['ITEM_NAME'] . '</a>' . '</td></tr>';
    echo '</table>';
}
```

The final view is generated when the item parameter is provided and displays a single product's information. The record is retrieved from the database and displayed. Also, this is where the `ShoppingCart` object is referenced, as there should be a link to add or remove the item from the shopping cart. If the product is not found in the cart, then the link should direct the user to add it by pointing to `cart.php?add`. Otherwise, the link would point to `cart.php?remove` so the shopper may remove it.

```php
echo '<table>';
echo '<tr><td rowspan="3">';
echo '<img src="' . $row['ITEM_IMAGE'] . '"/></td>';
echo '<td><b>' . $row['ITEM_NAME'] . '</b></td></tr>';
echo '<tr><td>' . nl2br($row['ITEM_DESCRIPTION']) . '</td></tr>';
echo '<tr><td>$' . number_format($row['PRICE'], 2) . '<br/>';

if (!$cart->qtyItem($row['ITEM_ID']))
{
    echo '<a href="cart.php?add&item=' . $row['ITEM_ID'] . '">';
    echo '<img src="img/cartadd.gif" alt="Add to Cart"/></a>';
}
else
{
    echo '<a href="cart.php?remove&item=' . $row['ITEM_ID'] . '">';
    echo '<img src="img/cartremove.gif" alt="Remove from Cart"/></a>';
}
echo '</td></tr>';
echo '</table>';
```

Figure 8-4 shows an item's individual product page.

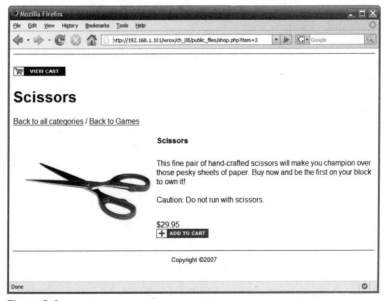

Figure 8-4

213

You may have noticed in each figure links to view the contents of the shopping cart and to return to either the full category listing or, if suitable, a specific category's products. The code to generate the links for the category's product listing page must provide a `category` parameter to `cart.php` so it can reciprocate an appropriate back link. The link to view all the categories simply points to `shop.php` with no parameters so it will display its default view.

```
echo '<p><a href="cart.php?category=' . $id . '">';
echo '<img src="img/cartview.gif" alt="View Cart"/></a></p>';
echo '<p><a href="shop.php">Back to all categories</a></p>';
```

The links for the individual product's view should also include a `category` parameter that is obtained in the query to validate the `item` parameter it received. Here is the code to generate the links to the shopping cart, all categories view, and the category listing under which the item is organized.

```
echo '<p><a href="cart.php?category=' . $row['CATEGORY_ID'] . '">';
echo '<img src="img/cartview.gif" alt="View Cart"/></a></p>';

echo '<p><a href="shop.php">Back to all categories</a> / ';
echo '<a href="shop.php?category=' . $row['CATEGORY_ID']. '">Back to ' .
    $row['CATEGORY_NAME'] . '</a></p>';
```

Here is the complete code listing for `public_files/shop.php`. Because I didn't discuss the file's logic linearly, please take extra time to read through it so you have an understanding of how the pieces I've discussed in this section come together.

```
<?php
include '../lib/common.php';
include '../lib/db.php';
include '../lib/ShoppingCart.php';

// create or resume session and retrieve shopping cart
session_start();
if (isset($_SESSION['cart']))
{
    $cart = unserialize($_SESSION['cart']);
}
else
{
    $cart = new ShoppingCart();
}

// display sales page for a particular item
if (isset($_GET['item']))
{
    // verify item exists
    $query = sprintf('
        SELECT
            ITEM_ID, ITEM_NAME, ITEM_DESCRIPTION, PRICE, ITEM_IMAGE,
            C.CATEGORY_ID, CATEGORY_NAME
        FROM
            %sSHOP_INVENTORY I
                JOIN %sSHOP_CATEGORY C ON I.CATEGORY_ID = C.CATEGORY_ID
        WHERE
```

```
                 ITEM_ID = %d',
         DB_TBL_PREFIX,
         DB_TBL_PREFIX,
         $_GET['item']);
     $result = mysql_query($query, $GLOBALS['DB']);

     // item does not exist so redirect to main categories list
     if (!mysql_num_rows($result))
     {
         mysql_free_result($result);
         header('Location: shop.php');
         exit();
     }

     $row = mysql_fetch_assoc($result);

     ob_start();
     echo '<p><a href="cart.php?category=' . $row['CATEGORY_ID'] . '">';
     echo '<img src="img/cartview.gif" alt="View Cart"/></a></p>';

     echo '<h1>' . $row['ITEM_NAME'] . '</h1>';

     echo '<p><a href="shop.php">Back to all categories</a> / ';
     echo '<a href="shop.php?category=' . $row['CATEGORY_ID']. '">Back to ' .
         $row['CATEGORY_NAME'] . '</a></p>';

     echo '<table>';
     echo '<tr><td rowspan="3">';
     echo '<img src="' . $row['ITEM_IMAGE'] . '"/></td>';
     echo '<td><b>' . $row['ITEM_NAME'] . '</b></td></tr>';
     echo '<tr><td>' . nl2br($row['ITEM_DESCRIPTION']) . '</td></tr>';
     echo '<tr><td>$' . number_format($row['PRICE'], 2) . '<br/>';

     // show link to either add or remove item from cart
     if (!$cart->qtyItem($row['ITEM_ID']))
     {
         echo '<a href="cart.php?add&item=' . $row['ITEM_ID'] . '">';
         echo '<img src="img/cartadd.gif" alt="Add to Cart"/></a>';
     }
     else
     {
         echo '<a href="cart.php?remove&item=' . $row['ITEM_ID'] . '">';
         echo '<img src="img/cartremove.gif" alt="Remove from Cart"/></a>';
     }
     echo '</td></tr>';
     echo '</table>';

     $GLOBALS['TEMPLATE']['content'] = ob_get_clean();
}

// display list of items in category
else if (isset($_GET['category']))
```

(continued)

(continued)

```
{
    // verify if category parameter is valid
    $query = sprintf('SELECT CATEGORY_ID, CATEGORY_NAME FROM ' .
        '%sSHOP_CATEGORY WHERE CATEGORY_ID = %d',
        DB_TBL_PREFIX,
        $_GET['category']);
    $result = mysql_query($query, $GLOBALS['DB']);

    // category does not exist so redirect to main categories list
    if (!mysql_num_rows($result))
    {
        mysql_free_result($result);
        header('Location: shop.php');
        exit();
    }

    $row = mysql_fetch_assoc($result);
    $id = $row['CATEGORY_ID'];
    $name = $row['CATEGORY_NAME'];
    mysql_free_result($result);

    ob_start();
    echo '<p><a href="cart.php?category=' . $id . '">';
    echo '<img src="img/cartview.gif" alt="View Cart"/></a></p>';

    echo '<h1>Products in ' . $name . '</h1>';

    echo '<p><a href="shop.php">Back to all categories</a></p>';

    // retrieve items
    $query = sprintf('SELECT ITEM_ID, ITEM_NAME, ITEM_IMAGE ' .
        'FROM %sSHOP_INVENTORY WHERE CATEGORY_ID = %d ORDER BY ITEM_NAME ASC',
        DB_TBL_PREFIX,
        $id);
    $result = mysql_query($query, $GLOBALS['DB']);

    while ($row = mysql_fetch_assoc($result))
    {
        echo '<table>';
        echo '<tr><td><img src="' . $row['ITEM_IMAGE'] .
            '" style="width:50px;height:50px;"/></td>';
        echo '<td><a href="shop.php?item=' . $row['ITEM_ID'] . '">' .
            $row['ITEM_NAME'] . '</a>' . '</td></tr>';
        echo '</table>';
    }

    $GLOBALS['TEMPLATE']['content'] = ob_get_clean();
}

// display main list of categories and the number of products within each
else
```

```
    {
        ob_start();
        echo '<p><a href="cart.php">' .
            '<img src="img/cartview.gif" alt="View Cart"/></a></p>';

        echo '<h1>All Categories</h1>';

        // Note: LEFT JOIN not specified so any categories without products will
        // not be included in the results
        $query = sprintf('
            SELECT
                C.CATEGORY_ID, CATEGORY_NAME, COUNT(ITEM_ID) AS ITEM_COUNT
            FROM
                %sSHOP_CATEGORY C
                    JOIN %sSHOP_INVENTORY I ON C.CATEGORY_ID = I.CATEGORY_ID
            GROUP BY
                C.CATEGORY_ID
            ORDER BY
                CATEGORY_NAME ASC',
            DB_TBL_PREFIX,
            DB_TBL_PREFIX);
        $result = mysql_query($query, $GLOBALS['DB']);

        echo '<ul>';
        while ($row = mysql_fetch_assoc($result))
        {
            printf('<li><a href="shop.php?category=%d">%s</a> (%d %s)</li>',
                $row['CATEGORY_ID'],
                $row['CATEGORY_NAME'],
                $row['ITEM_COUNT'],
                (($row['ITEM_COUNT'] == 1) ? 'product' : 'products'));
        }
        mysql_free_result($result);
        echo '</ul>';

        $GLOBALS['TEMPLATE']['content'] = ob_get_clean();
    }

// display the page
include '../templates/template-page.php';
?>
```

Adding Inventory

The administrative portion of the shopping cart allows you to manage the store's inventory. You are able to add, edit, and delete product categories and add, edit, and delete products within the categories. By applying the Ajax paradigm with JavaScript, the interface becomes easier and more intuitive to use.

HTML Structure of the Forms

The form to allow category management will consist of a `select` list populated with all the possible categories and an option to create a new category. When users select an option from the list they are presented a text field in which they can enter the category's name. In the case of editing an existing entry, a check box to delete the category is also presented.

Another `select` list will also be displayed to create or select an existing product. A text field is needed to accept the product's name, price and an image URL as well as a `textarea` element for the item's description.

The form elements can all be coded on to the same page and hidden or shown at the appropriate times with JavaScript. Initially, however, the section of the category form other than its `select` list and both the `select` and item sections of the product form should be hidden using `style="display:none;"`. Here is the HTML code that creates the forms and which I have saved as `inventory.html`:

```html
<html>
 <head>
  <title>Inventory</title>
  <style type="text/css"><!-- td { vertical-align: top; } --></style>
  <script type="text/javascript" src="js/ajax.js"></script>
  <script type="text/javascript" src="js/shop_inventory.js"></script>
 </head>
 <body>
  <h1>Store Inventory</h1>
  <form>
   <table id="cat_select_tbl">
    <tr>
     <td><label for="cat_select">Category</label></td>
     <td id="cat_select_cell"></td>
    </tr>
   </table>
   <table id="cat_form_tbl" style="display:none;">
    <tr>
     <td><label for="cat_name">Category</label></td>
     <td><input type="text" name="cat_name" id="cat_name"/></td>
    </tr>
    <tr id="cat_delete_row">
     <td></td>
     <td><input type="checkbox" name="cat_delete" id="cat_delete"/>
      <label for="cat_delete">Delete</label>
     </td>
    </tr><tr>
     <td></td>
     <td><input type="button" id="cat_submit" value="Save"/>
      <input type="button" id="cat_cancel" value="Cancel"/></td>
    </tr>
   </table>
   <table id="item_select_tbl" style="display:none;">
    <tr>
     <td><label for="item_select">Item</label></td>
     <td id="item_select_cell"></td>
    </tr>
   </table>
   <table id="item_form_tbl" style="display:none;">
    <tr>
     <td><label for="item_name">Item</label></td>
     <td><input type="text" name="item_name" id="item_name"/></td>
    </tr><tr>
     <td><label for="item_description">Description</label></td>
     <td><textarea name="item_description" id="item_description"
```

```
         cols="50" rows="5"></textarea></td>
      </tr><tr>
       <td><label for="item_price">Price</label></td>
       <td><input type="text" name="item_price" id="item_price"/></td>
      </tr><tr>
       <td><label for="item_image">Image</label></td>
       <td><input type="text" name="item_image" id="item_image"/></td>
      </tr>
      <tr id="item_delete_row">
       <td></td>
       <td><input type="checkbox" name="item_delete" id="item_delete"/>
        <label for="item_delete">Delete</label>
       </td>
      </tr><tr>
       <td></td>
       <td><input type="button" id="item_submit" value="Save"/>
        <input type="button" id="item_cancel" value="Cancel"/></td>
      </tr>
    </table>
   </form>
  </body>
</html>
```

Figure 8-5 shows all the elements (without applying the `display:none` styles). Note that the two `select` fields are missing; in the HTML they are represented as `div` elements. The actual `select` elements will be retrieved via Ajax and inserted into their respective placeholders when necessary.

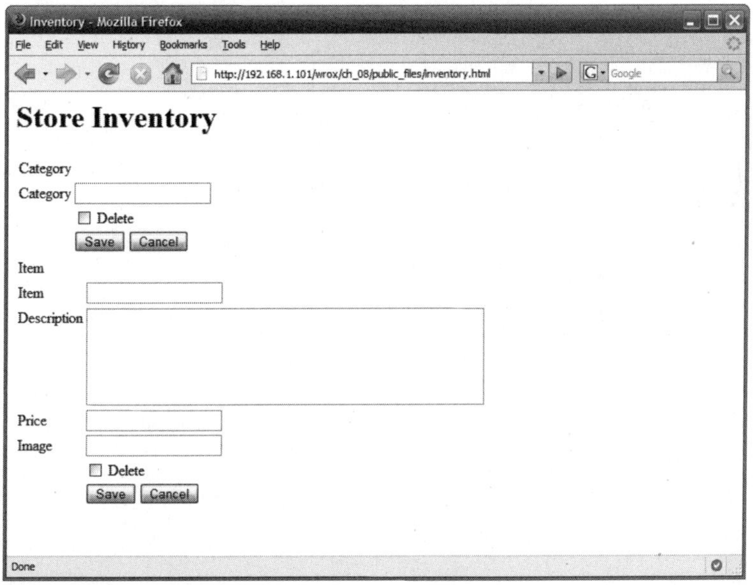

Figure 8-5

Server-Side Processing

The PHP code responsible for processing the Ajax requests must be written to handle various actions; this is denoted with a parameter passed in the calling URL:

- ❏ `retrieve_category_select`: Query the database to retrieve the list of product categories and return them in the form of an HTML `select` list.

- ❏ `retrieve_category`: Fetch the requested category's record from the database and return it as a JSON encoded string.

- ❏ `save_category`: Accept a post of category information and create, update or delete the database record

- ❏ `retrieve_item_select`: Query the database to retrieve the list of products within the categories and return them in the form of an HTML `select` list.

- ❏ `retrieve_item`: Fetch the requested product's record from the database and return it as a JSON encoded string.

- ❏ `save_item`: Accept a post of product information and create, update or delete the item's database record

There's no sense in discussing each action individually as the code is simple data retrieval or update processing. I would, however, like to touch on the SQL used to retrieve the list of categories. Like the statement used to pull the categories in `shop.php`, the names and the number of items within each category can be retrieved at the same time. At this point, however, it is advisable to use a `LEFT JOIN` instead of `JOIN` so that categories without products will still be included in the list.

Here is the complete code for `public_files/inventory_process.php`:

```php
<?php
include '../lib/common.php';
include '../lib/db.php';

// return HTML for category select list
if (isset($_GET['retrieve_category_select']))
{
    echo '<select id="cat_select" name="cat_select">';
    echo '<option>Select</option>';
    echo '<option value="new">Create New Category</option>';

    $query = sprintf('
        SELECT
            C.CATEGORY_ID, CATEGORY_NAME, COUNT(ITEM_ID) AS ITEM_COUNT
        FROM
            %sSHOP_CATEGORY C
                LEFT JOIN %sSHOP_INVENTORY I ON C.CATEGORY_ID = I.CATEGORY_ID
        GROUP BY
            C.CATEGORY_ID
        ORDER BY
            CATEGORY_NAME ASC',
        DB_TBL_PREFIX,
        DB_TBL_PREFIX);
```

```php
    $result = mysql_query($query, $GLOBALS['DB']);

    while ($row = mysql_fetch_assoc($result))
    {
        printf('<option value="%d">%s   (%s)</option>',
            $row['CATEGORY_ID'], $row['CATEGORY_NAME'], $row['ITEM_COUNT']);
    }
    mysql_free_result($result);

    echo '</select>';
}

// return JSON-encoded string with category information
else if (isset($_GET['retrieve_category']))
{
    $query = sprintf('SELECT CATEGORY_NAME FROM %sSHOP_CATEGORY WHERE ' .
        'CATEGORY_ID = %d',
        DB_TBL_PREFIX,
        $_GET['id']);
    $result = mysql_query($query, $GLOBALS['DB']);

    $row = mysql_fetch_assoc($result);
    echo json_encode(array('cat_name' => $row['CATEGORY_NAME']));

    mysql_free_result($result);
}

// process save request for category information
else if (isset($_GET['save_category']))
{
    // create a new record
    if ($_POST['id'] == 'new')
    {
        $query = sprintf('INSERT INTO %sSHOP_CATEGORY (CATEGORY_NAME) ' .
            'VALUES ("%s")',
            DB_TBL_PREFIX,
            mysql_real_escape_string($_POST['name'], $GLOBALS['DB']));
    }
    else
    {
        // delete an existing record
        if (isset($_POST['delete']))
        {
            $query = sprintf('DELETE FROM %sSHOP_CATEGORY WHERE ' .
                'CATEGORY_ID = %d',
                DB_TBL_PREFIX,
                $_POST['id']);
        }
        // update an existing record
        else
```

(continued)

221

(continued)

```
            {
                $query = sprintf('UPDATE %sSHOP_CATEGORY SET ' .
                    'CATEGORY_NAME = "%s" WHERE CATEGORY_ID = %d',
                    DB_TBL_PREFIX,
                    mysql_real_escape_string($_POST['name'], $GLOBALS['DB']),
                    $_POST['id']);
            }
        }
        mysql_query($query, $GLOBALS['DB']);
    }

    // return HTML for item select list
    else if (isset($_GET['retrieve_item_select']))
    {
        echo '<select id="item_select" name="item_select">';
        echo '<option>Select</option>';
        echo '<option value="new">Create New Item</option>';

        $query = sprintf('SELECT ITEM_ID, ITEM_NAME FROM %sSHOP_INVENTORY ' .
            'WHERE CATEGORY_ID = %d ORDER BY ITEM_NAME ASC',
            DB_TBL_PREFIX,
            $_GET['id']);
        $result = mysql_query($query, $GLOBALS['DB']);

        while ($row = mysql_fetch_assoc($result))
        {
            echo '<option value="' . $row['ITEM_ID'] . '">' . $row['ITEM_NAME'] .
                '</option>';
        }
        mysql_free_result($result);

        echo '</select>';
    }

    // return JSON-encoded string with item information
    else if (isset($_GET['retrieve_item']))
    {
        $query = sprintf('SELECT ITEM_NAME, ITEM_DESCRIPTION, PRICE, ' .
            'ITEM_IMAGE FROM %sSHOP_INVENTORY WHERE ITEM_ID = %d',
            DB_TBL_PREFIX,
            $_GET['id']);
        $result = mysql_query($query, $GLOBALS['DB']);

        $row = mysql_fetch_assoc($result);
        echo json_encode(array(
            'item_name' => $row['ITEM_NAME'],
            'item_description' => $row['ITEM_DESCRIPTION'],
            'item_price' => $row['PRICE'],
            'item_image' => $row['ITEM_IMAGE']));

        mysql_free_result($result);
    }
```

```php
    // process save request for item information
    else if (isset($_GET['save_item']))
    {
        // create a new record
        if ($_POST['id'] == 'new')
        {
            $query = sprintf('INSERT INTO %sSHOP_INVENTORY (ITEM_NAME, ' .
                'ITEM_DESCRIPTION, PRICE, ITEM_IMAGE, CATEGORY_ID) VALUES ' .
                '("%s", "%s", %02f, %d)',
                DB_TBL_PREFIX,
                mysql_real_escape_string($_POST['name'], $GLOBALS['DB']),
                mysql_real_escape_string($_POST['description'], $GLOBALS['DB']),
                $_POST['price'],
                mysql_real_escape_string($_POST['image'], $GLOBALS['DB']),
                $_POST['cat_id']);
        }
        else
        {
            // delete an existing record
            if (isset($_POST['delete']))
            {
                $query = sprintf('DELETE FROM %sSHOP_INVENTORY WHERE ' .
                    'ITEM_ID = %d',
                    DB_TBL_PREFIX,
                    $_POST['id']);
            }
            // update an existing record
            else
            {
                $query = sprintf('UPDATE %sSHOP_INVENTORY SET ' .
                    'ITEM_NAME = "%s", ITEM_DESCRIPTION = "%s", ' .
                    'PRICE = %02d, ITEM_IMAGE = "%s", CATEGORY_ID = %d ' .
                    'WHERE ITEM_ID = %d',
                    DB_TBL_PREFIX,
                    mysql_real_escape_string($_POST['name'], $GLOBALS['DB']),
                    mysql_real_escape_string($_POST['description'], $GLOBALS['DB']),
                    $_POST['price'],
                    mysql_real_escape_string($_POST['image'], $GLOBALS['DB']),
                    $_POST['cat_id'],
                    $_POST['id']);
            }
        }
        mysql_query($query, $GLOBALS['DB']);
    }
?>
```

Client-Side Support

JavaScript is used to bind the interface forms in `inventory.html` to the back-end processing of `inventory_process.php`.

The first event triggered when the page has finished loading in the user's browser is the `window` object's `onload` event and as such is typically the best place to assign event handlers. Wiring events like this instead of mixing on events in the HTML elements allows you to keep everything separate and easier to maintain.

```
window.onload = function()
{
    document.getElementById('cat_delete').onclick = warnCategoryDelete;
    document.getElementById('cat_cancel').onclick = resetCategoryForm;
    document.getElementById('cat_submit').onclick = submitCategoryForm;

    document.getElementById('item_delete').onclick = warnItemDelete;
    document.getElementById('item_cancel').onclick = resetItemForm;
    document.getElementById('item_submit').onclick = submitItemForm;

    resetCategoryForm();
}
```

When the product information form is shown the controls in the category form should be disabled. This gives the user a visual cue that even after drilling down to the product level in the category the focus is on the category form. It also prevents any accidental submissions of the category form. Consequently, when the category form is reset, it is important to make sure the elements have been enabled again. The resetCategoryForm() resets the category form by making sure the appropriate elements are enabled and hides the sub-forms. It also calls retrieveCategorySelect(), which issues the Ajax call to pull in the category select list.

```
function resetCategoryForm()
{
    document.getElementById('cat_name').disabled = false;
    document.getElementById('cat_delete').disabled = false;
    document.getElementById('cat_submit').disabled = false;
    document.getElementById('cat_cancel').disabled = false;

    document.getElementById('cat_form_tbl').style.display = 'none';
    document.getElementById('item_select_tbl').style.display = 'none';
    document.getElementById('item_form_tbl').style.display = 'none';

    document.getElementById('cat_delete').checked = false;
    document.getElementById('cat_submit').style.backgroundColor = '';

    retrieveCategorySelect();
    document.getElementById('cat_select_tbl').style.display = '';
}
```

The retrieveCategorySelect() function uses an XMLHttpObject object to communicate with inventory_process.php. It attaches the retrieve_category_select parameter to the URL as well as a nocache timestamp to avoid caching by the browser or any intermediate proxies. The response is set in the cat_select_celltd to be displayed to the user. The code must also wire the onchange event handler to the select list once it is in place so that is functional for the user.

```
function retrieveCategorySelect()
{
    var url = 'inventory_process.php?retrieve_category_select&nocache=' +
        (new Date()).getTime();

    window.httpObj = createXMLHTTPObject();
    window.httpObj.onreadystatechange = function()
```

```
    {
        if (window.httpObj.readyState == 4)
        {
            document.getElementById('cat_select_cell').innerHTML =
                window.httpObj.responseText;

            // assign select list's event handler
            document.getElementById('cat_select').onchange = showCategoryForms;
        }
    }

    window.httpObj.open('GET', url, false);
    window.httpObj.send(null);
}
```

The `showCategoryForms()` function displays the category form which was initially set hidden. A call is made to `retrieveCategoryValues()` to populate the field with the category's name and `retrieveItemSelect()` to sync the product list to the selected category.

```
function showCategoryForms()
{
    document.getElementById('cat_select_tbl').style.display = 'none';

    var select = document.getElementById('cat_select');
    retrieveCategoryValues(select.options[select.selectedIndex].value);

    if (select.options[select.selectedIndex].value != 'new')
    {
        retrieveItemSelect(select.options[select.selectedIndex].value);
        document.getElementById('item_select_tbl').style.display = '';
    }

    document.getElementById('cat_form_tbl').style.display = '';
}
```

`retrieveCategoryValues()` is responsible for populating the `cat_name` field. If the Create New option is selected from the list, then the field is shown empty and ready to accept user input. Otherwise the function issues an Ajax call and pre-fills the field.

```
function retrieveCategoryValues(value)
{
    if (value == 'new')
    {
        // clear fields if creating a new record
        document.getElementById('cat_name').value = '';
        document.getElementById('cat_delete_row').style.display = 'none';
    }
    else
    {
        var url = 'inventory_process.php?retrieve_category&id=' + value +
            '&nocache=' + (new Date()).getTime();

        window.httpObj = createXMLHTTPObject();
        window.httpObj.onreadystatechange = function()
```

(continued)

(continued)

```
        {
            if (window.httpObj.readyState == 4)
            {
                var r = eval('(' + window.httpObj.responseText + ')');
                document.getElementById('cat_name').value = r.cat_name;
                document.getElementById('cat_delete_row').style.display = '';
            }
        }

        window.httpObj.open('GET', url, false);
        window.httpObj.send(null);
    }
}
```

When a user is editing an existing category, an option to delete the record is presented in the form of a check box. Because it is irreversible, it is nice to provide extra notification to the severity of the action. The `warnCategoryDelete()` function highlights the submit button red when the check box is selected.

```
function warnCategoryDelete()
{
    var btn = document.getElementById('cat_submit');
    if (document.getElementById('cat_delete').checked)
    {
        btn.style.backgroundColor = '#FF0000';
    }
    else
    {
        btn.style.backgroundColor = '';
    }
}
```

The submit button for the item form should be highlighted red just like the category form's when the record is marked for deletion. `warnItemDelete()` handles this and is essentially the same as `warnCategoryDelete()` with the exception of the button being affected, so I will not show the code here.

`submitCategoryForm()` is responsible for sending the form data to `inventory_process.php`. It first verifies whether the delete check box has been selected, and if so it displays a confirmation message as an extra precaution. The data is sent via Ajax using the POST method and the form is cleared.

Only a relatively small amount of information can be passed in a URL parameter with the GET method, but larger amounts can be passed using POST. Because of this, POST is more suitable for sending the product information since the descriptive text could be quite lengthy. Although the category information can easily be sent via GET, I've decided to send it as POST just for the sake of consistency in my code.

```
function submitCategoryForm()
{
    if (document.getElementById('cat_delete').checked)
    {
        if (!confirm('Deleting a category will delete the inventory items ' +
            'it contains as well. Are you sure you wish to proceed?'))
```

```
        {
            return;
        }
    }

    // prepare the url and data
    var url = 'inventory_process.php?save_category&nocache=' +
        (new Date()).getTime();

    var select = document.getElementById('cat_select');
    var data = 'id=' + select.options[select.selectedIndex].value +
        '&name=' + escape(document.getElementById('cat_name').value);

    if (document.getElementById('cat_delete').checked)
    {
        data += '&delete=true';
    }

    window.httpObj = createXMLHTTPObject();
    window.httpObj.onreadystatechange = function()
    {
        if (window.httpObj.readyState == 4)
        {
            // reset the form when submission is complete
            resetCategoryForm();
        }
    }

    window.httpObj.open('POST', url, false);
    window.httpObj.setRequestHeader('Content-type',
        'application/x-www-form-urlencoded');
    window.httpObj.setRequestHeader('Content-length', data.length);
    window.httpObj.setRequestHeader('Connection', 'close');
    window.httpObj.send(data);
}
```

The `resetItemForm()` resets the product form by making sure the controls in the category form are disabled for safety reasons, hides the product's information fields and makes a call to `retrieveItemSelect()` to sync the list to the viewed category.

```
function resetItemForm()
{
    document.getElementById('cat_name').disabled = true;
    document.getElementById('cat_delete').disabled = true;
    document.getElementById('cat_submit').disabled = true;
    document.getElementById('cat_cancel').disabled = true;

    document.getElementById('item_form_tbl').style.display = 'none';

    document.getElementById('item_delete').checked = false;
    document.getElementById('item_submit').style.backgroundColor = '';
```

(continued)

(continued)

```
        var select = document.getElementById('cat_select');
        retrieveItemSelect(select.options[select.selectedIndex].value);
        document.getElementById('item_select_tbl').style.display = '';
}
```

retrieveItemSelect(), like its category counterpart, is responsible for retrieving a select list from inventory_process.php, but the category's id is passed as a URL parameter so that the products included are only those associated with the currently viewed category. It also assigns the onchange event handler to the list once it is in place so that is functional for the user.

```
function retrieveItemSelect(id)
{
    var url = 'inventory_process.php?retrieve_item_select&id=' + id +
        '&nocache=' + (new Date()).getTime();

    window.httpObj = createXMLHTTPObject();
    window.httpObj.onreadystatechange = function()
    {
        if (window.httpObj.readyState == 4)
        {
            document.getElementById('item_select_cell').innerHTML =
                window.httpObj.responseText;

            // assign select list's event handler
            document.getElementById('item_select').onchange = showItemForm;
        }
    }

    window.httpObj.open('GET', url, false);
    window.httpObj.send(null);
}
```

The showItemForm() function displays the hidden form fields for the product item form. It also makes a call to retrieveItemValues() to populate the fields with product information.

```
function showItemForm()
{
    var select = document.getElementById('item_select');

    retrieveItemValues(select.options[select.selectedIndex].value);

    document.getElementById('item_select_tbl').style.display = 'none';
    document.getElementById('item_form_tbl').style.display = '';
    document.getElementById('item_submit').style.backgroundColor = '';
}
```

retrieveItemValues() is responsible for populating the product fields. If the user selected the Create New option, then all the fields will be empty. However, if an existing product is chosen, then an Ajax call is issued to inventory_process.php. The resulting JSON-encoded string is parsed and used to fill in the field values.

```
function retrieveItemValues(value)
{
    if (value == 'new')
    {
        document.getElementById('item_name').value = '';
        document.getElementById('item_description').value = '';
        document.getElementById('item_price').value = '';
        document.getElementById('item_image').value = '';
        document.getElementById('item_delete_row').style.display = 'none';
    }
    else
    {
        var url = 'inventory_process.php?retrieve_item&id=' + value +
            '&nocache=' + (new Date()).getTime();

        window.httpObj = createXMLHTTPObject();
        window.httpObj.onreadystatechange = function()
        {
            if (window.httpObj.readyState == 4)
            {
                var r = eval('(' + window.httpObj.responseText + ')');
                document.getElementById('item_name').value = r.item_name;
                document.getElementById('item_description').value =
                    r.item_description;
                document.getElementById('item_price').value = r.item_price;
                document.getElementById('item_image').value = r.item_image;
                document.getElementById('item_delete_row').style.display = '';
            }
        }

        window.httpObj.open('GET', url, false);
        window.httpObj.send(null);
    }
}
```

The final function, `submitCategoryForm()`, is responsible for sending the form data to `inventory_process.php` after it verifies whether the delete check box has been selected. The data is sent via Ajax using the POST method.

```
function submitItemForm()
{
    if (document.getElementById('item_delete').checked)
    {
        if (!confirm('You are about to delete an inventory item. ' +
            'Are you sure you wish to proceed?'))
        {
            return;
        }
    }

    var url = 'inventory_process.php?save_item&nocache=' +
        (new Date()).getTime();
```

(continued)

(continued)

```javascript
    var i_select = document.getElementById('item_select');
    var c_select = document.getElementById('cat_select');
    var data = 'id=' + i_select.options[i_select.selectedIndex].value +
        '&name=' + escape(document.getElementById('item_name').value) +
        '&description=' +
            escape(document.getElementById('item_description').value) +
        '&price=' + document.getElementById('item_price').value +
        '&image=' + escape(document.getElementById('item_image').value) +
        '&cat_id=' + c_select.options[c_select.selectedIndex].value;

    if (document.getElementById('item_delete').checked)
    {
        data += '&delete=true';
    }

    window.httpObj = createXMLHTTPObject();
    window.httpObj.onreadystatechange = function()
    {
        if (window.httpObj.readyState == 4)
        {
            // reset the form when submission is complete
            resetItemForm();
        }
    }

    window.httpObj.open('POST', url, false);
    window.httpObj.setRequestHeader('Content-type',
        'application/x-www-form-urlencoded');
    window.httpObj.setRequestHeader('Content-length', data.length);
    window.httpObj.setRequestHeader('Connection', 'close');
    window.httpObj.send(data);
}
```

Whew! That is a lot of JavaScript code, isn't it? Here is the full code listing for the client-side functionality which I have saved as `public_files/js/inventory.js`:

```javascript
// register event handlers and set initial view
window.onload = function()
{
    document.getElementById('cat_delete').onclick = warnCategoryDelete;
    document.getElementById('cat_cancel').onclick = resetCategoryForm;
    document.getElementById('cat_submit').onclick = submitCategoryForm;

    document.getElementById('item_delete').onclick = warnItemDelete;
    document.getElementById('item_cancel').onclick = resetItemForm;
    document.getElementById('item_submit').onclick = submitItemForm;

    resetCategoryForm();
}

// reset the category form
function resetCategoryForm()
```

```
{
    // make sure all controls are enabled
    document.getElementById('cat_name').disabled = false;
    document.getElementById('cat_delete').disabled = false;
    document.getElementById('cat_submit').disabled = false;
    document.getElementById('cat_cancel').disabled = false;

    // hide sub forms
    document.getElementById('cat_form_tbl').style.display = 'none';
    document.getElementById('item_select_tbl').style.display = 'none';
    document.getElementById('item_form_tbl').style.display = 'none';

    // reset the submit button's background color and the delete option
    document.getElementById('cat_delete').checked = false;
    document.getElementById('cat_submit').style.backgroundColor = '';

    // populate the category select list and make visible
    retrieveCategorySelect();
    document.getElementById('cat_select_tbl').style.display = '';
}

// populate the category select list via AJAX
function retrieveCategorySelect()
{
    var url = 'inventory_process.php?retrieve_category_select&nocache=' +
        (new Date()).getTime();

    window.httpObj = createXMLHTTPObject();
    window.httpObj.onreadystatechange = function()
    {
        if (window.httpObj.readyState == 4)
        {
            document.getElementById('cat_select_cell').innerHTML =
                window.httpObj.responseText;

            // assign select list's event handler
            document.getElementById('cat_select').onchange = showCategoryForms;
        }
    }

    window.httpObj.open('GET', url, false);
    window.httpObj.send(null);
}

// display the category's form and possibly a synced item list
function showCategoryForms()
{
    // hide the category select list
    document.getElementById('cat_select_tbl').style.display = 'none';

    var select = document.getElementById('cat_select');
    retrieveCategoryValues(select.options[select.selectedIndex].value);

    if (select.options[select.selectedIndex].value != 'new')
```

(continued)

(continued)

```
    {
        // populate the item list for this category and make visible
        retrieveItemSelect(select.options[select.selectedIndex].value);
        document.getElementById('item_select_tbl').style.display = '';
    }

    document.getElementById('cat_form_tbl').style.display = '';
}

// populate the category form via AJAX
function retrieveCategoryValues(value)
{
    if (value == 'new')
    {
        // clear fields if creating a new record
        document.getElementById('cat_name').value = '';
        document.getElementById('cat_delete_row').style.display = 'none';
    }
    else
    {
        var url = 'inventory_process.php?retrieve_category&id=' + value +
            '&nocache=' + (new Date()).getTime();

        window.httpObj = createXMLHTTPObject();
        window.httpObj.onreadystatechange = function()
        {
            if (window.httpObj.readyState == 4)
            {
                var r = eval('(' + window.httpObj.responseText + ')');
                document.getElementById('cat_name').value = r.cat_name;
                document.getElementById('cat_delete_row').style.display = '';
            }
        }

        window.httpObj.open('GET', url, false);
        window.httpObj.send(null);
    }
}

// highlight the submit button if it will cause records to be deleted
function warnCategoryDelete()
{
    var btn = document.getElementById('cat_submit');
    if (document.getElementById('cat_delete').checked)
    {
        btn.style.backgroundColor = '#FF0000';
    }
    else
    {
        btn.style.backgroundColor = '';
    }
}
```

```
    // submit the category form via AJAX
    function submitCategoryForm()
    {
        // warn if the submit will cause records to be deleted
        if (document.getElementById('cat_delete').checked)
        {
            if (!confirm('Deleting a category will delete the inventory items ' +
                'it contains as well. Are you sure you wish to proceed?'))
            {
                return;
            }
        }

        // prepare the url and data
        var url = 'inventory_process.php?save_category&nocache=' +
            (new Date()).getTime();

        var select = document.getElementById('cat_select');
        var data = 'id=' + select.options[select.selectedIndex].value +
            '&name=' + escape(document.getElementById('cat_name').value);

        if (document.getElementById('cat_delete').checked)
        {
            data += '&delete=true';
        }

        window.httpObj = createXMLHTTPObject();
        window.httpObj.onreadystatechange = function()
        {
            if (window.httpObj.readyState == 4)
            {
                // reset the form when submission is complete
                resetCategoryForm();
            }
        }

        // set headers and send content
        window.httpObj.open('POST', url, false);
        window.httpObj.setRequestHeader('Content-type',
            'application/x-www-form-urlencoded');
        window.httpObj.setRequestHeader('Content-length', data.length);
        window.httpObj.setRequestHeader('Connection', 'close');
        window.httpObj.send(data);
    }

    // reset the item form
    function resetItemForm()
    {
        // make sure all category controls are disable
        document.getElementById('cat_name').disabled = true;
        document.getElementById('cat_delete').disabled = true;
```

(continued)

233

(continued)

```
        document.getElementById('cat_submit').disabled = true;
        document.getElementById('cat_cancel').disabled = true;

        // hide sub form
        document.getElementById('item_form_tbl').style.display = 'none';

        // reset the submit button's background color and the delete option
        document.getElementById('item_delete').checked = false;
        document.getElementById('item_submit').style.backgroundColor = '';

        // populate the item list and make it visible
        var select = document.getElementById('cat_select');
        retrieveItemSelect(select.options[select.selectedIndex].value);
        document.getElementById('item_select_tbl').style.display = '';
    }

    // populate the item select list for the selected category via AJAX
    function retrieveItemSelect(id)
    {
        var url = 'inventory_process.php?retrieve_item_select&id=' + id +
            '&nocache=' + (new Date()).getTime();

        window.httpObj = createXMLHTTPObject();
        window.httpObj.onreadystatechange = function()
        {
            if (window.httpObj.readyState == 4)
            {
                document.getElementById('item_select_cell').innerHTML =
                    window.httpObj.responseText;

                // assign select list's event handler
                document.getElementById('item_select').onchange = showItemForm;
            }
        }

        window.httpObj.open('GET', url, false);
        window.httpObj.send(null);
    }

    // display the item's form
    function showItemForm()
    {
        var select = document.getElementById('item_select');

        // populate the item list for this category and make visible
        retrieveItemValues(select.options[select.selectedIndex].value);

        // hide item select list and make item form visible
        document.getElementById('item_select_tbl').style.display = 'none';
        document.getElementById('item_form_tbl').style.display = '';
        document.getElementById('item_submit').style.backgroundColor = '';
    }
```

```
// populate the item form via AJAX
function retrieveItemValues(value)
{
    if (value == 'new')
    {
        // clear fields if creating a new record
        document.getElementById('item_name').value = '';
        document.getElementById('item_description').value = '';
        document.getElementById('item_price').value = '';
        document.getElementById('item_image').value = '';
        document.getElementById('item_delete_row').style.display = 'none';
    }
    else
    {
        var url = 'inventory_process.php?retrieve_item&id=' + value +
            '&nocache=' + (new Date()).getTime();

        window.httpObj = createXMLHTTPObject();
        window.httpObj.onreadystatechange = function()
        {
            if (window.httpObj.readyState == 4)
            {
                var r = eval('(' + window.httpObj.responseText + ')');
                document.getElementById('item_name').value = r.item_name;
                document.getElementById('item_description').value =
                    r.item_description;
                document.getElementById('item_price').value = r.item_price;
                document.getElementById('item_image').value = r.item_image;
                document.getElementById('item_delete_row').style.display = '';
            }
        }

        window.httpObj.open('GET', url, false);
        window.httpObj.send(null);
    }
}

// highlight the submit button if it will cause records to be deleted
function warnItemDelete()
{
    var btn = document.getElementById('item_submit');
    if (document.getElementById('item_delete').checked)
    {
        btn.style.backgroundColor = '#FF0000';
    }
    else
    {
        btn.style.backgroundColor = '';
    }
}

// submit the item form via AJAX
function submitItemForm()
```

(continued)

(continued)

```
    {
        // warn if the submit will cause records to be deleted
        if (document.getElementById('item_delete').checked)
        {
            if (!confirm('You are about to delete an inventory item. ' +
                'Are you sure you wish to proceed?'))
            {
                return;
            }
        }

        // prepare the url and data
        var url = 'inventory_process.php?save_item&nocache=' +
            (new Date()).getTime();

        var i_select = document.getElementById('item_select');
        var c_select = document.getElementById('cat_select');
        var data = 'id=' + i_select.options[i_select.selectedIndex].value +
            '&name=' + escape(document.getElementById('item_name').value) +
            '&description=' +
                escape(document.getElementById('item_description').value) +
            '&price=' + document.getElementById('item_price').value +
            '&image=' + escape(document.getElementById('item_image').value) +
            '&cat_id=' + c_select.options[c_select.selectedIndex].value;

        if (document.getElementById('item_delete').checked)
        {
            data += '&delete=true';
        }

        window.httpObj = createXMLHTTPObject();
        window.httpObj.onreadystatechange = function()
        {
            if (window.httpObj.readyState == 4)
            {
                // reset the form when submission is complete
                resetItemForm();
            }
        }

        // set headers and send content
        window.httpObj.open('POST', url, false);
        window.httpObj.setRequestHeader('Content-type',
            'application/x-www-form-urlencoded');
        window.httpObj.setRequestHeader('Content-length', data.length);
        window.httpObj.setRequestHeader('Connection', 'close');
        window.httpObj.send(data);
    }
```

Now you should be able to populate the store's inventory and offer products for sale. Figure 8-6 shows adding a new category through the interface and Figure 8-7 shows adding a new product.

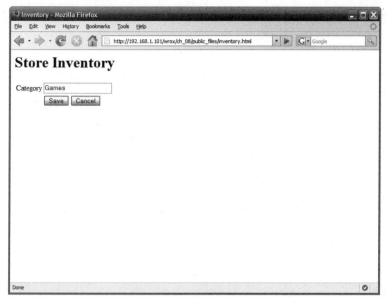

Figure 8-6

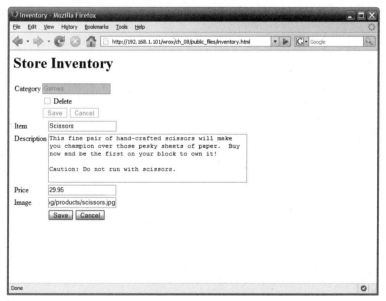

Figure 8-7

Summary

In this chapter, I've guided you through writing an application to allow shoppers to view products you're selling and to keep track of the ones they're interested in within their session until they're ready for checkout. It's up to you to integrate a payment processor so they can actually submit their order (and you can make some money). There are a lot of different factors that come into play when choosing a processor and you would do well to read John Conde's article on the subject titled *Solve the Payment Processing Problem* and available online at www.sitepoint.com/article/merchant-account-review.

In the next chapter, I'll discuss how you can collect and analyze page hits to generate a website statistic report. Such reports can be used to better understand the effectiveness of a site and to make better business decisions.

9

Web Site Statistics

People like to collect access statistics for different reasons. Perhaps you've been asked by a supervisor to prepare a report showing the traffic your company's web site receives, or maybe you're just curious yourself as to how many people are visiting. People like to see if their site is growing in popularity. Aside from satisfying curiosity though, statistics can be used to make informed business decisions as well. Such reports can be correlated against times when new promotions were rolled out and show whether visits increase because of them. They can even provide a snapshot of a site's state of health by showing how popular certain pages are compared to others in the site. Tracking can even be mandated by policy for a variety of reasons.

In this chapter, you'll collect and analyze page hits to generate a web site statistic report. Such reports can be used to better understand the effectiveness of a site and to make better business decisions.

Determining What to Collect

Before starting on a project like this, you need to identify what purpose gathering the statistics will serve. Why they're needed will affect what information needs to be collected. For example, a report generated for a company's marketing department might show the most popular pages for visitors to enter or exit the site on. A web development team might be more interested in seeing a report showing what browsers the visitors are using.

After you've identified what will be included in the report, you then check if that information is something that can easily be retrieved or calculated. Sometimes it can be extracted right from an environment variable or the HTTP request but other times you will have to extrapolate the information. Using the entrance and exit pages as an example again, page requests aren't explicitly marked as an entrance or exit — but if you collect a list of pages a user visits and sort them in chronological order, then obviously the first is the entry and the last is the exit.

HTTP is a stateless protocol so there is no real foolproof way to identify users and track their session. You can track the IP address, but a visitor could be behind an anonymizing proxy server, which presents a new address for each request, or multiple users may be behind a gateway and all share one publically visible IP address. The page may even be retrieved from a proxy's cache in which case the request would never hit your server to be tallied. Even cookies and sessions can be manipulated to skew tracking results. It is important for you and those reading your reports to keep in mind that only general trends can be presented. There will always be some margin of error.

So what's available? First check PHP's `$_SERVER` super global array (`http://us.php.net/manual/en/reserved.variables.php`). `PHP_SELF`, `REQUEST_URI`, `REQUEST_TIME`, `HTTP_USER_AGENT`, and `REMOTE_ADDR` may be helpful. You can also use JavaScript to determine other values such as the client's screen resolution and send it back to your server.

The raw data for the report in this chapter will be the users' IP addresses, what pages they viewed, and the access time. The report will then present the following information for both the current month and the current year:

- ❏ The total number of unique visitors accessing the site
- ❏ The top 10 IP addresses
- ❏ The top 5 most popular pages
- ❏ The 5 least popular pages that have been visited

I'm not concerned much about the effects of proxies or gateways and will consider any request from the same IP address within the same day part of a user's visit.

Although numbers are great, sometimes it's helpful to see information presented graphically as well. You will use the GD functions to add graphs to the reports. The charts will show traffic breakdown for the month and year.

Figure 9-1 shows this project in action as the report displayed in a web browser.

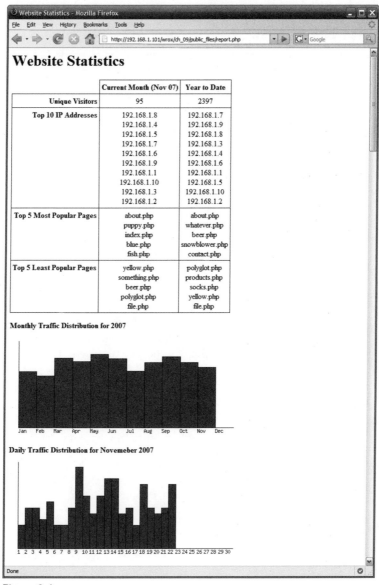

Figure 9-1

Designing the Database

The database table will be required to store the name of a requested page, the time it was accessed, and which IP address requested it.

```
+-------------+-------------------+------+-----+-------------------+
| Field       | Type              | Null | Key | Default           |
+-------------+-------------------+------+-----+-------------------+
| ACCESS_TIME | timestamp         | NO   | PRI | CURRENT_TIMESTAMP |
| IP_ADDRESS  | int(10) unsigned  | NO   | PRI |                   |
| REQ_PAGE    | varchar(255)      | NO   |     |                   |
+-------------+-------------------+------+-----+-------------------+
```

Perhaps you are wondering why I chose to store the user's IP address as INTEGER UNSIGNED instead of CHAR(15). Certainly storing the value as a string would work fine, but it is more efficient for computers to store a work with integer values. MySQL offers two built-in functions to convert an address to and from an integer. The INET_ATON() function converts a network address represented as a dotted-quad into an 8-byte integer value. INET_NTOA() converts the integer value back to its string representation. When storing addresses in this manner, the MySQL documentation recommends using UNSIGNED INTEGER as the column type to avoid potential problems. Addresses with a first octet greater than 127 would not be stored correctly if the column were signed.

ACCESS_TIME is not a suitable primary key by itself and prevent duplication (and subsequent errors) so I needed to include the IP address as part of the key as well.

I prefer to specify the InnoDB storage engine for a project of this type. MyISAM is slower when performing INSERT statements than InnoDB and locks the entire table when performing an INSERT or UPDATE statements. InnoDB locks just the affected row for INSERT and UPDATE statements. I'm not so much concerned about retrieval speed since that will only be done periodically to retrieve a report. I would rather have better performance when adding records so users will see less of a performance impact in a high-load environment.

Here is the SQL code for WROX_SITE_ACCESS:

```sql
CREATE TABLE WROX_SITE_ACCESS (
    ACCESS_TIME  TIMESTAMP         NOT NULL  DEFAULT CURRENT_TIMESTAMP,
    IP_ADDRESS   INTEGER UNSIGNED  NOT NULL,
    REQ_PAGE     VARCHAR(255)      NOT NULL,

    PRIMARY KEY (ACCESS_TIME, IP_ADDRESS)
)
ENGINE=InnoDB DEFAULT CHARACTER SET latin1
    COLLATE latin1_general_cs;
```

Obtaining Data

Adding tracking entries to the database is nothing more complicated than a simple INSERT statement. ACCESS_TIME will default to the current timestamp when the record in first created so I do not need to explicitly provide it in the query.

It would make sense however to encapsulate the logic as its own function. I've done so as log_page_hit() which appears below. You can really save it in any file you want, although I save mine in lib/functions.php:

```
function log_page_hit()
{
    $query = sprintf('INSERT INTO %sSITE_ACCESS (IP_ADDRESS, ' .
        'REQ_PAGE) VALUES (INET_ATON("%s"), "%s")', DB_TBL_PREFIX,
        $_SERVER['REMOTE_ADDR'],
        mysql_real_escape_string($_SERVER['SCRIPT_NAME'], $GLOBALS['DB']));

    return mysql_query($query, $GLOBALS['DB']);
}
```

All you need to do is call the logging function from any file you want to track access of. If you want to target your tracking for just a handful of files then it's perfectly acceptable to place the function call directly in them. Otherwise, it might be a better idea to call the function at the end of a template file so any script that is based on it will then be generating log entries and you don't have to touch each individual file.

Collecting the statistics is pretty easy and straightforward. The real challenge (and fun) comes when it's time to analyze the data and produce the report with useful information. Now you can look at different queries to retrieve information for the reports and charts.

The total number of unique visitors (defined by their IP addresses) accessing the site as well as the top 10 IP addresses can be found using the same query:

```
SELECT
    INET_NTOA(IP_ADDRESS) AS IP_ADDRESS
FROM
    WROX_SITE_ACCESS SA
GROUP BY
    SA.IP_ADDRESS
ORDER BY
    COUNT(IP_ADDRESS) DESC;
```

A GROUP BY clause in the query effectively collapses the records sharing the same IP addresses so you are returned one row for each address. By ordering the results in descending order by the number IP addresses in each group, we can make sure the most active addresses appear first. mysql_num_rows() will be used in PHP to determine the total number of unique addresses. A WHERE clause can appear before GROUP BY to narrow the results down between a certain period of time.

The query to determine the top five most popular pages is similar:

```
SELECT
    REQ_PAGE, COUNT(REQ_PAGE) AS TOTAL
FROM
    WROX_SITE_ACCESS
GROUP BY
    REQ_PAGE
ORDER BY
    TOTAL DESC;
```

Again the GROUP BY clause collapses the returned records, this time on the REQ_PAGE column so we obtain one row per page. ORDER BY sorts the results in descending order so more active pages appear first.

To retrieve the least active pages we could set the result's cursor to the last record using `mysql_data_seek()` and read five records backward, however it's easier to just issue another query but change ORDER BY to ASC.

The third query retrieves the distribution of page hits between a start and end date.

```
SELECT
    UNIX_TIMESTAMP(ACCESS_TIME) AS ATIME, COUNT(REQ_PAGE) AS TOTAL
FROM
    WROX_SITE_ACCESS
WHERE
    DATE(ACCESS_TIME) BETWEEN
        '2007-01-01' AND
        DATE('2007-01-01') + INTERVAL 1 WEEK - INTERVAL 1 DAY
GROUP BY
    ATIME;
```

The DATE(ACCESS_TIME) appearing in the WHERE clause widens the timestamp's resolution from seconds to a day. You may want to change it retrieve different time spans instead. REQ_PAGE = 'pagename' may be added to the WHERE clause to restrict results for a particular page.

Code and Code Explanation

Now you should have an understanding of what information will be collected and how to retrieve it in a meaningful way so it's time to turn your attention to writing the project's code. You have the ability to create charts and graphs by using PHP's GD functions. Here you'll build two common types: a bar chart and a pie chart. Both will be coded as classes so they can easily be extended and reused in future projects. First I will take a look at the pie chart and then the bar chart. They can be incorporated into the report to augment the presentation of information in a visual way. Then I will present the code for the report itself.

Pie Chart

A pie chart is a circular graph that is divided into section. Each section represents how much a data member consumes of the aggregate total. In other words, a pie chart might be a good choice when you want to visually present percentage data. The PieChart class will offer three public methods, as shown in Table 9-1.

Table 9-1: PieChart **Methods**

Method	Description
_construct(width)	Initializes a new PieChart object with the specified width
flushImage([filename])	Sends the chart image to the browser or saves to a file if filename is provided
graphData(data, colors)	Graphs an array of data and uses colors as the corresponding colors for the data segments

The class has three private properties: One to store the image handle of the graph, one to store the width of the graph, and then the center of the chart. The constructor initializes a new instance of `PieChart` by creating a new true color image using `imagecreatetruecolor()` and flood fills the image canvas using `imagefill()`. The image's width is divided in half and stored for later use so you'll be able to easily determine the image's center point.

```
class PieChart
{
    private $center;
    private $width;
    private $image;

    public function __construct($width)
    {
        $this->image = imagecreatetruecolor($width, $width);

        $this->width = $width;
        $this->center = $width / 2;

        $white = imagecolorallocate($this->image, 0xFF, 0xFF, 0xFF);
        imagefill($this->image, 0,0, $white);
    }
    ...
}
```

The `flushImage()` method encapsulates the logic of outputting an image to the browser. It sends the appropriate HTTP header and then flushes the image from memory. This behavior can change, however, if a file name is passed as an argument, in which case it will save the image as the provided name.

```
public function flushImage($filename = '')
{
    if ($filename)
    {
        imagepng($this->image, $filename);
    }
    else
    {
        header('Content-type: image/png');
        imagepng($this->image);
    }
}
```

`graphData()` accepts two related arrays and is where the majority of the drawing routines takes place. The first array is the sequence of data to graph and the second is which colors the segments will be. Each color is represented as an array with r, g, and b representing the individual RGB values.

Each arc is drawn twice — once for the filled segment and a second time for a black outline. Set the starting angle of the first slice at –90 degrees so it starts at the circle's top (the 12 o'clock position if it were a clock), although this is nothing more than personal preference. The default 0 value for `imagefilledarc()` would start slice at the circle's right (3 o'clock).

```php
public function graphData($data, $colors)
{
    $black = imagecolorallocate($this->image, 0x00, 0x00, 0x00);

    $sum = array_sum($data);

    $start = -90;

    for ($i = 0; $i < count($data); $i++)
    {
        $color = imagecolorallocate($this->image, $colors[$i]['r'],
            $colors[$i]['g'], $colors[$i]['b']);

        $stop = (100 * $data[$i] / $sum * 3.6) + $start;

        imagefilledarc($this->image, $this->center, $this->center,
            $this->width, $this->width, $start, $stop, $color,
            IMG_ARC_PIE);
        imagefilledarc($this->image, $this->center, $this->center,
            $this->width, $this->width, $start, $stop, $black,
            IMG_ARC_NOFILL | IMG_ARC_EDGED);

        $start = $stop;
    }
}
```

To generate a new pie chart you must first instantiate a new object of the `PieChart` class, feed `graphData()` some values and colors, and call `flushImage()`. Figure 9-2 shows the sample's output.

```php
<?php
include '../lib/PieChart.php';

$data = array(150, 302, 250);
$colors = array(
    array('r' => 0x33, 'g' => 0xCC, 'b' => 0xFF),
    array('r' => 0xFF, 'g' => 0x33, 'b' => 0xCC),
    array('r' => 0xCC, 'g' => 0xFF, 'b' => 0x33));

$chart = new PieChart(150);
$chart->graphData($data, $colors);
$chart->flushImage();
?>
```

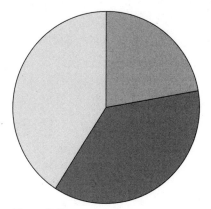

Figure 9-2

Here is the complete code for `lib/PieChart.php`.

```php
<?php
class PieChart
{
    private $center;  // center point
    private $width;   // width of chart
    private $image;   // image reference

    // initialize new object
    public function __construct($width)
    {
        // create a new image
        $this->image = imagecreatetruecolor($width, $width);

        // determine center of image
        $this->center = $width / 2;
        $this->width = $width;

        // fill image background white
        $white = imagecolorallocate($this->image, 0xFF, 0xFF, 0xFF);
        imagefill($this->image, 0,0, $white);
    }

    // dump image to browser or save
    public function flushImage($filename = '')
    {
        if ($filename)
        {
            imagepng($this->image, $filename);
        }
        else
        {
            header('Content-type: image/png');
```

(continued)

247

(continued)

```php
                imagepng($this->image);
        }
    }

    // graph the data using the associated colors
    public function graphData($data, $colors)
    {
        // allocate black for slice outline
        $black = imagecolorallocate($this->image, 0x00, 0x00, 0x00);

        // sum of all values
        $sum = array_sum($data);

        // starting angle of pie slice
        $start = -90;

        for ($i = 0; $i < count($data); $i++)
        {
            $color = imagecolorallocate($this->image, $colors[$i]['r'],
                $colors[$i]['g'], $colors[$i]['b']);

            // stop angle of pie slice
            $stop = (100 * $data[$i] / $sum * 3.6) + $start;

            // draw arc twice - once for filled area and again for outline
            imagefilledarc($this->image, $this->center, $this->center,
                $this->width, $this->width, $start, $stop, $color,
                IMG_ARC_PIE);
            imagefilledarc($this->image, $this->center, $this->center,
                $this->width, $this->width, $start, $stop, $black,
                IMG_ARC_NOFILL | IMG_ARC_EDGED);

            // increment to next starting point
            $start = $stop;
        }
    }
}
?>
```

Bar Chart

A bar chart places multiple values for a visual side-by-side comparison. Because pieces of data appear alongside one other against an x-y axis, bar charts are useful for showing trends over a given period of time. The `BarChart` class will also offer three public methods, as shown in Table 9-2.

The `BarChart` class's methods and their purposes are similar to the ones in the `PieChart` class. The constructor is responsible for initializing a new object and preparing the image in memory. `flushImage()` outputs the graph image and the drawing logic is contained in `graphData()`.

Table 9-2: BarChart Methods

Method	Description
_construct(width, height)	Initializes a new BarChart object with the specified width and height
flushImage([filename])	Sends the chart image to the browser or save to a file if filename is provided
graphData(data, colors, labels)	Graphs an array of data and using colors as the corresponding colors for the data segments and labels the segments with values in array labels

The class has three private properties: One property stores the image handle of the graph and two other properties store the width and height of the graph. Because the color black used in several places in the code, it makes sense to only allocate it once in the image and store a handle to it as a property as well.

The constructor initializes a new instance of BarChart by creating a new true color image using imagecreatetruecolor() and flood fills the image canvas using imagefill(). The image's width and height are stored to the corresponding property. The black color is allocated and used to draw the chart's axis lines.

```
class BarChart
{
    private $width;
    private $height;
    private $image;
    private $black;

    public function __construct($width, $height)
    {
        $this->image = imagecreatetruecolor($width, $height);
        $this->width = $width;
        $this->height = $height;

        $white = imagecolorallocate($this->image, 0xFF, 0xFF, 0xFF);
        imagefill($this->image, 0,0, $white);

        $this->black = imagecolorallocate($this->image, 0x00, 0 x00, 0 x00);
        imageline($this->image, 20, 0, 20, $height - 20, $this->black);
        imageline($this->image, 20, $height - 20, $width - 20, $height - 20,
            $this->black);
    }
    ...
}
```

The `flushImage()` method encapsulates the logic of outputting an image to the browser. It sends the appropriate HTTP header and then flushes the image from memory. This behavior can change, however, if a file name is passed as an argument, in which case it will save the image as the provided name.

```php
public function flushImage($filename = '')
{
    if ($filename)
    {
        imagepng($this->image, $filename);
    }
    else
    {
        header('Content-type: image/png');
        imagepng($this->image);
    }
}
```

Unlike its `PieChart` counterpart, `BarChart`'s `graphData()` method accepts an additional argument. Besides the arrays of data and corresponding colors, the elements' labels for the graph's x-axis are provided as a third array. The method places these labels underneath the dataset. Again, the data segments are drawn twice — once for the color and again to provide a black outline.

```php
public function graphData($data, $colors, $labels)
{
    $x = 20;
    $y = $this->height - 20;

    $bar_width = ($this->width - $x - 20) / count($data);

    $ymax = max($data);
    for ($i = 0; $i < count($data); $i++)
    {
        $bar_height = ($data[$i] / $ymax) * ($this->height - 30);
        $color = imagecolorallocate($this->image, $colors[$i]['r'],
            $colors[$i]['g'], $colors[$i]['b']);

        imagefilledrectangle($this->image, $x, $y, $x + $bar_width,
            $y - $bar_height, $color);
        imagerectangle($this->image, $x, $y, $x + $bar_width,
            $y - $bar_height, $this->black);
        imagestring($this->image, 2, $x, $y, $labels[$i], $this->black);

        $x += $bar_width;
    }
}
```

Here's the example usage of the `BarChart` class. Figure 9-3 shows the sample's output.

```php
<?php
include '../lib/BarChart.php';

$data = array(100, 150, 70, 130, 190, 160);
$colors = array_fill(0, count($data),
```

```
        array('r' => 0x33, 'g' => 0xCC, 'b' => 0xFF));
$labels = array('ABC', 'EFG', 'IJK', 'MNO', 'QRS', 'UVW');

$chart = new BarChart(400, 175);
$chart->graphData($data, $colors, $labels, 10);
$chart->flushImage();
?>
```

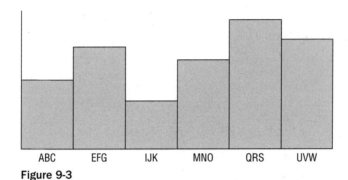

Figure 9-3

Here is the complete listing for lib/BarChart.php:

```
<?php
class BarChart
{
    private $width;    // width of chart
    private $height;   // height of chart
    private $image;    // image reference
    private $black;    // allocated color black

    // initialize new object
    public function __construct($width, $height)
    {
        // create new image
        $this->image = imagecreatetruecolor($width, $height);
        $this->width = $width;
        $this->height = $height;

        // fill image background white
        $white = imagecolorallocate($this->image, 0xFF, 0xFF, 0xFF);
        imagefill($this->image, 0,0, $white);

        // draw axis
        $this->black = imagecolorallocate($this->image, 0x00, 0x00, 0x00);
        imageline($this->image, 20, 0, 20, $height - 20, $this->black);
        imageline($this->image, 20, $height - 20, $width - 20, $height - 20,
            $this->black);
    }

    // dump image to browser or save
```

(continued)

(continued)

```php
        public function flushImage($filename = '')
        {
            if ($filename)
            {
                imagepng($this->image, $filename);
            }
            else
            {
                header('Content-type: image/png');
                imagepng($this->image);
            }
        }

        // graph the data using the associated colors and labels
        public function graphData($data, $colors, $labels)
        {
            // start point
            $x = 20;
            $y = $this->height - 20;

            // calculate bar width
            $bar_width = ($this->width - $x - 20) / count($data);


            $ymax = max($data);
            for ($i = 0; $i < count($data); $i++)
            {
                // calculate height of bar
                $bar_height = ($data[$i] / $ymax) * ($this->height - 30);
                $color = imagecolorallocate($this->image, $colors[$i]['r'],
                    $colors[$i]['g'], $colors[$i]['b']);
                // draw bar twice - once for filled area and again for outline

                imagefilledrectangle($this->image, $x, $y, $x + $bar_width,
                    $y - $bar_height, $color);
                imagerectangle($this->image, $x, $y, $x + $bar_width,
                    $y - $bar_height, $this->black);
                imagestring($this->image, 2, $x, $y, $labels[$i], $this->black);

                // increment starting point
                $x += $bar_width;
            }
        }
    }
?>
```

The chart classes presented in this chapter are basic and prove sufficient enough to meet your needs. However, to make them truly useful you may want to expand them. Some possible suggestions are adding titles, centering the axis labels, drawing the bars or pie slices so they appear three-dimensional, or whatever else you may think of.

The Report

The information you collect from the database will be displayed in a report page. However, before any data is pulled from the database, it might be a good idea to retrieve some date values that would be useful in constructing queries or to be displayed in the report. This can be done conveniently with the date(), list(), and explode() functions.

```
list($full_month, $full_year, $short_month, $num_month, $short_year) =
    explode('/', date('F/Y/M/m/y'));
```

This first portion of the report will show the top 10 unique IP addresses for the current month and current year. Retrieving the unique IP addresses for the current month can be done like this:

```
$query = sprintf('
    SELECT
        INET_NTOA(IP_ADDRESS) AS IP_ADDRESS
    FROM
        %sSITE_ACCESS
    WHERE
        DATE(ACCESS_TIME) BETWEEN
            "%d-%02d-01" AND
            "%d-%02d-01" + INTERVAL 1 MONTH - INTERVAL 1 DAY
    GROUP BY
        IP_ADDRESS
    ORDER BY
        COUNT(IP_ADDRESS) DESC',
    DB_TBL_PREFIX,
    $full_year,
    $num_month,
    $full_year,
    $num_month);
```

After the addresses have been retrieved, the top 10 results can be stored in an array. As I chose not to use a LIMIT clause in my SQL statement, I must use a for loop to obtain the first 10 addresses but also check against the total number of records in case less than 10 were returned. This allows me to retrieve the total number of unique visitors for the month at the same time which will also appear in the report.

```
$result = mysql_query($query, $GLOBALS['DB']);

$mo_total = mysql_num_rows($result);

for ($i = 0; $i < 10 && $i < $mo_total; $i++)
{
    $row = mysql_fetch_assoc($result);
    $mo_addrs[] = $row['IP_ADDRESS'];
}
```

The same logic applies to retrieving the top IP addresses for the year, although the comparison in the query's WHERE clause is adjusted to retrieve the entire year's addresses.

```php
$query = sprintf('
    SELECT
        INET_NTOA(IP_ADDRESS) AS IP_ADDRESS
    FROM
        %sSITE_ACCESS
    WHERE
        DATE(ACCESS_TIME) BETWEEN
            "%d-01-01" AND
            "%d-01-01" + INTERVAL 1 YEAR - INTERVAL 1 DAY
    GROUP BY
        IP_ADDRESS
    ORDER BY
        COUNT(IP_ADDRESS) DESC',
    DB_TBL_PREFIX,
    $full_year,
    $full_year);
$result = mysql_query($query, $GLOBALS['DB']);

$yr_total = mysql_num_rows($result);

for ($i = 0; $i < 10 && $i < $yr_total; $i++)
{
    $row = mysql_fetch_assoc($result);
    $yr_addrs[] = $row['IP_ADDRESS'];
}
```

Once the number of unique visitors for the month and year and the list of top 10 addresses have been collected, they can easily displayed in the report.

```html
<table>
 <tr>
  <th>Unique Visitors</th>
  <td>MONTH: <?php echo $mo_total;?></td>
  <td>YEAR: <?php echo $yr_total;?></td>
 </tr><tr>
  <th>Top 10 IP Addresses</th>
  <td>MONTH<br/>
   <?php foreach ($mo_addrs as $addr) echo $addr . '<br/>';?></td>
  <td>YEAR<br/>
   <?php foreach ($yr_addrs as $addr) echo $addr . '<br/>';?></td>
 </tr>
</table>
```

Unlike the IP addresses, the total number of pages isn't needed so a LIMIT clause may be used in the query to retrieve the top five requested pages for the month and year. This code retrieves the pages for the current month. The query to retrieve pages for the year is only different within the WHERE clause.

```
$query = sprintf('
    SELECT
        REQ_PAGE, COUNT(REQ_PAGE) AS TOTAL
    FROM
        %sSITE_ACCESS
    WHERE
        DATE(ACCESS_TIME) BETWEEN
            "%d-%02d-01" AND
            "%d-%02d-01" + INTERVAL 1 MONTH - INTERVAL 1 DAY
    GROUP BY
        REQ_PAGE
    ORDER BY
        TOTAL DESC
    LIMIT 5',
    DB_TBL_PREFIX,
    $full_year,
    $num_month,
    $full_year,
    $num_month);
$result = mysql_query($query, $GLOBALS['DB']);

while ($row = mysql_fetch_assoc($result))
{
    $mo_pages_most[] = $row['REQ_PAGE'];
}
mysql_free_result($result);
```

When the LIMIT clause is used though you must issue another query with the sort order reversed to retrieve the least popular pages. Perhaps a more convenient way to do things would be to omit the LIMIT clause so that all pages are returned. A for loop can be used to retrieve the first five as shown previously, but then the results pointer can be set to the end of the set with mysql_data_seek() and a loop reads the results in reverse for the least five popular. Which method you choose is a matter of taste and clarity.

```
// assume the query omits LIMIT clause

$total = mysql_num_rows($result);

// retrieve the 5 most popular pages for the month
for ($i = 0; $i < 5 && $i < $total; $i++)
{
    $row = mysql_fetch_assoc($result);
    $mo_pages_most [] = $row['REQ_PAGE'];
}

// retrieve the 5 least popular pages
for ($i = $total; $i > $total - 5 && $i > 0; $i--)
{
    mysql_data_seek($GLOBALS['DB'], $i - 1);
    $row = mysql_fetch_assoc($result);
    $mo_pages_least[] = $row['REQ_PAGE'];
}
```

After the most popular and least popular pages have been retrieved for the month and year, they, too, can be displayed in the report. It's then time to pull in the traffic distribution charts. Another file (in my case img/chart.php) will make use of the BarChart class to output the graphic, so it can be referenced with an img tag.

```
<p><strong>Monthly Traffic Distribution for
  <?php echo $full_year; ?></strong></p>
<p><img src="img/chart.php?month" alt="monthly traffic distribution"></p>

<p><strong>Daily Traffic Distribution for <?php echo $full_month . ' ' .
  $full_year; ?></strong></p>
<p><img src="img/chart.php?day" alt="daily traffic distribution"></p>
```

Here's the complete code for public_files/report.php:

```php
<?php
include '../lib/common.php';
include '../lib/db.php';

// determine useful date values
list($full_month, $full_year, $short_month, $num_month, $short_year) =
    explode('/', date('F/Y/M/m/y'));
?>
<html>
 <head>
  <title>Website Statistics</title>
  <style type="text/css">
table {
    border-collapse: collapse;
}
th.blank {
    border: none;
}
th, td {
    text-align: center;
    vertical-align: top;
    border: 1px solid black;
    padding: 4px;
}
th.label {
    text-align: right;
}
  </style>
 </head>
 <body>
  <h1>Website Statistics</h1>
  <table>
   <tr>
    <th class="blank"> </th>
    <th>Current Month (<?php echo $short_month . ' ' . $short_year; ?>)</th>
    <th>Year to Date</th></th>
   </tr>
<?php
```

```
// retrieve the unique IP addresses for the current month
$query = sprintf('
    SELECT
        INET_NTOA(IP_ADDRESS) AS IP_ADDRESS
    FROM
        %sSITE_ACCESS SA
    WHERE
        DATE(ACCESS_TIME) BETWEEN
            "%d-%02d-01" AND
            "%d-%02d-01" + INTERVAL 1 MONTH - INTERVAL 1 DAY
    GROUP BY
        SA.IP_ADDRESS
    ORDER BY
        COUNT(IP_ADDRESS) DESC',
    DB_TBL_PREFIX,
    $full_year,
    $num_month,
    $full_year,
    $num_month);
$result = mysql_query($query, $GLOBALS['DB']);

// total addresses
$mo_total = mysql_num_rows($result);

// collect the top 10 IP addresses from the result set
for ($i = 0; $i < 10 && $i < $mo_total; $i++)
{
    $row = mysql_fetch_assoc($result);
    $mo_addrs[] = $row['IP_ADDRESS'];
}
mysql_free_result($result);

// retrieve the unique IP addresses for the current year
$query = sprintf('
    SELECT
        INET_NTOA(IP_ADDRESS) AS IP_ADDRESS
    FROM
        %sSITE_ACCESS
    WHERE
        DATE(ACCESS_TIME) BETWEEN
            "%d-01-01" AND
            "%d-01-01" + INTERVAL 1 YEAR - INTERVAL 1 DAY
    GROUP BY
        IP_ADDRESS
    ORDER BY
        COUNT(IP_ADDRESS) DESC',
    DB_TBL_PREFIX,
    $full_year,
    $full_year);
$result = mysql_query($query, $GLOBALS['DB']);

// total addresses
```

(continued)

(continued)

```php
$yr_total = mysql_num_rows($result);

// collect the top 10 IP addresses from the result set
for ($i = 0; $i < 10 && $i < $yr_total; $i++)
{
    $row = mysql_fetch_assoc($result);
    $yr_addrs[] = $row['IP_ADDRESS'];
}
mysql_free_result($result);
?>
    <tr>
    <th class="label">Unique Visitors</th>
    <td><?php echo $mo_total;?></td>
    <td><?php echo $yr_total;?></td>
    </tr><tr>
    <th class="label">Top 10 IP Addresses</th>
    <td><?php foreach ($mo_addrs as $addr) echo $addr . '<br/>';?></td>
    <td><?php foreach ($yr_addrs as $addr) echo $addr . '<br/>';?></td>
    </tr>
<?php
// retrieve the top 5 pages accessed during the current month
$query = sprintf('
    SELECT
        REQ_PAGE, COUNT(REQ_PAGE) AS TOTAL
    FROM
        %sSITE_ACCESS
    WHERE
        DATE(ACCESS_TIME) BETWEEN
            "%d-%02d-01" AND
            "%d-%02d-01" + INTERVAL 1 MONTH - INTERVAL 1 DAY
    GROUP BY
        REQ_PAGE
    ORDER BY
        TOTAL DESC
    LIMIT 5',
    DB_TBL_PREFIX,
    $full_year,
    $num_month,
    $full_year,
    $num_month);
$result = mysql_query($query, $GLOBALS['DB']);

// collect the pages from the result set
while ($row = mysql_fetch_assoc($result))
{
    $mo_pages_most[] = $row['REQ_PAGE'];
}
mysql_free_result($result);

// retrieve the top 5 pages accessed during the current year
$query = sprintf('
    SELECT
```

```
            REQ_PAGE, COUNT(REQ_PAGE) AS TOTAL
     FROM
         %sSITE_ACCESS
     WHERE
         DATE(ACCESS_TIME) BETWEEN
             "%d-01-01" AND
             "%d-01-01" + INTERVAL 1 YEAR - INTERVAL 1 DAY
     GROUP BY
         REQ_PAGE
     ORDER BY
         TOTAL DESC
     LIMIT 5',
     DB_TBL_PREFIX,
     $full_year,
     $full_year);
$result = mysql_query($query, $GLOBALS['DB']);

// collect the pages from the result set
while ($row = mysql_fetch_assoc($result))
{
     $yr_pages_most[] = $row['REQ_PAGE'];
}
mysql_free_result($result);
?>
    <tr>
    <th class="label">Top 5 Most Popular Pages</th>
    <td><?php foreach ($mo_pages_most as $addr) echo $addr . '<br/>';?></td>
    <td><?php foreach ($yr_pages_most as $addr) echo $addr . '<br/>';?></td>
    </tr>
<?php
// reverse sort order to retrieve the 5 least popular pages
$query = sprintf('
    SELECT
         REQ_PAGE, COUNT(REQ_PAGE) AS TOTAL
     FROM
         %sSITE_ACCESS
     WHERE
         DATE(ACCESS_TIME) BETWEEN
             "%d-%02d-01" AND
             "%d-%02d-01" + INTERVAL 1 MONTH - INTERVAL 1 DAY
     GROUP BY
         REQ_PAGE
     ORDER BY
         TOTAL ASC
     LIMIT 5',
     DB_TBL_PREFIX,
     $full_year,
     $num_month,
     $full_year,
     $num_month);
$result = mysql_query($query, $GLOBALS['DB']);

// collect the least popular pages from the result set
```

(continued)

(continued)

```php
    while ($row = mysql_fetch_assoc($result))
    {
        $mo_pages_least[] = $row['REQ_PAGE'];
    }
    mysql_free_result($result);

    $query = sprintf('
        SELECT
            REQ_PAGE, COUNT(REQ_PAGE) AS TOTAL
        FROM
            %sSITE_ACCESS
        WHERE
            DATE(ACCESS_TIME) BETWEEN
                "%d-01-01" AND
                "%d-01-01" + INTERVAL 1 YEAR - INTERVAL 1 DAY
        GROUP BY
            REQ_PAGE
        ORDER BY
            TOTAL ASC
        LIMIT 5',
        DB_TBL_PREFIX,
        $full_year,
        $full_year);
    $result = mysql_query($query, $GLOBALS['DB']);

    // collect the least popular pages
    while ($row = mysql_fetch_assoc($result))
    {
        $yr_pages_least[] = $row['REQ_PAGE'];
    }
    mysql_free_result($result);
?>
    <tr>
    <th class="label">Top 5 Least Popular Pages</th>
    <td><?php foreach ($mo_pages_least as $addr) echo $addr . '<br/>';?></td>
    <td><?php foreach ($yr_pages_least as $addr) echo $addr . '<br/>';?></td>
    </tr>
    </table>

    <p><strong>Monthly Traffic Distribution for
     <?php echo $full_year; ?></strong></p>
    <p><img src="chart.php?month" alt="monthly traffic distribution"></p>

    <p><strong>Daily Traffic Distribution for <?php echo $full_month . ' ' .
      $full_year; ?></strong></p>
    <p><img src="chart.php?day" alt="daily traffic distribution"></p>
    </body>
</html>
```

Another file is needed to use the BarChart class and output the chart. Since it will output an image, I've chosen to store the file in the public_files/img directory.

The script is passed a parameter so it can determine the correct query to execute. If an appropriate parameter is not received, then the script terminates as there is no sense in continuing forward and the img element will present a broken image. A day parameter will retrieve the total number of page hits for a given month and display them by day. A month parameter will retrieve the total number of hits for the year and display them by month.

A word of caution: You must initialize the data arrays you pass to BarChart first. If the data set has any missing dates and you just read in the database records and assign them, then the missing values would be skipped over in the chart as shown in Figure 9-4. Sometimes you may want this behavior. Typically, however, this isn't desired and space for the missing value should still be allocated as shown in Figure 9-5.

Here's one way you can initialize the data set prior to querying the database for month values as an example:

```
// initialize arrays
for ($i = 1; $i < 13; $i++)
{
    $data[$i] = 0;
    $labels[$i] = date("M", mktime(0,0,0,$i));
    $colors[$i] = array('r' => 0xCC, 'g' => 0x33, 'b' => 0x33);
}
```

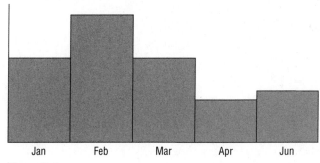

Figure 9-4

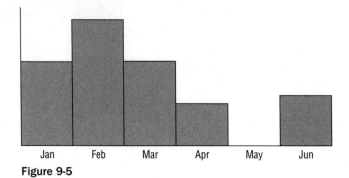

Figure 9-5

Here is the complete code listing for `public_files/img/chart.php`:

```php
<?php
include '../../lib/common.php';
include '../../lib/db.php';
include '../../lib/BarChart.php';

// get current month and year
list($month, $year) = explode('/', date('m/Y'));

// determine which query to execute
if (isset($_GET['day']))
{
    // initialize arrays
    $num_days = date("t", mktime(0, 0, 0, $month, 1, $year));
    for ($i = 1; $i < $num_days + 1; $i++)
    {
        $data[$i] = 0;
        $labels[$i] = $i;
        $colors[$i] = array('r' => 0xCC, 'g' => 0x33, 'b' => 0x33);
    }

    // retrieve total hits
    $query = sprintf('
        SELECT
            DAY(ACCESS_TIME) AS ATIME, COUNT(IP_ADDRESS) AS TOTAL
        FROM
            %sSITE_ACCESS
        WHERE
            DATE(ACCESS_TIME) BETWEEN
                "%d-%02d-01" AND
                "%d-%02d-01" + INTERVAL 1 MONTH - INTERVAL 1 DAY
        GROUP BY
            ATIME
        ORDER BY
            ATIME ASC',
        DB_TBL_PREFIX,
        $year,
        $month,
```

```php
            $year,
            $month);

    $result = mysql_query($query, $GLOBALS['DB']);
    while ($row = mysql_fetch_assoc($result))
    {
        $data[$row['ATIME']] = $row['TOTAL'];
    }
    mysql_free_result($result);
}
else if (isset($_GET['month']))
{
    // initialize arrays
    for ($i = 1; $i < 13; $i++)
    {
        $data[$i] = 0;
        $labels[$i] = date("M", mktime(0,0,0,$i));
        $colors[$i] = array('r' => 0xCC, 'g' => 0x33, 'b' => 0x33);
    }

    // retrieve total hits
    $query = sprintf('
        SELECT
            MONTH(ACCESS_TIME) AS ATIME, COUNT(IP_ADDRESS) AS TOTAL
        FROM
            %sSITE_ACCESS
        WHERE
            DATE(ACCESS_TIME) BETWEEN
                "%d-01-01" AND
                "%d-12-31"
            GROUP
                BY ATIME
            ORDER BY
                ATIME ASC',
            DB_TBL_PREFIX,
            $year,
            $year);
    $result = mysql_query($query, $GLOBALS['DB']);

    while ($row = mysql_fetch_assoc($result))
    {
        $data[$row['ATIME']] = $row['TOTAL'];
    }
    mysql_free_result($result);
}
else
{
    die();
}

// present bar chart
$chart = new BarChart(500, 200);
$chart->graphData($data, $colors, $labels);
$chart->flushImage();
?>
```

Summary

In this chapter, you've collected access data and generated a web site statistic report. Such reports can be used to better understand the effectiveness of a site and to make business decisions.

Depending on your location and what type of site you run, you may be required to disclose what information you collect and how you intend to use it. This is a good thing to do even if you're not legally required to do so.

In the next chapter, you'll explore writing a news or blog system with comments and an RSS feed.

10

News/Blog System

The word *blog* comes from a shortening of *web log* and since its inception, it has become synonymous with any type of online journal. A blogger — someone who authors the blog — posts his or her ideas or experiences and invites readers to leave comments starting a dialog around a certain topic. Few of us predicted the popularity and impact blogs would have on the web; writing blogs is an activity that has swept the Web by storm so much that few of us can recall what the Web was like before they appeared. You can find all sorts of blogs ranging from "a day in the life" type recounts to pundit comments which become the impetus for political action.

With its comment feature disabled, a blog is suitable as a news system. Posts can let visitors know what's going on behind the scenes at the web site or summarize changes that have recently been made to the site's content.

In this chapter, you will build a basic blog system. It will have an administrative page to allow the blog author to create new, modify and delete existing posts. A JavaScript-powered rich text edit control will be integrated so the author can easily format the entry. Visitors, however, need only be allowed to post plain text comments (although if you wanted you could just as easily allow them to format comments using BBCode mark up as discussed in Chapter 2). The system should also automatically generate an RSS feed showing the most recent posts so visitors can subscribe to the blog.

Tables

The database requirements for this project are rather simple. You need two database tables: one to store the blog posts made by the author and another table to store visitor comments.

```
+-------------+-------------------+------+-----+-------------------+----------------+
| Field       | Type              | Null | Key | Default           | Extra          |
+-------------+-------------------+------+-----+-------------------+----------------+
| POST_ID     | int(10) unsigned  | NO   | PRI | NULL              | auto_increment |
| POST_TITLE  | varchar(50)       | NO   |     |                   |                |
| POST_TEXT   | text              | NO   |     |                   |                |
| POST_DATE   | timestamp         | NO   |     | CURRENT_TIMESTAMP |                |
+-------------+-------------------+------+-----+-------------------+----------------+


+--------------+-------------------+------+-----+-------------------+
| Field        | Type              | Null | Key | Default           |
+--------------+-------------------+------+-----+-------------------+
| POST_ID      | int(10) unsigned  | NO   | MUL |                   |
| PERSON_NAME  | varchar(50)       | NO   |     |                   |
| POST_COMMENT | varchar(255)      | NO   |     |                   |
| COMMENT_DATE | timestamp         | NO   |     | CURRENT_TIMESTAMP |
+--------------+-------------------+------+-----+-------------------+
```

If you want to require visitors to register before leaving a comment, you could change PERSON_NAME to reference the USER_ID in some user table and then make the appropriate checks before saving the comment to the database. I simply store their names in a VARCHAR column since I am not planning on requiring my visitors to be site members.

Here is the SQL code for the database tables:

```
CREATE TABLE WROX_BLOG_POST (
    POST_ID         INTEGER UNSIGNED  NOT NULL  AUTO_INCREMENT,
    POST_TITLE      VARCHAR(50)       NOT NULL,
    POST_TEXT       TEXT              NOT NULL,
    POST_DATE       TIMESTAMP         DEFAULT CURRENT_TIMESTAMP,

    PRIMARY KEY (POST_ID)
)
ENGINE=MyISAM DEFAULT CHARACTER SET latin1
    COLLATE latin1_general_cs AUTO_INCREMENT=0;

CREATE TABLE WROX_BLOG_COMMENT (
    POST_ID         INTEGER UNSIGNED  NOT NULL,
    PERSON_NAME     VARCHAR(50)       NOT NULL,
    POST_COMMENT    VARCHAR(255)      NOT NULL,
    COMMENT_DATE    TIMESTAMP         DEFAULT CURRENT_TIMESTAMP,

    FOREIGN KEY (POST_ID)
        REFERENCES WROX_BLOG_POST(POST_ID)
)
ENGINE=MyISAM DEFAULT CHARACTER SET latin1
    COLLATE latin1_general_cs;
```

Adding Posts

Figure 10-1 shows the form with a new post entry.

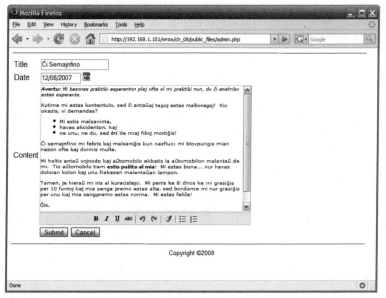

Figure 10-1

The admin page will be where the blog author will enter his posts. The `401.php` file should be included at the start of it since the functionality of this page should only be allowed to the author after he's identified himself by logging in.

The page initially displays a list of available blog posts in a `select` control, although over time the number of posts will undoubtedly grow and presenting them this way may become cumbersome. You may want to consider listing them some other way — perhaps by first narrowing the list by month or year or as a data grid similar to the one I presented in the file manager project. Then the form through which the blogger will enter his post should offer fields to enter the post's date, title, and main content. Two third-party components are used in the form, a rich text edit box and a pop-up calendar component.

The edit box used is TinyMCE and is available from `http://tinymce.moxiecode.com` under the GNU Lesser Public License, which means you can freely use it in your applications. TinyMCE is popular for its ease of integration. After uploading the control's code to the server, just a little bit of JavaScript can be added to the top of a page and any HTML `textarea` can be converted into a rich text editor. The minimal amount of code required for pulling in the TinyMCE code and instructing transforming `textareas` is:

```
<script type="text/javascript" src="js/tinymce/tiny_mce.js"></script>
<script type="text/javascript">
    tinyMCE.init({mode : "textareas"});
</script>
```

Other options may be passed to tinyMCE.init() which affects how the control appears and behaves. I've given it a width of 450px and a reduce set of formatting options as specified in the simple theme.

The calendar component I used is part of the Yahoo! User Interface (YUI) library, freely available under the BSD license from http://developer.yahoo.com/yui. The calendar is just one of many components that make up the YUI library, so be sure to spend some time exploring what else is available to you to integrate into future products. Figure 10-2 highlights the date field with the calendar component expanded and in action.

Figure 10-2

Although not overwhelmingly difficult, a bit more effort is required to integrate the calendar nicely as a pop-up control. The initial code tasked with pulling in the YUI dependency files is:

```
<script type="text/javascript" src="js/yui/yahoo-dom-event/yahoo-dom-event.js">
</script>
<script type="text/javascript" src="js/yui/calendar/calendar-min.js"></script>
<link rel="stylesheet" type="text/css" href="css/calendar.css" />
```

I've also included additional CSS directives to set the calendar div element hidden and a z-index so when the calendar is shown, it will appear to pop up on top of the other page content.

```
#calendar {
    display: none;
    position: absolute;
    z-index: 1;
}
```

Custom JavaScript code to initialize the control and wire the appropriate even handlers is placed in public_files/js/blog_admin.js. Setting the initial view of the form and calendar widget and registering the handlers is placed in code attached to the onload event:

```
window.onload = function()
{
    document.getElementById('form_select').style.display = '';
    document.getElementById('form_fields').style.display = 'none';

    document.getElementById('post_id').onchange = show_form;
```

```
document.getElementById('form_submit').onclick = submit_form;
document.getElementById('form_reset').onclick = reset_form;
document.getElementById('delete').onclick = submit_warning;

window.cal1 = new YAHOO.widget.Calendar("cal1", "calendar",
    { mindate: '1/1/2007',
    maxdate: '12/31/2015',
    title: 'Select Date',
    close: true
    });
window.cal1.selectEvent.subscribe(updatePostDate, cal1, true);
YAHOO.util.Event.addListener("show_calendar", "click",
    window.cal1.show, window.cal1, true);
updateCalendar();
document.getElementById('post_date').onchange = updateCalendar;
}
```

The updatePostDate() and updateCalendar() functions are designed to help link the post_date input field and the calendar so they can update each other; changing the date entered in the text field will modify the date in the calendar, and changing the calendar date will be reflected in the text field.

```
function updatePostDate(type,args,obj)
{
    var month = (args[0][0][1] < 10) ? '0' + args[0][0][1] : args[0][0][1];
    var day = (args[0][0][2] < 10) ? '0' + args[0][0][2] : args[0][0][2];
    var year = args[0][0][0];

    document.getElementById('post_date').value = month + '/' + day + '/' + year;
    window.cal1.hide();
}

function updateCalendar()
{
    var field = document.getElementById('post_date');

    if (field.value)
    {
        window.cal1.select(field.value);
        var selectedDates = window.cal1.getSelectedDates();
        if (selectedDates.length > 0)
        {
            var firstDate = selectedDates[0];
            window.cal1.cfg.setProperty('pagedate',
                (firstDate.getMonth() + 1) + '/' + firstDate.getFullYear());
        }
    }
    window.cal1.render();
}
```

At this point the calendar control is successfully integrated. The remaining code in blog_admin.js is responsible adding functionality to the form itself.

The editing form is initially hidden until the author chooses to create a new one or modify an existing blog post. If the author is editing an existing entry, an Ajax call is made using the XMLHttpRequest object discussed in Chapter 6 to fetch content and pre-populate the fields.

```
function show_form()
{
    fetch_info();
    document.getElementById('form_select').style.display = 'none';
    document.getElementById('form_fields').style.display = '';
    if (document.getElementById('post_id').value == 'new')
    {
        document.getElementById('delete_field').style.display = 'none';
    }
    else
    {
        document.getElementById('delete_field').style.display = '';
    }
}

function fetch_info()
{
    var select = document.getElementById('post_id');
    if (select.options[select.selectedIndex].value == 'new')
    {
        return;
    }

    var url = 'fetch_admin.php?post_id=' +
        select.options[select.selectedIndex].value + "&nocache=" +
        (new Date()).getTime();

    window.httpObj = createXMLWindow.httpObject();
    window.httpObj.open('GET', url, true);
    window.httpObj.onreadystatechange = function()
    {
        if (window.httpObj.readyState == 4 && window.httpObj.responseText)
        {
            var r = eval('(' + window.httpObj.responseText + ')');

            document.getElementById('post_title').value = r.post_title;
            document.getElementById('post_date').value = r.post_date;
            updateCalendar();
            document.getElementById('post_text').value = r.post_text;
            tinyMCE.updateContent(
                tinyMCE.getInstanceById('mce_editor_0' ).formElement.id);
        }
    }
    window.httpObj.send(null);
}
```

Code is also included to confirm the author truly desires to delete an entry if the delete check box is marked or to reset the form.

```
function submit_form()
{
    if (document.getElementById('delete').checked)
    {
        return confirm('Are you sure you wish to delete this entry?');
    }
}

function submit_warning()
{
    if (document.getElementById('delete').checked)
    {
        document.getElementById('form_submit').style.backgroundColor =
                '#FF9999';
    }
    else
    {
        document.getElementById('form_submit').style.backgroundColor = '';
    }
}

function reset_form()
{
    if (!confirm('Are you sure you wish to cancel?')) return false;

    document.getElementById('form_fields').style.display = 'none';
    document.getElementById('form_select').style.display = '';

    // manually clear the RTE area
    document.getElementById('post_text').value = '';
    tinyMCE.updateContent(tinyMCE.getInstanceById('mce_editor_0').formElement.id);

    // default action of reset button will clear fields and reset select index
    // so an explicit clearing is not needed so long as we return true to not
    // break that bubble
    return true;
}
```

Here is the full code listing for public_files/admin.php:

```
<?php
// include shared code
include '../lib/common.php';
include '../lib/db.php';

// must be logged in
include '401.php';

// generate extra elements for HTML head section
ob_start();
?>
```

(continued)

(continued)

```
<script type="text/javascript" src="js/yui/yahoo-dom-event/yahoo-dom-event.js">
</script>
<script type="text/javascript" src="js/yui/calendar/calendar-min.js"></script>
<script type="text/javascript" src="js/tinymce/tiny_mce.js"></script>
<script type="text/javascript" src="js/helper.js"></script>
<script type="text/javascript" src="js/blog_admin.js"></script>

<script type="text/javascript">
    tinyMCE.init({mode : "textareas", theme : "simple", width : "450" });
</script>
<link rel="stylesheet" type="text/css" href="css/calendar.css" />
<style type="text/css">
#calendar {
    display: none;
    position: absolute;
    z-index: 1;
}
</style>
<?php
$GLOBALS['TEMPLATE']['extra_head'] = ob_get_contents();
ob_clean();

// Generate entry form
?>
<form action="post_admin.php"
 method="post">
 <div id="form_select">
  <table>
   <tr>
    <td class="label"><label for="post_id">Blog Post</label></td>
    <td>
     <select name="post_id" id="post_id"/>
       <option value="select">SELECT</option>
       <option value="new">Add New</option>
<?php
// retrieve list of post titles
$query = sprintf('SELECT POST_ID, POST_TITLE, UNIX_TIMESTAMP(POST_DATE) ' .
    'AS POST_DATE FROM %sBLOG_POST ORDER BY POST_DATE DESC, POST_TITLE ASC',
    DB_TBL_PREFIX);

$result = mysql_query($query, $GLOBALS['DB']);
while ($record = mysql_fetch_assoc($result))
{
    echo '<option value="' . $record['POST_ID'] . '">';
    echo '(' . date('m/d/Y', $record['POST_DATE']) . ') ' .
        $record['POST_TITLE'];
    echo '</option>';
}
mysql_free_result($result);
?>
     </select>
    </td>
   </tr>
  </table>
```

```
    </div>
    <div id="form_fields" style="display:none;">
     <table>
      <tr>
       <td class="label"><label for="post_title">Title</label></td>
       <td><input type="text" name="post_title" id="post_title"/></td>
      </tr><tr>
       <td class="label"><label for="post_date">Date</label></td>
       <td class="yui-skin-sam"><input type="text" name="post_date" id="post_date"
        maxlength="10" size="10" value="<?php echo date('m/d/Y'); ?>"/>
        <img id="show_calendar" src="img/calendar.jpg" alt="Show Calendar" />
        <div id="calendar"></div>
 </td>
      </tr><tr>
       <td class="label"><label for=news_content>Content</label></td>
       <td>
        <textarea id="post_text" name="post_text" rows="15" cols="60"></textarea>
       </td>
      </tr><tr id="delete_field">
       <td> </td>
       <td style="text-align: right;">
        <input type="checkbox" id="delete" name="delete"/>
        <label for="delete">Delete Entry</label></td>
      </tr><tr>
       <td> </td>
       <td>
        <input type="submit" value="Submit" id="form_submit" class="button"/>
        <input type="reset" value="Cancel" id="form_reset" class="button"/></td>
      </tr>
     </table>
    </div>
   </form>
   <?php
   $GLOBALS['TEMPLATE']['content'] = ob_get_clean();
   include '../templates/template-page.php';
   mysql_close($GLOBALS['DB']);
   ?>
```

And here is the full code listing for `public_files/js/blog_admin.js`:

```
// set initial view and register event handlers
window.onload = function()
{
    document.getElementById('form_select').style.display = '';
    document.getElementById('form_fields').style.display = 'none';

    window.cal1 = new YAHOO.widget.Calendar("cal1", "calendar",
        { mindate: '1/1/2007',
        maxdate: '12/31/2015',
        title: 'Select Date',
        close: true
        });
```

(continued)

(continued)

```
        window.cal1.selectEvent.subscribe(updatePostDate, cal1, true);
        YAHOO.util.Event.addListener("show_calendar", "click",
            window.cal1.show, window.cal1, true);
        updateCalendar();
        document.getElementById('post_date').onchange = updateCalendar;

        document.getElementById('post_id').onchange = show_form;
        document.getElementById('form_submit').onclick = submit_form;
        document.getElementById('form_reset').onclick = reset_form;
        document.getElementById('delete').onclick = submit_warning;
    }

    // update the post_date field when the user changes the calendar's date
    function updatePostDate(type,args,obj)
    {
        var month = (args[0][0][1] < 10) ? '0' + args[0][0][1] : args[0][0][1];
        var day = (args[0][0][2] < 10) ? '0' + args[0][0][2] : args[0][0][2];
        var year = args[0][0][0];

        document.getElementById('post_date').value = month + '/' + day + '/' + year;
        window.cal1.hide();
    }

    // update the calendar's date when the user changes the post_date field
    function updateCalendar()
    {
        var field = document.getElementById('post_date');

        if (field.value)
        {
            window.cal1.select(field.value);
            var selectedDates = window.cal1.getSelectedDates();
            if (selectedDates.length > 0)
            {
                var firstDate = selectedDates[0];
                window.cal1.cfg.setProperty('pagedate',
                    (firstDate.getMonth() + 1) + '/' + firstDate.getFullYear());
            }
        }
        window.cal1.render();
    }

    // unhide the form when the user choses to modify a page
    function show_form()
    {
        fetch_info();
        document.getElementById('form_select').style.display = 'none';
        document.getElementById('form_fields').style.display = '';
        if (document.getElementById('post_id').value == 'new')
        {
            document.getElementById('delete_field').style.display = 'none';
        }
```

```
        else
        {
            document.getElementById('delete_field').style.display = '';
        }
    }

    // confirm is user checked delete
    function submit_form()
    {
        if (document.getElementById('delete').checked)
        {
            return confirm('Are you sure you wish to delete this entry?');
        }
    }

    // highlight the submit button if record will be deleted
    function submit_warning()
    {
        if (document.getElementById('delete').checked)
        {
            document.getElementById('form_submit').style.backgroundColor =
                    '#FF9999';
        }
        else
        {
            document.getElementById('form_submit').style.backgroundColor = '';
        }
    }

    // clear form
    function reset_form()
    {
        if (!confirm('Are you sure you wish to cancel?')) return false;

        document.getElementById('form_fields').style.display = 'none';
        document.getElementById('form_select').style.display = '';

        // manually clear the RTE area
        document.getElementById('post_text').value = '';
        tinyMCE.updateContent(tinyMCE.getInstanceById('mce_editor_0').formElement.id);

        // default action of reset button will clear fields and reset select index
        // so an explicit clearing is not needed so long as we return true to not
        // break that bubble
        return true;
    }

    // retrieve existing information via "AJAX"
    var httpObj;
    function fetch_info()
    {
        var select = document.getElementById('post_id');
        if (select.options[select.selectedIndex].value == 'new')
        {
```

(continued)

(continued)

```
            return;
    }

    var url = 'fetch_admin.php?post_id=' +
        select.options[select.selectedIndex].value + "&nocache=" +
        (new Date()).getTime();

    httpObj = createXMLHTTPObject();
    httpObj.open('GET', url, true);
    httpObj.onreadystatechange = function()
    {
        // populate the fields
        if (httpObj.readyState == 4 && httpObj.responseText)
        {
            var r = eval('(' + httpObj.responseText + ')');

            document.getElementById('post_title').value = r.post_title;
            document.getElementById('post_date').value = r.post_date;
            updateCalendar();
            document.getElementById('post_text').value = r.post_text;

tinyMCE.updateContent(tinyMCE.getInstanceById('mce_editor_0').formElement.id);
        }
    }
    httpObj.send(null);
}
```

The `fetch_info()` function sends the Ajax request to `fetch_admin.php`, which is responsible for retrieving the date, title, and content for the appropriate blog entry. Here is the full code listing for `public_files/fetch_admin.php`:

```php
<?php
// include shared code
include '../lib/common.php';
include '../lib/db.php';

// retrieve blog entry content
$query = sprintf('SELECT POST_ID, POST_TITLE, POST_TEXT, ' .
    'UNIX_TIMESTAMP(POST_DATE) AS POST_DATE FROM %sBLOG_POST WHERE ' .
    'POST_ID = "%d"',
    DB_TBL_PREFIX, $_GET['post_id']);
$result = mysql_query($query, $GLOBALS['DB']);
$record = mysql_fetch_assoc($result);

// output blog entry
$data = array(
'post_id' => $record['POST_ID'],
'post_title' => $record['POST_TITLE'],
'post_text' => $record['POST_TEXT'],
'post_date' => date('m/d/Y', $record['POST_DATE']));
echo json_encode($data);
mysql_free_result($result);
mysql_close($GLOBALS['DB']);
?>
```

The form contents are posted to post_admin.php, which in turn accepts the incoming data and saves it to the database. When the entry is saved, the author is redirected to the form so he or she may either write or edit another entry. Here is the code for public_files/post_admin.php:

```php
<?php
// include shared code
include '../lib/common.php';
include '../lib/db.php';
include '../lib/functions.php';

// this should not be available unless the user has logged in
include '401.php';

// insert a new blog entry
if ($_POST['post_id'] == 'new')
{
    $query = sprintf('INSERT INTO %sBLOG_POST SET POST_TITLE = "%s", ' .
        'POST_DATE = "%s", POST_TEXT = "%s"',
        DB_TBL_PREFIX,
        mysql_real_escape_string($_POST['post_title'], $GLOBALS['DB']),
        mysql_format_date($_POST['post_date']),
        mysql_real_escape_string($_POST['post_text'], $GLOBALS['DB']));

    mysql_query($query, $GLOBALS['DB']);
}
else
{
    // delete entry
    if (isset($_POST['delete']))
    {
        $query = sprintf('DELETE FROM %sBLOG_POST WHERE POST_ID = %d',
            DB_TBL_PREFIX, $_POST['post_id']);

        mysql_query($query, $GLOBALS['DB']);
    }
    // update entry
    else    {
        $query = sprintf('UPDATE %sBLOG_POST SET POST_TITLE = "%s", ' .
            'POST_DATE = "%s", POST_TEXT = "%s" WHERE POST_ID = %d',
            DB_TBL_PREFIX,
            mysql_real_escape_string($_POST['post_title'], $GLOBALS['DB']),
            mysql_format_date($_POST['post_date']),
            mysql_real_escape_string($_POST['post_text'], $GLOBALS['DB']),
            $_POST['post_id']);

        mysql_query($query, $GLOBALS['DB']);
    }
}

mysql_close($GLOBALS['DB']);
header('Location: admin.php');
?>
```

277

Generating the RSS

Really Simple Syndication (RSS) is an easy way to notify others of content changes. RSS feeds are used to publicize new blog posts, news events, new product additions to e-commerce sites and more. Visitors typically will subscribe to a feed you make available and are then able to automatically review updates directly from within their favorite aggregator without having to visit the site in a browser.

For historical reasons there are several different RSS formats. They are all XML-based although they aren't necessarily compatible with one another. I've chosen RSS 2.0 to publicize the new posts.

The root element of the feed is `rss`. Information about the site is placed in a `channel` section using `title`, `link`, and `description` elements. Any number of `item` elements follow the `channel` section, one for each post you want to publicize, each with `title`, `link`, and `description` elements.

Here is `public_files/rss.php`:

```php
<?php header('Content-Type: text/xml'); ?>
<?xml version="1.0"?>
<rss version="2.0">
<channel>
  <title>My Blog</title>
  <link>http://www.example.com/myBlog</link>
  <description>
   My Blog is a place where I write my innermost thoughts and feelings for
   all the world to read.
  </description>
 </channel>
<?php
// include the 5 most recent entries
$query = sprintf('SELECT POST_ID, POST_TITLE, POST_TEXT, ' .
    'UNIX_TIMESTAMP(POST_DATE) AS POST_DATE FROM %sBLOG_POST ' .
    'ORDER BY POST_DATE DESC', DB_TBL_PREFIX);
$result = mysql_query($query, $GLOBALS['DB']);

$count = 0;
while (($row = mysql_fetch_array($result)) && $count++ < 5)
{
    echo '<item>';
    echo '<title>' . htmlspecialchars($row['POST_TITLE']) . '</title>';
    printf('<link>http://www.example.com/myBlog/view.php?m=%d&y=%d</link>',
        date('n', $row['POST_DATE']), date('Y', $row['POST_DATE']));
    echo '<description>' . htmlspecialchars($row['POST_TEXT']) . '</description>';
    echo '</item>';
}
?>
</rss>
```

I've included only the required elements in my feed, but there are others you can include to provide more information. Table 10-1 shows a listing of all elements for the RSS 2.0 specification.

Table 10-1: RSS Elements

Element	Description	Example

rss	Root element.	`<rss version="2.0">`
		`  <channel> ... </channel>`
		`</rss>`

channel	Section that contains information about the feed's originating website and item elements.	`<channel>`
		`  <title>...</title>`
		`<link>...</link>`
		`  <description>`
		`  ... </description>`
		`<item> ... </item>`
		`  <item> ... </item>`
		`  ...`
		`</channel>`

item	Individual item entries.	`<item>`
		`  <title>...</title>`
		`<link>...</link>`
		`  <description>`
		`  ...`
		`  </description>`
		`</item>`

channel Elements		
category	(Optional) Specifies one or more site categories.	`<category domain="syndic8">` `  Web Log</category>`

cloud	(Optional) Indicates the cloud to be notified of updates.	`<cloud domain="www.example.com`
		`"port="80" path="/RPC" protocol="xml-rpc"`
		`  registerProcedure="NotifyMe" />`

copyright	(Optional) Specifies copyright statement.	`<copyright>`
		`  Copyright 2007`
		`</copyright>`

description	(Optional) Provides web site description/summary.	`<description>`
		`  My Blog is a place where I write my`
		`innermost thoughts and feelings for all`
		`the world to read.`
		`</description>`

docs	(Optional) Provides documentation address for the RSS format used.	`<docs>`
		`  http://blogs.law.harvard.edu/tech/rss`
		`</docs>`

Table continued on following page

Element	Description	Example
generator	(Optional) Determines which program was used to generate the feed.	`<generator>PHP</generator>`

image	(Optional) Specifies an image to associate with the feed. Has required child elements url, title and link.	`<image>`
		`<url>`
		`http://www.example.com/img/logo.png`
		`</url>`
		`<title>My Blog</title>`
		`<link>http://www.example.com</link>`
		`</image>`

language	(Optional) Indicates in which language the feed is written.	`<language>en-us</language>`

lastBuildDate	(Optional) Indicates RFC 822-formatted date the feed was last modified.	`<pubDate>`
		`Wed, 21 Nov 2007 21:55:00 EST`
		`</pubDate>`

link	Specifies web site address.	`<link>http://www.example.com</link>`

managingEditor	(Optional) Specifies e-mail address of the feed's managing editor.	`<managingEditor>`
		`m.editor@example.com`
		`</managingEditor>`

pubDate	(Optional) Provides RFC 822-formatted date the feed was published.	`<pubDate>`
		`Wed, 21 Nov 2007 21:55:00 EST`
		`</pubDate>`

rating	(Optional) Shows Platform for Internet Content Selection (PICS) rating for the feed.	`<rating>`
		`(PICS-1.1 "http://www.classify.org/`
		`safesurf/" L  gen true for "http://www`
		`.example.com"  r (SS~~000 6 SS~~001 2`
		`SS~~002 2  SS~~003 2 SS~~004 2 SS~~005 1`
		`SS~~009 1))`
		`</rating>`

skipDays	(Optional) Specifies which days the RSS aggregator should skip updating the feed	`<skipDays>Saturday</skipDays>`
`<skipHours>`	(Optional) Specifies which hours the RSS aggregator should skip updating the feed (24-hour, 0 represents midnight).	`<skipHours>0</skipHours>`

Element	Description	Example
title	Specifies the name of web site.	`<title>My Blog</title>`
ttl	(Optional) Specifies cache time to live in minutes.	`<ttl>120</ttl>`

webMaster	(Optional) Specifies e-mail address of the site's webmaster.	`<webMaster>`
		`webmaster@example.com`
		`</webMaster>`

item Elements		

author	(Optional) Specifies e-mail address of the item's author.	`<author>`
		`me@example.com`
		`</author>`

category	(Optional) Specifies one or more item categories.	`<category domain="syndic8">` `Web Log</category>`

comments	(Optional) Provides link to comments about the item.	`<comments>`
		`http://www.example.com/comments.php`
		`</comments>`

description	Specifies item description/ summary.	`<description>`
		`Once upon a time...`
		`</description>`

enclosure	(Optional) Links a media file to the item. Has required child elements length, type and url.	`<enclosure url="http://www.example.com/`
		`vid.mov" length="659435" type="video/`
		`quicktime" />`

guid	(Optional) Provides a Globally Unique Identifier for the item.	`<guid>`
		`http://www.example.com/item123456`
		`</guid>`

link	Links to item.	`<link>`
		`http://www.example.com/view.php?m=11&`
		`y=2007`
		`</link>`

pubDate	(Optional) Indicates RFC 822-formatted date the item was published.	`<pubDate>`
		`Wed, 21 Nov 2007 21:55:00 EST`
		`</pubDate>`

source	(Optional) Provides third-party source for item.	`<source url="http://example.org">` `example.org</source>`

title	Indicates the name of the item.	`<title>`
		`My First Blog Entry`
		`</title>`

Displaying Posts

I've written the following code and saved it as `public_files/view.php` to display the blog posts. Posts are ordered in descending date order so newer posts appear first. The current month's posts are displayed first and links are placed at the bottom of the page to traverse other months.

I can pass a timestamp as a parameter to display various months, just like was done in the calendar application in Chapter 5. If the requested month isn't within reason or if the parameters weren't provided, the current month and year are assumed. The script can then determine whichever information it needs from the timestamp using PHP's `date()` function.

```
$timestamp = (isset($_GET['t'])) ? $_GET['t'] : time();
list($day, $year) = explode('/', date('m/Y', $timestamp));
```

After displaying the contents of the month's posts, previous and next links can be generated to traverse to other months. Again, as in Chapter 5, the timestamp can be easily be modified using `strtotime()`. Although you don't want to provide links beyond the oldest and newest dates, you should check the dates of the oldest and newest entries stored in the database.

```
$query = sprintf('SELECT UNIX_TIMESTAMP(POST_DATE) AS POST_DATE ' .
    'FROM %sBLOG_POST ORDER BY POST_DATE DESC',
    DB_TBL_PREFIX);
$result = mysql_query($query, $GLOBALS['DB']);
if (mysql_num_rows($result))
{

    // determine date of newest post
    $row = mysql_fetch_assoc($result);
    $newest = $row['POST_DATE'];

    // determine date of oldest post
    mysql_data_seek($result, mysql_num_rows($result) - 1);
    $row = mysql_fetch_assoc($result);
    $oldest = $row['POST_DATE'];

    if ($timestamp > $oldest)
    {
        echo '<a href="' . htmlspecialchars($_SERVER['PHP_SELF']) .
            '?t=' . strtotime('-1 month', $timestamp) . '">Prev</a> ';
    }

    if ($timestamp < $newest)
    {
        echo ' <a href="' . htmlspecialchars($_SERVER['PHP_SELF']) .
            '?t=' . strtotime('+1 month', $timestamp) . '">Next</a>';
    }

}
mysql_free_result($result);
```

Here is the full code for `public_files/view.php`:

```php
<?php
// include shared code
include '../lib/common.php';
include '../lib/db.php';

// determine current viewed month and year
$timestamp = (isset($_GET['t'])) ? $_GET['t'] : time();
list($day, $year) = explode('/', date('m/Y', $timestamp));

// retrieve entries for currently viewed month
$query = sprintf('
    SELECT
        POST_ID, POST_TITLE, POST_TEXT,
        UNIX_TIMESTAMP(POST_DATE) AS POST_DATE
    FROM
        %sBLOG_POST
    WHERE
        DATE(POST_DATE) BETWEEN
            "%d-%02d-01" AND
            DATE("%d-%02d-01") + INTERVAL 1 MONTH - INTERVAL 1 DAY
    ORDER BY
        POST_DATE DESC',
    DB_TBL_PREFIX,
    $year, $month,
    $year, $month);
$result = mysql_query($query, $GLOBALS['DB']);

ob_start();
while ($record = mysql_fetch_assoc($result))
{
    echo '<h2>' . $record['POST_TITLE'] . '</h2>';
    echo '<p>' . date('m/d/Y', $record['POST_DATE']) . '</p>';
    echo $record['POST_TEXT'];
    echo '<hr/>';
}
mysql_free_result($result);

// generate link to view previous month if appropriate
$query = sprintf('SELECT UNIX_TIMESTAMP(POST_DATE) AS POST_DATE ' .
    'FROM %sBLOG_POST ORDER BY POST_DATE DESC',
    DB_TBL_PREFIX);
$result = mysql_query($query, $GLOBALS['DB']);
if (mysql_num_rows($result))
{

    // determine date of newest post
    $row = mysql_fetch_assoc($result);
    $newest = $row['POST_DATE'];

    // determine date of oldest post
    mysql_data_seek($result, mysql_num_rows($result) - 1);
    $row = mysql_fetch_assoc($result);
```

(continued)

(continued)

```
        $oldest = $row['POST_DATE'];

        if ($timestamp > $oldest)
        {
            echo '<a href="' . htmlspecialchars($_SERVER['PHP_SELF']) .
                '?t=' . strtotime('-1 month', $timestamp) . '">Prev</a> ';
        }

        if ($timestamp < $newest)
        {
            echo ' <a href="' . htmlspecialchars($_SERVER['PHP_SELF']) .
                '?t=' . strtotime('+1 month', $timestamp) . '">Next</a>';
        }

}
mysql_free_result($result);

// link to RSS feed
$GLOBALS['TEMPLATE']['head_extra'] = '<link rel="alternate" ' .
    'type="application/rss+xml" href="rss.php" title="My Blog">';

echo '<p><a href="rss.php">RSS Feed</a></p>';

$GLOBALS['TEMPLATE']['content'] = ob_get_clean();


include '../templates/template-page.php';
mysql_close($GLOBALS['DB']);
?>
```

Figure 10-3 shows the blog posts for a given month.

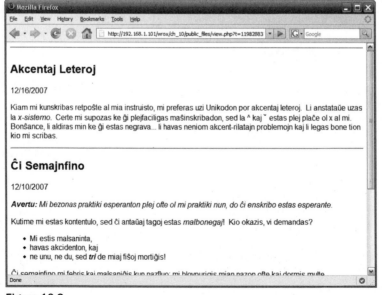

Figure 10-3

Adding Comments

As it stands now, what has been built functions well as a news system. Typically news posts will be short messages informing visitors as to what's new at the site or what's going on behind the scenes. Blogs, however, typically will have longer posts and invite the readers to leave their comments on the topic. I've decided to use the Ajax paradigm again to add comments.

Code must be added to `view.php` which will reference external JavaScript code and provides a Show Comments link:

```
// Javascript references
$GLOBALS['TEMPLATE']['extra_head'] = <<<ENDHTML
<script src="js/helper.js" type="text/javascript"></script>
<script src="js/blog.js" type="text/javascript">
ENDHTML;

...

while ($record = mysql_fetch_assoc($result))
{
    echo '<h2>' . $record['POST_TITLE'] . '</h2>';
    echo '<p>' . date('m/d/Y', $record['POST_DATE']) . '</p>';
    echo $record['POST_TEXT'];
    echo '<div style="display:none;" id="comments_' . $record['POST_ID'] .
        '"></div>';
    echo '<p><a href="#" onclick="toggleComments(' . $record['POST_ID'] .
        ', this);return false;">Show Comments</a></p>';
    echo '<hr/>';
}
```

The JavaScript code to toggle the comments display, retrieve comments for a particular post and submit new comments is then placed in `public_files/js/blog.js`:

```
// toggle the comments display of a particular post
function toggleComments(id, link)
{
    var div = document.getElementById('comments_' + id);

    if (div.style.display == 'none')
    {
        link.innerHTML = 'Hide Comments';
        fetchComments(id);
        div.style.display = '';
    }
    else
    {
        link.innerHTML = 'Show Comments';
        div.style.display = 'none';
    }
}
```

(continued)

285

(continued)

```
// retrieve existing comments via "AJAX"
window.httpObj;
function fetchComments(id)
{
    var div = document.getElementById('comments_' + id);

    var url = 'fetch.php?post_id=' + id + "&nocache=" +
        (new Date()).getTime();

    window.httpObj = createXMLHTTPObject();
    window.httpObj.open('GET', url , true);
    window.httpObj.onreadystatechange = function()
    {
        // populate the fields
        if (window.httpObj.readyState == 4 && httpObj.responseText)
        {
            div.innerHTML = httpObj.responseText;
        }
    }
    window.httpObj.send(null);
}

// submit a comment via "AJAX"
function postComment(id, form)
{
    var url = form.action + "&nocache=" + (new Date()).getTime();
    var data = 'person_name=' + escape(form.person_name.value) +
        '&post_comment=' + escape(form.post_comment.value);

    window.httpObj = createXMLHTTPObject();
    window.httpObj.open('POST', url , true);
    window.httpObj.setRequestHeader('Content-type',
        'application/x-www-form-urlencoded');
    window.httpObj.setRequestHeader('Content-length', data.length);
    window.httpObj.setRequestHeader('Connection', 'close');

    window.httpObj.onreadystatechange = function()
    {
        // populate the fields
        if (window.httpObj.readyState == 4 && window.httpObj.responseText)
        {
            if (window.httpObj.responseText == 'OK')
            {
                fetchComments(id);
            }
            else
            {
                alert('Error posting comment.');
            }
        }
    }
    window.httpObj.send(data);
    return false;
}
```

The HTML markup displaying existing comments and the form to submit new comments is retrieved with a call from `fetchComments()` to `public_files/fetch.php`. If there are no comments, a message is included saying there are no comments for the requested post.

```php
<?php
// include shared code
include '../lib/common.php';
include '../lib/db.php';

// retrieve comments for this post
$id = (int)$_GET['post_id'];
$query = sprintf('SELECT PERSON_NAME, POST_COMMENT, ' .
    'UNIX_TIMESTAMP(COMMENT_DATE) AS COMMENT_DATE FROM %sBLOG_COMMENT ' .
    'WHERE POST_ID = %d ORDER BY COMMENT_DATE ASC',
    DB_TBL_PREFIX, $id);
$result = mysql_query($query, $GLOBALS['DB']);

if (mysql_num_rows($result))
{
    while($row = mysql_fetch_assoc($result))
    {
        echo '<p>' . htmlspecialchars($row['POST_COMMENT']) . '<br/>';
        echo htmlspecialchars($row['PERSON_NAME']) . ' ' .
            date('m/d/Y', $row['COMMENT_DATE']) . '</p>';
    }
}
else
{
    echo '<p>There are no comments for this post.</p>';
}

// form to add comments
?>
<form action="post.php?id=<?php echo $id; ?>" method="post"
onsubmit="postComment(<?php echo $id; ?>, this); return false;">
<div>
 <label for="name_<?php echo $id; ?>">Name: </label>
 <input type="text" name="person_name" id="name_<?php echo $id; ?>"/><br />
 <label for="comment_<?php echo $id; ?>">Comment: </label>
 <textarea type="text" name="post_comment"
  id="comment_<?php echo $id; ?>"/></textarea></br>
 <input type="submit" value="submit" />
</form>

<?php
mysql_free_result($result);
mysql_close($GLOBALS['DB']);
?>
```

The `postComment()` function calls `post.php` to post a comment. Unlike other Ajax calls we've seen, this one is sent using the POST method because the comment can potentially contain a large amount of data and we wouldn't want to be restricted by the length limitations of GET.

`public_files/post.php` will return either OK if the comment is saved successfully or ERR if not.

```php
<?php
// include shared code
include '../lib/common.php';
include '../lib/db.php';

// validate incoming values
$name = (isset($_POST['person_name'])) ? trim($_POST['person_name']) : '';
$comment = (isset($_POST['post_comment'])) ? trim($_POST['post_comment']) : '';

if ($name && $comment)
{
    // add comment
    $query = sprintf('INSERT INTO %sBLOG_COMMENT (POST_ID, PERSON_NAME, ' .
        'POST_COMMENT) VALUES (%d, "%s", "%s")',
        DB_TBL_PREFIX,
        $_GET['id'],
        htmlspecialchars($name),
        htmlspecialchars($comment));
    mysql_query($query, $GLOBALS['DB']);
    echo 'OK';
}
else
{
    echo 'ERR';
}
mysql_close($GLOBALS['DB']);
?>
```

Figure 10-4 shows a post with the comment area expanded.

Figure 10-4

Summary

This chapter presented the foundation upon which you can build up a custom news or blogging application. It integrates two third-party JavaScript components to make entering new and modifying existing posts easier on the blog author. You've also seen how to provide an RSS 2.0 feed to publicize new posts.

In the next chapter, you'll develop command-line scripts to assist in setting up a consistent development environment and performing general maintenance activities.

11

Shell Scripts

The mailing list project presented in Chapter 3 demonstrates how PHP can be used for more than just generating web pages. Certainly that is the area where PHP shines the brightest, but PHP really is a capable language flexible enough for tackling most any programming task. In this chapter, I will discuss using PHP to write shell scripts.

The impetus for this project comes from the realization that many applications share the same basic layout. For example, the directory structure and shared code files first discussed in Chapter 1 have appeared in other projects throughout the entire book. Directories such as `lib`, `public_files` and `sql` keep the project organized and shared code such as `common.php` and `db.php` provide the project's configuration.

The Rails framework that has gained widespread acceptance in the Ruby programming community and really put Ruby on the map offers more functionality than just setting up a common skeleton for a project, but this is often the first service it performs for the developer. Similarly, Django initially assists a Python programmer to create an application structure. Sure you're using PHP, but there's no reason why you can't "borrow" good ideas just because it's not the same language.

So in this chapter, you will be writing a shell script to help set up a well organized directory layout and copy basic code files into it to start a new application. It will run from the command line and prompt the developer for important values such as the database connection information and use them to fill in the relevant parts of the shared code. Along the way you will code a library useful for writing future shell scripts to assist reading in user input.

To give you a better idea of how the script will be used, here's a sample execution. The script is named `startproject` and is called with a target path provided as the argument.

```
$ ./startproject -o /srv/apache/example.com/test

Database host [localhost]:
Database schema [TEST]: WROX_DATABASE
Database user [TESTUSR]: username
Database password: password
Database table prefix []:

The following information will be used to generate the site layout:
----------------------------------------------------------------
Database host:          localhost
Database schema:        WROX_DATABASE
Database user:          username
Database password:      password
Database table prefix:  WROX_

Is this correct? [yes]:
Congratulations!  Your project layout has been deployed to
/srv/apache/example.com/test.
```

Designing the Script

The prompts shown in the sample execution will be the same ones that I will require here: database host, schema, user, password and table prefix. Some questions might suggest a default answer if one is appropriate (such as localhost for the database host). When they do, the suggestion appears alongside their prompt in square brackets. The developer can choose to either type the response or leave the prompt blank to accept the default.

If valid options or the directory are not given when the script is called from the command line then proper usage instructions should be shown to help guide the user.

```
$ ./startproject
Usage: startproject [-options] -o target
Setup project directory and copy basic files into it.
```

startproject will be written to support the following command line arguments:

❏   -c and --copy-only only copy the project skeleton to the target directory, but do not replace placeholders or delete .tmp files

❏   -h and --help display usage information and exit

❏   -o target and --output=target specify the directory to where the files will be copied

❏   -p and --preserve don't delete .tmp files after replacing placeholders

❏   -v and --version display version information and exit

I use a custom set-up script not unlike the example. However, over time my needs have grown and the prompts and options have become considerably more complex. After you have written your set-up script and created a basic site skeleton you can augment either any way you see fit. Perhaps you may have it copy over JavaScript utilities files like the Rich Text Edit control or elements of the Yahoo! User Interface Library introduced in Chapter 10.

General Shell Scripting Advice

Before I delve into the project I first want to provide some general tips you should keep in mind when writing shell scripts:

❑ Provide usage instructions and help options.

❑ Be sure to provide guidance on how to use your scripts. A good summary of what the script does and its argument list is mandatory if you plan on sharing them with others, but should still be included even if you're the only person who will ever use it. I've written several utility scripts and have come back months later and have forgotten how to use them.

❑ Comment your code.

❑ Writing code to perform common activities solidifies them into procedures and reduces some possibility of human error. Still, just because something is "taken care of" doesn't mean it can be forgotten. Comments can document the steps taken in a human readable format and compliance regulations may require you to comment your code depending on your environment.

❑ Know under which account the script will run.

❑ In general, shell scripts run with the same privileges of the user account that initiated it. This means the script may not be able to change a file's owner or permissions or to perform other activities typically reserved for a super user. You may need to escalate your privileges using su or sudo to run the script.

❑ Direct error messages to STDERR.

❑ Command line utilities have a rich tradition and power users have come to expect certain behavior. One such behavior is respecting the use of the standard Unix file descriptors standard-input, standard-output, and standard-error. Competent shell users feel comfortable redirecting and piping the output of one command to the input of another.

❑ PHP automatically opens streams to the standard Unix file descriptors standard-input, standard-output, and standard-error and makes the references available through the magic constants STDIN, STDOUT, and STDERR respectively. PHP also closes these streams automatically as well when the script's execution terminates, saving you the effort of explicitly having to manage these streams yourself with fopen() and fclose().

❑ Because output from an echo or print statement is eventually directed to STDOUT, you will most likely never have to direct it to that stream yourself. You may find STDIN more useful, however, since it is used to read in user input from a prompt. It's a good idea to send error messages to STDERR, separate from output sent to STDOUT. This allows the developer running the script to send error messages to a separate file using redirection for later review, like this:

❑ `$ ./startproject -o /srv/apache/example.com/test 2>errors.txt`

❑ Supply default values for prompts when appropriate.

❑ Providing default values for a prompt offers the user guidance as to what type of information the script expects. If the value applies to the current project, then the developer has to type less and has a lesser chance of entering a typo. This all helps to make the script easier to use.

❑ Validate user input.

❏ Input should be properly validated and escaped regardless if the execution of a script is initiated at the command line or a web request. Never trust user input — people can (and will) provide all sorts of crazy and unexpected input. Sometimes this is accidental but other times it's malicious. Malformed input could be potentially even more dangerous for a shell script than a web page depending on the code's activities.

❏ Write code with portability in mind.

❏ Unless the script only performs a platform-specific function, don't expect it to be used only on just one particular platform. You might develop it on Unix, but people you share the script with run it on Windows. Or perhaps you write it on AIX and then the production server migrates to Novel. Use PHP functions when they are available and avoid using `exec()`, `passthru()`, and `system()`.

Code and Code Explanation

It's time to discuss the actual code for the project. First, I will cover creating a reusable `CommandLine` class to assist in obtaining user input. Then I will cover the `startproject` script, which uses it.

The CommandLine Class

The `CommandLine` class will contain static methods to ease getting outside information. This can be either in the form of command-line arguments or values provided in a configuration file. It will also help reading information in from the user interactively with a prompt. Table 11-1 shows the methods and properties `CommandLine` will expose.

Table 11-1: CommandLine Properties and Methods

Property	Description
CONFIG_TYPE_PLAIN	Represents a basic configuration file format
CONFIG_TYPE_INI	Represents a ini-style configuration file format
Method	
parseOptions(args[, allowed])	Parses command-line arguments and returns them as an array
parseConfigFile(file[, type])	Parses a configuration file and returns the options as an array
prompt(label[, length[, callback]])	Displays a prompt and reads keyboard input
promtDefault(label[, default[, length[, callback]]])	Displays a prompt with suggested response and reads keyboard input

Command-Line Arguments

When the PHP script is run from the command line, the `$_SERVER['argc']` and `$_SERVER['argv']` variables are populated with the number of arguments passed, and the arguments themselves respectively to the script an array of the arguments. Simple scripts may interpret these values directly, although more complex scripts may want to parse them into options and arguments. Parsing them can prove invaluable by saving the user from having to enter information in any one particular order. You can think of passing information this way as defining key/value pairs, where the key is the option and value the argument.

Keep in mind the script name itself is considered an argument, so if you were to run `startproject` with no arguments then `$_SERVER['argc']` would be 1 and `$_SERVER['argv'][0]` would be "`./startproject`".

There are several syntax styles commonly used by command line utilities when it comes to accepting arguments:

❑   `-a` is a single-character option that assumes a Boolean value (acts as a switch for turning script options on or off)

❑   `-a -b -c` are a series of single-character options, may also be condensed as `-abc`

❑   `-a foo` is a single-character option with an assigned argument

❑   `-abc foo` are single-character options condensed with an argument assigned to the last option (a and b would assume `true` while c would be assigned `foo`)

❑   `--abc` is an option provided as a multiple-character string

❑   `--abc=foo` is a multiple-character option with an assigned argument

Although not all programs use the same values to represent the same options, over time certain standard values have emerged. The two most popular options are `-h` and `--help` to return usage information and `-v` and `--version` to return the utility's version number. See the Linux Documentation Project's Advanced Bash-Scripting Guide for a list of common options (`http://tldp.org/LDP/abs/html/standard-options.html`).

The logic to parse arguments can be encapsulated in either a function or a class with static members and saved in its own file for inclusion in other command line scripts. I've chosen to go with a class.

The `parseOptions()` method accepts the array of arguments passed in from the command line and optionally an array containing a list of options to consider valid. If the white list is supplied, the method will throw an exception when it encounters an unrecognized option. Internally, `parseOptions()` initializes a new array (`$options`) which it will return populated with the value/key pairs it parses.

Probably the easiest way to find long-options with assigned values is by using a regular expression. The option and argument portions can be captured with `preg_match()` and placed into the `$options` array.

When a compacted set of single-character options is detected, all characters are set as options with an implied Boolean argument except for the last one. The following argument must be inspected to determine if it has a value assignable to the last option or if the option should also be an implied Boolean.

295

```php
class CommandLineOptionException extends Exception { }

class CommandLine
{
    static public function parseOptions($args, $allowed = array())
    {
        $options = array();
        $count = count($args);

        for ($i = 1; $i < $count; $i++)
        {
            // retrieve arguments in form of --abc=foo
            if (preg_match('/^--([-A-Z0-9]+)=(.+)$/i', $args[$i], $matches))
            {
                if (empty($allowed) || in_array($matches[1], $allowed))
                {
                    $options[$matches[1]] = $matches[2];
                }
                else
                {
                    throw new CommandLineOptionException(
                        'Unrecognized option ' . $matches[1]);
                }
            }

            // retrieve --abc arguments
            else if (substr($args[$i], 0, 2) == '--')
            {
                $tmp = substr($args[$i], 2);
                if (empty($allowed) || in_array($tmp, $allowed))
                {
                    $options[$tmp] = true;
                }
                else
                {
                    throw new CommandLineOptionException(
                        'Unrecognized option ' . $tmp);
                }
            }

            // retrieve -abc foo, -abc, -a foo and -a arguments
            else if ($args[$i][0] == '-' && strlen($args[$i]) > 1)
            {
                // set all arguments to true except for last in sequence
                for ($j = 1; $j < strlen($args[$i]) - 1; $j++)
                {
                    if (empty($allowed) || in_array($args[$i][$j], $allowed))
                    {
                        $options[$args[$i][$j]] = true;
                    }
```

```
                else
                {
                    throw new CommandLineOptionException(
                        'Unrecognized option ' . $args[$i][$j]);
                }
            }

            // set last argument in compressed sequence
            $tmp = substr($args[$i], -1, 1);
            if (empty($allowed) || in_array($tmp, $allowed))
            {
                if ($i + 1 < $count && $args[$i + 1][0] != '-')
                {
                    $options[$tmp] = $args[$i + 1];
                    $i++;
                }
                else
                {
                    $options[$tmp] = true;
                }
            }
            else
            {
                throw new CommandLineOptionException(
                    'Unrecognized option ' . $tmp);
            }
        }
        else
        {
            throw new CommandLineOptionException(
                'Invalid option format at ' . $args[$i]);
        }
    }
    return $options;
}
...
}
```

The method can be tested with the following code:

```
try
{
    print_r(CommandLine::parseOptions($_SERVER['argv']));
}
catch (CommandLineOptionException $e)
{
    fwrite(STDERR, 'Error: ' . $e->getMessage() . "\n");
    exit(1);
}
```

Reading a Configuration File

A configuration file is an external file, usually in a plain text format although it can also be in a binary format. It is read by a program or script upon startup and the values within the file influences how the program behaves.

Probably the simplest form of a configuration file for a PHP script to handle is built with PHP code itself. Many applications will have a dedicated file containing define statements, which are included into other files. In fact, this is essentially what db.php is in applications throughout this book.

Sometimes, however, it is desirable for the configuration file to not contain any code. When this is the case, another choice is to list options and their corresponding values. A good example of this type of configuration file is the one used to compile a Linux kernel. Each line that starts with a hash is considered a comment and should be disregarded by the script. Other lines list options that are set to desired values.

```
# ATA/IDE/MFM/RLL support
#
CONFIG_IDE=y


#
# IDE, ATA and ATAPI Block devices
#
CONFIG_BLK_DEV_IDE=y
CONFIG_BLK_DEV_IDEDISK=y
CONFIG_BLK_DEV_IDECD=n
```

Another type of configuration file is commonly referred to as the ini file. This style is commonly seen on older versions of Windows and uses a semicolon to delimit comments. The file can also be structured into sections identified by braced headers. PHP offers the `parse_ini_file()` function to process this type of configuration file.

The logic for processing configuration files can be encapsulated in a `readConfig()` method. Class constants can represent the different types of configuration files and be passed to `readConfig()` to differentiate between the two.

```php
const CONFIG_TYPE_PLAIN = 1;
const CONFIG_TYPE_INI = 2;

static public function parseConfigFile($file, $type = CONFIG_TYPE_PLAIN)
{
    $options = array();

    if ($type == CONFIG_TYPE_PLAIN)
    {
        $fp = fopen($file, 'r');
        while (!feof($fp))
        {
            $line = trim(fgets($fp));
            // skip blank lines and comments
            if ($line && !preg('^#', $line))
            {
                $pieces = explode('=', $line);
                $opt = trim($pieces[0]);
                $value = trim($pieces[1]);

                $options[$opt] = $value;
```

```
            }
        }
        fclose($fp);
    }

    else if ($type == CONFIG_TYPE_INI)
    {
        $options = parse_ini_file($file);
    }

    return $options;
}
```

Prompting for Input

Besides supplying arguments on the command line or through a configuration file, user input can be read in at prompts while the script is running. The code to display the prompt and then accept the input can be incorporated into the CommandLine class as well for reusability purposes.

The prompt() method displays the prompt's label and reads data from STDIN. The trailing newline from when the user presses Enter or Return on a keyboard to submit the input is included so I strip it using trim(). The value may then be passed to a user-provided callback function for validation.

```
static public function prompt($label, $length = 255, $callback = null)
{
    echo $label . ': ';
    $value = trim(fread(STDIN, $length));

    return ($callback) ? call_user_func($callback, $value) : $value;
}
```

The promptDefault() method performs essentially the same task as prompt() and actually relies on it to take in user input. The difference, however, is that promptDefault() makes a suggested default value available to the user.

```
static public function promptDefault($label, $default = null,
    $length = 255, $callback = null)
{
    $label .= ' [' . $default .']';
    $value = self::prompt($label, $length);
    if (!$value)
    {
        $value = $default;
    }

    return ($callback) ? call_user_func($callback, $value) : $value;
}
```

The methods can be tested with the following code:

```php
$value = CommandLine::prompt('First Name', 20, 'ucfirst');
echo 'Nice to meet you, ' . $value . "!\n";

$value = CommandLine::promptDefault('Subnet Mask', '255.255.255.0', 15);
echo 'Subnet mask entered was ' . $value . "\n";
```

Here is the entire contents of `lib/CommandLine.php`:

```php
<?php
// extend Exception class for custom exception type
class CommandLineOptionException extends Exception { }

class CommandLine
{
    // define different configuration file types
    const CONFIG_TYPE_PLAIN = 1;
    const CONFIG_TYPE_INI = 2;

    // accept array of command line arguments, optional array of
    // valid/whitelist options
    static public function parseOptions($args, $allowed = array())
    {
        $options = array();
        $count = count($args);

        // retrive arguments and populate $options array
        for ($i = 1; $i < $count; $i++)
        {
            // retrieve arguments in form of --abc=foo
            if (preg_match('/^--([-A-Z0-9]+)=(.+)$/i', $args[$i], $matches))
            {
                if (empty($allowed) || in_array($matches[1], $allowed))
                {
                    $options[$matches[1]] = $matches[2];
                }
                else
                {
                    throw new CommandLineOptionException(
                        'Unrecognized option ' . $matches[1]);
                }
            }

            // retrieve --abc arguments
            else if (substr($args[$i], 0, 2) == '--')
            {
                $tmp = substr($args[$i], 2);
                if (empty($allowed) || in_array($tmp, $allowed))
                {
                    $options[$tmp] = true;
                }
```

```
            else
            {
                throw new CommandLineOptionException(
                    'Unrecognized option ' . $tmp);
            }
        }

        // retrieve -abc foo, -abc, -a foo and -a arguments
        else if ($args[$i][0] == '-' && strlen($args[$i]) > 1)
        {
            // set all arguments to true except for last in sequence
            for ($j = 1; $j < strlen($args[$i]) - 1; $j++)
            {
                if (empty($allowed) || in_array($args[$i][$j], $allowed))
                {
                    $options[$args[$i][$j]] = true;
                }
                else
                {
                    throw new CommandLineOptionException(
                        'Unrecognized option ' . $args[$i][$j]);
                }
            }

            // set last argument in compressed sequence
            $tmp = substr($args[$i], -1, 1);
            if (empty($allowed) || in_array($tmp, $allowed))
            {
                // assign next $args value if is value
                if ($i + 1 < $count && $args[$i + 1][0] != '-')
                {
                    $options[$tmp] = $args[$i + 1];
                    $i++;
                }
                // assign option as boolean
                else
                {
                    $options[$tmp] = true;
                }
            }
            else
            {
                throw new CommandLineOptionException(
                    'Unrecognized option ' . $tmp);
            }
        }

        // invalid option format
        else
        {
            throw new CommandLineOptionException(
                    'Invalid option format at ' . $args[$i]);
```

(continued)

(continued)

```php
            }
        }
        return $options;
    }

    // process a configuration file and return its options as an array
    static public function parseConfigFile($file, $type = CONFIG_TYPE_PLAIN)
    {
        $options = array();

        // process plain configuration file
        if ($type == CONFIG_TYPE_PLAIN)
        {
            $fp = fopen($file, 'r');
            while (!feof($fp))
            {
                $line = trim(fgets($fp));
                // skip blank lines and comments
                if ($line && !preg('^#', $line))
                {
                    $pieces = explode('=', $line);
                    $opt = trim($pieces[0]);
                    $value = trim($pieces[1]);

                    $options[$opt] = $value;
                }
            }
            fclose($fp);
        }

        // process ini configuration file
        else if ($type == CONFIG_TYPE_INI)
        {
            $options = parse_ini_file($file);
        }
        return $options;
    }

    // prompt for user input, accept optional maximum input length and
    // callback function for validation
    static public function prompt($label, $length = 255, $callback = null)
    {
        echo $label . ': ';
        $value = trim(fread(STDIN, 255));

        return ($callback) ? call_user_func($callback, $value) : $value;
    }

    // prompt for user input, accept optional default value, maximum input
    // length and callback function for validation
    static public function promptDefault($label, $default = null,
        $length = 255, $callback = null)
```

```
        {
            $label .= ' [' . $default .']';
            $value = self::prompt($label, $length);

            if (!$value)
            {
                $value = $default;
            }

            return ($callback) ? call_user_func($callback, $value) : $value;
        }

    }
?>
```

startproject

With the CommandLine class handling the heavy work for parsing arguments and accepting user input
through prompts, the code in startproject can focus on interpreting the information and acting
accordingly.

First Actions

Some arguments can be handled immediately such as -h/--help or -v/--version, whereas others
are checked later to determine the correct course for processing. The most important argument is
-o/ --output because it provides the target location for the new project.

The beginning of startproject should define the location of the skeleton files, provide functions to
handle -h/--help and -v/--version and identify the target provided with -o/--output.

```
#! /usr/bin/php
<?php
include '../lib/CommandLine.php';

define('SKEL_FILES', '/path/to/skeleton/layout');

function show_version()
{
    echo basename($_SERVER['argv'][0]) . ' version 1.0' . "\n";
}

function show_help($display = true)
{
    $script = basename($_SERVER['argv'][0]);
    $help =  <<<ENDHELP
Usage: {$script} [OPTIONS]
Setup project directory and copy basic files into it.

-c, --copy-only      copy project skeleton to TARGET but do not replace
                     Placeholders or delete .tmp files
-h, --help           display this help and exit
```

(continued)

(continued)

```
     -o, --output=TARGET  specify directory where the files will be copied
     -p, --preserve       don't delete .tmp files after replacing placeholders
     -v, --version        print version information and exit

ENDHELP;
    if ($display)
    {
        echo $display;
    }
    else
    {
        return $help;
    }
}

if ($_SERVER['argc'] == 1)
{

    fwrite(STDERR, show_help(false));
    exit(1);
}
else
{
    $allowed = array('c', 'copy-only', 'h', 'help', 'o', 'output',
        'p', 'preserve', 'v', 'version');
    try
    {
        $options = CommandLine::parseOptions($argv, $allowed);
    }
    catch (CommandLineOptionException $e)
    {

        fwrite(STDERR, $e->getMessage() . "\n" . show_help(false));
        exit(1);
    }
}

if (isset($options['h']) || isset($options['help']))
{
    show_help();
    exit();
}

if (isset($options['v']) || isset($options['version']))
{
    show_version();
    exit();
}

if (isset($options['o']) && isset($options['output']))
```

```
{
    fwrite(STDERR, 'ERROR: Unable to determine target. To prevent ' .
        'potential ' . "\n" . 'conflicts please use either -o or ' .
        '--output, not both.' . "\n");
    exit(1);
}
else if (isset($options['o']) || isset($options['output']))
{
    $output = (isset($options['o'])) ? $options['o'] : $options['output'];
}
else
{
    fwrite(STDERR, 'ERROR: Target location was not specified with -o ' .
        'or --output.' . "\n");
    exit(1);
}
```

The script should also determine the absolute path of the target argument. This affords the developer using `startproject` the flexibility to provide the project's directory either as a relative path or absolute path. It should also check if the target can be created and doesn't already exist and if not then display an error message.

```
$dir = basename($output);
$path = realpath(substr($output, 0, strlen($output) - strlen($dir)));

clearstatcache();
if (!file_exists($path) || !is_dir($path) || !is_writable($path))
{
    fwrite(STDERR, 'ERROR: Parent of target directory either does ' .
        'not exist or is' . "\n" . 'not writable.' . "\n");
    exit(1);
}
if (file_exists($path . '/' . $dir))
{
    fwrite(STDERR, 'ERROR: Requested target already exists.' . "\n");
    exit(1);
}
```

Continuing forward, the database connection values are then read from the developer using the static `CommandLine::prompt()` and `CommandLine::promptDefault()` methods. When all the necessary values are collected, they are displayed to the developer for review. It's a good idea to give the user a chance to go back and re-enter information if a mistake was made. When everything appears correct, the user can then type **yes** to proceed and `startproject` will begin copying the skeleton files to the project's destination.

```
do
{
    $db_host = CommandLine::promptDefault('Database host', 'localhost');
    $db_schema = CommandLine::promptDefault('Database schema', 'TEST');
    $db_user = CommandLine::promptDefault('Database user', 'TESTUSR');
    $db_pass = CommandLine::prompt('Database password');
```

(continued)

(continued)

```
        $db_tbl_prefix = CommandLine::promptDefault('Database table prefix', '');

        echo str_repeat('-', 70) . "\n";
        echo 'Database host:          ' . $db_host . "\n";
        echo 'Database schema:        ' . $db_schema . "\n";
        echo 'Database user:          ' . $db_user . "\n";
        echo 'Database password:      ' . $db_pass . "\n";
        echo 'Database table prefix:  ' . $db_tbl_prefix . "\n";

        $ok = CommandLine::promptDefault('Is this correct?', 'yes', 3,
            'strtolower');
    }
while ($ok != 'yes' && $ok != 'y');
echo "\n";
```

Copying Files

Unfortunately, PHP's `copy()` function doesn't perform a recursive copy, so you must write your own to duplicate the entire set of skeleton files. I uncovered a user-submitted function posted to the php.net manual that accomplishes this. It appears here as `dircopy_recurs()` with some minor alterations.

```
// function to recursively copy a directory, modified from code found
// at http://us2.php.net/manual/en/function.copy.php#77238
function dircopy_recurs($source, $dest)
{
    if (!$dir = opendir($source))
    {
        fwrite(STEDRR, 'ERROR: Unable to open ' . $source . "\n");
        exit(1);
    }

    while($file = readdir($dir))
    {
        if($file != '.' && $file != '..')
        {
            $path = $source . '/' . $file;

            // create directory and copy contents
            if (is_dir($path))
            {
                if(!mkdir($dest . '/' . $file))
                {
                    fwrite(STDERR, 'ERROR: Unable to create directory ' .
                        $file . '.' . "\n");
                    exit(1);
                }
                dircopy_recurs($path, $dest . '/' . $file);
            }
            // copy files
            else if(is_file($path))
            {
                if(!copy($path, $dest . '/' . $file))
```

```
                {
                    fwrite(STDERR, 'ERROR: Unable to copy file ' . $file .
                        '.' . "\n");
                    exit(1);
                }
            }
        }
    }
    closedir($dir);
}
```

`startproject` can create the project's destination directory and begin copying the skeleton files now that a recursive copy function is available.

```
if (!mkdir($path . '/' . $dir))
{
    fwrite(STDERR, 'ERROR: Unable to create target directory.' . "\n");
    exit(1);
}

dircopy_recurs(SKEL_FILES, $path . '/' . $dir);
```

Replacing the Placeholders

After the skeleton files have been copied to the target directory, `startproject` must then verify if the -c/--copy-only option was provided. If it was, then the script's task is complete. Otherwise, it must go through and replace placeholder found in the .tmp files with information collected from the prompts. The values are matched up to the appropriate tags and then the script loops through each file that needs to be updated.

For each file, a new file is written with the values in place. If the -p/--preserve option was not set when the script was called then .tmp files are deleted with `unlink()`.

```
if (!isset($options['c']) && !isset($options['copy-only']))
{
    $tags = array(
        '<tag::db_host>' => $db_host,
        '<tag::db_schema>' => $db_schema,
        '<tag::db_user>' => $db_user,
        '<tag::db_pass>' => $db_pass,
        '<tag::db_tbl_prefix>' => $db_tbl_prefix);

    $files = array(
        'lib/db.php.tmp');

    foreach ($files as $f)
    {
        $file_old = $path . '/' . $dir . '/' . $f;
        $file_new = substr($file_old, 0, -4);
        $newcontents = str_replace(array_keys($tags),
            array_values($tags),
            file_get_contents($file_old));
        if (!file_put_contents($file_new, $newcontents))
```

(continued)

307

(continued)

```php
        {
            fwrite(STDERR, 'ERROR: Unable to write ' . $file_new . '.' . "\n");

            exit(1);
        }

        if (!isset($options['p']) && !isset($options['preserve']))
        {
            if (!unlink($file_old))
            {
                fwrite(STDERR, 'ERROR: Unable to remove ' . $file_old . '.' .
                    "\n");
                fclose($fp);
                exit(1);
            }
        }
    }
}
```

There is only one file in this skeleton that needs attention (db.php.tmp), but I still structured my code as a loop so other files can be added easily in the future as requirements change. I use a custom set-up script not too unlike the one presented in this project and over time the number of files with placeholders has grown. After you have written your set-up script and created a basic site skeleton you can augment either anyway you see fit.

Finally, a message is shown to inform the developer his project's base has been successfully deployed to the target directory and is ready for him to start coding.

```php
echo 'Congratulations!  Your project has been deployed to ' . "\n" .
    $path . '/' . $dir . ".\n\n";
```

Here is the complete code for startproject:

```php
#! /usr/bin/php
<?php
// include shared code
include '../lib/CommandLine.php';

// define location of the skeleton layout
define('SKEL_FILES', '/path/to/skeleton/layout');

// function to output the version number
function show_version()
{
    echo basename($_SERVER['argv'][0]) . ' version 1.0' . "\n";
}

// function to output usage instructions
function show_help($display = true)
{
    $script = basename($_SERVER['argv'][0]);
    $help =   <<<ENDHELP
```

```
Usage: {$script} [OPTIONS]
Setup project directory and copy basic files into it.

-c, --copy-only      copy project skeleton to TARGET but do not replace
                     Placeholders or delete .tmp files
-h, --help           display this help and exit
-o, --output=TARGET  specify directory where the files will be copied
-p, --preserve       don't delete .tmp files after replacing placeholders
-v, --version        print version information and exit

ENDHELP;
    if ($display)
    {
        echo $help;
    }
    else
    {
        return $help;
    }
}

// function to recursively copy a directory, modified from code found
// at http://us2.php.net/manual/en/function.copy.php#77238
function dircopy_recurs($source, $dest)
{
    if (!$dir = opendir($source))
    {
        fwrite(STEDRR, 'ERROR: Unable to open ' . $source . "\n");
        exit(1);
    }

    while($file = readdir($dir))
    {
        if($file != '.' && $file != '..')
        {
            $path = $source . '/' . $file;

            // create directory and copy contents
            if (is_dir($path))
            {
                if(!mkdir($dest . '/' . $file))
                {
                    fwrite(STDERR, 'ERROR: Unable to create directory ' .
                        $file . '.' . "\n");
                    exit(1);
                }
                dircopy_recurs($path, $dest . '/' . $file);
            }
            // copy files
            else if(is_file($path))
```

(continued)

(continued)

```
                {
                    if(!copy($path, $dest . '/' . $file))
                    {
                        fwrite(STDERR, 'ERROR: Unable to copy file ' . $file .
                            '.' . "\n");
                        exit(1);
                    }
                }
            }
        }
    }
    closedir($dir);
}

// no arguments provided
if ($_SERVER['argc'] == 1)
{
    fwrite(STDERR, show_help(false));
    exit(1);
}

// Retrieve command-line arguments
else
{
    $allowed = array('c', 'copy-only', 'h', 'help', 'o', 'output',
        'p', 'preserve', 'v', 'version');
    try
    {
        $options = CommandLine::parseOptions($_SERVER['argv'], $allowed);
    }
    catch (CommandLineOptionException $e)
    {
        fwrite(STDERR, $e->getMessage() . "\n" . show_help(false));
        exit(1);
    }
}

// show help if requested
if (isset($options['h']) || isset($options['help']))
{
    show_help();
    exit();
}

// show version information if requested
if (isset($options['v']) || isset($options['version']))
{
    show_version();
    exit();
}

// retrieve target directory
if (isset($options['o']) && isset($options['output']))
```

```
{
    fwrite(STDERR, 'ERROR: Unable to determine target. To prevent ' .
        'potential ' . "\n" . 'conflicts please use either -o or ' .
        '--output, not both.' . "\n");
    exit(1);
}
else if (isset($options['o']) || isset($options['output']))
{
    $output = (isset($options['o'])) ? $options['o'] : $options['output'];
}
else
{
    fwrite(STDERR, 'ERROR: Target location was not specified with -o ' .
        'or --output.' . "\n");
    exit(1);
}

// determine absolute path to target
$dir = basename($output);
$path = realpath(substr($output, 0, strlen($output) - strlen($dir)));

// determine target can be created and doesn't already exist
clearstatcache();
if (!file_exists($path) || !is_dir($path) || !is_writable($path))
{
    fwrite(STDERR, 'ERROR: Parent of target directory either does ' .
        'not exist or is' . "\n" . 'not writable.' . "\n");
    exit(1);
}
if (file_exists($path . '/' . $dir))
{
    fwrite(STDERR, 'ERROR: Requested target already exists.' . "\n");
    exit(1);
}

do
{
    // Retrieve configuration information
    $db_host = CommandLine::promptDefault('Database host', 'localhost');
    $db_schema = CommandLine::promptDefault('Database schema', 'TEST');
    $db_user = CommandLine::promptDefault('Database user', 'TESTUSR');
    $db_pass = CommandLine::prompt('Database password');
    $db_tbl_prefix = CommandLine::promptDefault('Database table prefix', '');

    // Verify collected information is all correct
    echo str_repeat('-', 70) . "\n";
    echo 'Database host:         ' . $db_host . "\n";
    echo 'Database schema:       ' . $db_schema . "\n";
    echo 'Database user:         ' . $db_user . "\n";
    echo 'Database password:     ' . $db_pass . "\n";
    echo 'Database table prefix: ' . $db_tbl_prefix . "\n";

    $ok = CommandLine::promptDefault('Is this correct?', 'yes', 3,
```

(continued)

(continued)

```
            'strtolower');
    }
    while ($ok != 'yes' && $ok != 'y');
    echo "\n";

    // Create the target directory
    if (!mkdir($path . '/' . $dir))
    {
        fwrite(STDERR, 'ERROR: Unable to create target directory.' . "\n");
        exit(1);
    }

    // copy the skeleton files to the target directory
    dircopy_recurs(SKEL_FILES, $path . '/' . $dir);

    // match up placeholders with user provided values to replace them in the
    // temporary files and rename them as permanent
    if (!isset($options['c']) && !isset($options['copy-only']))
    {
        $tags = array(
            '<tag::db_host>' => $db_host,
            '<tag::db_schema>' => $db_schema,
            '<tag::db_user>' => $db_user,
            '<tag::db_pass>' => $db_pass,
            '<tag::db_tbl_prefix>' => $db_tbl_prefix);

        $files = array(
            'lib/db.php.tmp');

        foreach ($files as $f)
        {
            $file_old = $path . '/' . $dir . '/' . $f;
            $file_new = substr($file_old, 0, -4);
            $newcontents = str_replace(array_keys($tags),
                array_values($tags),
                file_get_contents($file_old));
            if (!file_put_contents($file_new, $newcontents))
            {
                fwrite(STDERR, 'ERROR: Unable to write ' . $file_new . '.' . "\n");
                exit(1);
            }

            // remove tmp files
            if (!isset($options['p']) && !isset($options['preserve']))
            {
                if (!unlink($file_old))
                {
                    fwrite(STDERR, 'ERROR: Unable to remove ' . $file_old . '.' .
                        "\n");
                    fclose($fp);
                    exit(1);
```

```
            }
        }
    }
}

echo 'Congratulations!  Your project has been deployed to ' . "\n" .
    $path . '/' . $dir . ".\n\n";
?>
```

Recall from Chapter 3 that `#! /usr/bin/php` provides the system with the location of the PHP interpreter. If your installation of PHP is not in `/usr/bin` then you must adjust the path accordingly. Also, ensure the execute permission is set or you may not be able to run it. On a Unix-based system, this can be done with a command like `chmod +x startproject`. Then the script can be called like any other system program.

The Skeleton

The script requires a layout to copy from when it creates a new project. I call this the site's skeleton because this layout consists of nothing more than the minimum directories, administration scripts, and configuration files necessary for a new project.

The directories for the skeleton will be: `lib`, `public_files`, `public_files/css`, `public_files/img`, `public_files/js`, `sql`, and `templates`. A copy of `common.php` and `db.php` should be placed in `lib`. You may want to review Chapter 1 if you aren't well versed in the purpose of each directory and support file at this point.

Rename `db.php` to `db.php.tmp` and replace its configuration values with placeholders. `startproject` will go through and update these placeholders with the values accepted from the developer at the prompts when it goes to copy the skeleton and resave the final file back as `db.php`.

```php
<?php
// database connection and schema constants
define('DB_HOST', '<tag::db_host>');
define('DB_USER', '<tag::db_user>');
define('DB_PASSWORD', '<tag::db_pass>');
define('DB_SCHEMA', '<tag::db_schema>');
define('DB_TBL_PREFIX', '<tag::db_tbl_prefix>');


...
?>
```

The skeleton should be saved in a safe place since it will serve as the authoritative blueprint for new projects created by `startproject`.

Summary

In this chapter you built a shell script to deploy basic directories and files to help make starting a new project easier. The skeleton files can be modified as your needs change over time. But more importantly, you also wrote reusable code, which eases development of other shell scripts in the future.

The `CommandLine` class encapsulates static methods to accept user input in the form of arguments, a configuration file or direct input in response to prompts. These prompts may even offer default values to the user making the script more user-friendly.

In the next chapter I'll discuss some common security concerns you should keep in mind when writing code and what you can do to protect your applications — definitely an important topic!

12

Security and Logging

I've reserved this last chapter to discuss the topics of security and logging. The applications you write are obviously intended to be used by others. Rarely do they exist in a vacuum and as such it is important to understand the security issues that face all PHP developers.

The aim of security is to prevent the misuse of your application in a way that could compromise data or even the system itself and minimize the effects if such a compromise were to happen. Logging can help support this by tracking usage and changes.

This chapter is a bit different from the previous ones in that I won't provide you with much reusable code in this chapter. Instead, I offer you the background necessary to develop your own. In this chapter you will gain an understanding of the following:

- ❑ Cross-site scripting (XSS)
- ❑ Path traversal
- ❑ Injection
- ❑ Weak authentication

You will also learn how to prevent accidental deletion of records in a database and conveniently log INSERT, UPDATE and DELETE queries.

Just because this chapter has been placed last in the book, don't think that security should be treated as an after-thought. Good programmers can protect their applications by keeping security in mind at all times.

Cross-Site Scripting

Cross-site scripting (XSS) is an attack method whereby a malicious user inserts specially crafted HTML or JavaScript into your page. The goal of such an attack is to trick a visitor into providing his sensitive information to the attacker while he thinks he is really providing it just to your site (phishing) or to outright steal the login credentials with which the attacker can later log in and legitimately retrieve the information. Identity theft in any form is a serious concern, but doubly so when personally identifiable or financial information is stolen.

The primary defense in protecting yourself, your applications and your users from XSS attacks is to properly escape user input and never display it unescaped in a web page. Consider the following example, exploit_01.php:

```
<html>
<?php
if (isset($_POST['submitted']))
{
    echo '<p>Hello, ' . $_POST['name'] . '</p>';
}
else
{
?>
<form action="<?php echo $_SERVER['PHP_SELF']; ?>" method="post">
 <div>
   Enter your name: <input type="text" name="name"/>
   <input type="submit" value="Submit"/>
   <input type="hidden" name="submitted" value="true"/>
 </div>
</form>
<?php
}
?>
</html>
```

The code displays a form to collect the user's name and posts the value back to the same page. The second viewing detects the form submission and displays a greeting. The code may look straight forward, but there are a couple of security vulnerabilities which a malicious user can take advantage of.

First, the input accepted from the form is inserted directly into the output HTML without any form of filtering. If an attacker were able to trick a user into putting HTML or JavaScript in the field, then the browser would parse the code when it processes the page. Suppose for a moment the following input was entered into the field:

```
<script>alert('Cracked!')</script>
```

The browser would detect the script tags and process the JavaScript code. Here the code does nothing more innocuous than display a message dialog as illustrated in Figure 12-1, but a malicious individual would be capable of crafting something more devious such as redirecting the user, changing the location the form posts its information to and more.

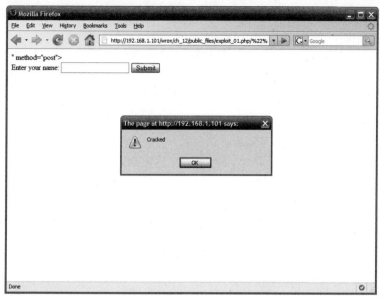

Figure 12-1

A good defense against the attack is to filter the input with `htmlentities()`, `htmlspecialchars()`, or `strip_tags()`. The `htmlentities()` and `htmlspecialchars()` functions will replace the special < and > characters with their respective entity definitions resulting in the browser displaying the input as plain text. `strip_tags()` will remove the `<script>` tags and any other HTML and PHP tags as well.

The second vulnerability which may not be as obvious is the unescaped use of `$_SERVER['PHP_SELF']`. Despite being a member of the `$_SERVER` array, the `PHP_SELF` value is considered user input because it reflects what was entered as the calling URL. Consider the following address:

```
www.example.com/exploit_01.php/%22%3E%3Cscript%3Ealert('Cracked!')%3C/script%3E
```

Apache will resolve the page request to `exploit_01.php` and pass the trailing fragment to the script for use as a parameter. The `%xx` values are actually URL encoded characters, which form the following:

```
"><script>alert('Cracked!')</script>
```

As PHP dutifully outputs the value of `$_SERVER['PHP_SELF']` the trailing attack vector is also included. The initial quote and closing angle bracket terminate the `form` tag. The browser then detects the `script` element and executes the JavaScript code.

To protect your application from this method of attack you should filter the value with `htmlspecialchars()`. Never trust user input no matter what the source.

Here is the same code but corrected to prevent these XSS attacks:

```
<html>
<?php
if (isset($_POST['submitted']))
{
    echo '<p>Hello, ' . htmlspecialchars($_POST['name']) . '</p>';
}
else
{
?>
<form action="<?php echo htmlspecialchars($_SERVER['PHP_SELF']); ?>"
 method="post">
 <div>
   Enter your name: <input type="text" name="name"/>
   <input type="submit" value="Submit"/>
   <input type="hidden" name="submitted" value="true"/>
 </div>
</form>
<?php
}
?>
</html>
```

Path Traversal

Web servers are typically set up to serve content from designated directories. Occasionally a vulnerability will be found in the server software itself which will allow files outside of designated areas to be accessed, but these are pretty much patched in more mature servers such as Apache. Web applications, however, can access the files in other directories, because they execute on the server machine behind the HTTP request. A path traversal attack tricks the script into displaying the contents of directories and files outside of the web root which may contain sensitive information.

Consider this vulnerable code, exploit_02.php:

```
<?php
define('TEMPLATE_DIR', '../templates/');

$GLOBALS['TEMPLATE']['content'] = '<p>Hello World!</p>';

if (isset($_GET['t']))
{
    $template = TEMPLATE_DIR . $_GET['t'];
}

if (isset($template) && file_exists($template))
{
    include $template;
}
else
{
    include TEMPLATE_DIR . 'default.php';
}
?>
```

The code accepts the name of a template file from the URL parameter t with which to display page content. A call to exploit_02.php?t=blue.php for example requests the file use ../templates/blue.php as its template when displaying the page. If blue.php doesn't exist it will default to ../templates/default.php. Well, at least that's what the intent is anyway.

The code is vulnerable because no checks are made on the $template variable to see if its value resides in the web root directory. Just as PHP uses ../ to back out of the public_files directory and reference files in the templates directory, an attacker can add .. and / to the parameter in order to traverse backwards in the file hierarchy into a different directory and access a more sensitive file. Consider the following address:

```
www.example.com/exploit_02.php?t=../../../../etc/passwd
```

With a t parameter of ../../../../etc/passwd, the value of $template becomes ../templates/../../../../etc/passwd. If the path didn't resolve to an existing file then the default.php file would still be used, but if the public_files folder resided in /srv/apache/example on the host server then PHP would include the system's password file that lists all the user accounts on the machine. Figure 12-2 shows the compromised web page displaying the contents of the system's passwd file.

Figure 12-2

The fix is again to properly verify user input. In this case you need to examine the created path to make sure it doesn't traverse into an undesired area of the file system. The realpath() function is useful for this because it accepts a relative path and returns it as an absolute path. You then know exactly which directory is being referenced and can perform a string comparison to make sure it's correct.

Here is the code with the vulnerability corrected:

```php
<?php
define(TEMPLATE_DIR, '/srv/apache/example/templates/');

if (isset($_GET['t']))
{
    $template = realpath(TEMPLATE_DIR . $_GET['t']);
}

if (isset($template) &&
    strpos($target, TEMPLATE_DIR) !== 0 &&
    file_exists($template))
{
    include $template;
}
else
{
    include TEMPLATE_DIR . 'default.php';
}
?>
```

Injection

Injection is where an attacker provides input to directly affect the execution of a command in his favor. I will actually talk about two types of injection attacks: SQL injection and command injection. This family of attacks can be quite devastating.

SQL Injection

The best way to explain SQL injection is jump right in with an illustration, so suppose you have a query, which should delete various records from the database that are older than a given date.

```php
$query = 'DELETE FROM WROX_CALENDAR WHERE TSTAMP < "' . $_POST['date'] . '"';
mysql_query($query, $GLOBALS['DB']);
```

In the desired scenario a user will submit an appropriate date, for example 2007-12-20. This would expand the query to:

```
DELETE FROM WROX_CALENDAR WHERE TSTAMP < "2007-12-20"
```

In this example, all events prior to December 20th would be deleted. However, what happens if the user were to enter the following string for the date value?

```
2007-12-20" OR 1=1 --
```

The query would then expand to:

```
DELETE FROM WROX_CALENDAR WHERE TSTAMP < "2007-12-20" OR 1=1 --"
```

Since a date is provided, records prior to December 20 would certainly be deleted, but the attacker injected extra information which found its way into query string: `" OR 1=1 --`. The double quote matches the opening quote prior to the date, but then another condition appears. Since a number equals itself this condition is always true. The final query would delete *all* records in the WROX_CALENDAR table. The trailing two dashes is how MySQL denotes a comment and is added to tell the database to ignore the closing quote in the original query so a syntax error isn't thrown. This is yet another case how trusting user input can lead to unexpected, and potentially disastrous, consequences.

To learn how to protect yourself, your application and your users' data, consider exploit_03.php:

```php
<?php
include "../lib/common.php";
include "../lib/db.php";

$query = 'SELECT USERNAME, EMAIL_ADDR FROM WROX_USER WHERE USER_ID = ' .
    $_POST['userid'];
$result = mysql_query($query, $GLOBALS['DB']);

echo '<p>Welcome!<br/>Here is the information we have on file for you:</p>';
echo '<table>';
while ($row = mysql_fetch_assoc($result))
{
    echo '<tr><td>Name:</td>';
    echo '<td>' . htmlspecialchars($row['USERNAME']) . '</td></tr>';
    echo '<tr><td>Email:</td>';
    echo '<td>' . htmlspecialchars($row['EMAIL_ADDR']) . '</td></tr>';
}
echo '</table>';
echo '<p>Is this correct?</p>';

mysql_free_result($result);
mysql_close($GLOBALS['DB']);
?>
```

The code pulls in a user id sent to it from an HTTP POST request and uses it in a query to retrieve the user's information. Figure 12-3 shows the script's expected output. The code displays the expected output but is still vulnerable.

Suppose now 1 OR 1=1 was passed as the value of $_POST['userid'], which would make the query:

```
SELECT USERNAME, EMAIL_ADDR FROM WROX_USER WHERE USER_ID = 1 OR 1=1
```

This would match every user record and return every user's e-mail address, as shown in Figure 12-4. The compromised page shows an attacker every user's personal information.

Figure 12-3

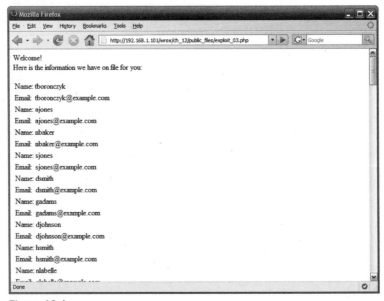

Figure 12-4

`htmlspecialchars()` is not suitable for protecting yourself against this type of attack as it deals specifically with HTML entities. Instead, you need to use the appropriate escape function for whichever database is used and what type of data is being incorporated into the query. Each database can have slightly different syntax and different special characters so you need to look up the appropriate function in the PHP documentation. For string data in MySQL you can use `mysql_real_escape_string()`, for PostgreSQL use `pgsql_escape_string()`, for SQLite use `sqlite_escape_string()`, and so forth. For numeric data or dates you can use `sprintf()` or type-casting. Ultimately how you escape the data depends on what the data is and what database you are using.

The data in the `exploit_03.php` page's query could be easily be escaped by forcing PHP to treat it as a number.

```
$query = sprintf('SELECT USERNAME, EMAIL_ADDR FROM WROX_USER WHERE ' .
    USER_ID = %d', $_POST['userid']);
```

If the attacker were to provide something like `1 OR 1=1`, PHP would cast the string first to an integer and then back to a string, making the query:

```
'SELECT USERNAME, EMAIL_ADDR FROM WROX_USER WHERE USER_ID = 1
```

The information for the user with id 1 may be compromised, but at least you have mitigated the effects of the exploit. To protect this user, simply make it policy to never start a database record with a numeric primary key value of 1.

If the query interpolated a string then you would use the appropriate escape function:

```
$query = sprintf('SELECT USER_ID, USERNAME, EMAIL_ADDR FROM WROX_USER WHERE ' .
    USERNAME = '%s' AND PASSWORD = '%s',
    mysql_real_escape_string($_POST['username'], $GLOBALS['DB']),
    sha1($_POST['password']));
```

You can find examples of using type-conversion and `mysql_real_escape_string()` to protect your queries in almost every chapter in this book.

Another potential vulnerability in `exploit_03.php` is the use of the `while` loop to display the user's record. It can be determined before hand that only one record should be shown, and that the `while` loop shouldn't be used. Querying a database and displaying the matching records is a common task and some programmers may have a code snippet or template they just cut and paste in place to do it. This may explain why the code used a `while` loop, but it doesn't justify it. Be sure to construct your code appropriately to help minimize the affects of an attack.

Here is the code with the vulnerabilities corrected:

```
<?php
include "../lib/common.php";
include "../lib/db.php";

$query = sprintf('SELECT USERNAME, EMAIL_ADDR FROM WROX_USER WHERE ' .
    'USER_ID = %d', $_POST['userid']);
```

(continued)

(continued)

```php
$result = mysql_query($query, $GLOBALS['DB']);

$row = mysql_fetch_assoc($result);
mysql_free_result($result);

echo '<p>Welcome!<br/>Here is the information we have on file for you:</p>';
echo '<table>';
echo '<tr><td>Name:</td>';
echo '<td>' . htmlspecialchars($row['USERNAME']) . '</td></tr>';
echo '<tr><td>Email:</td>';
echo '<td>' . htmlspecialchars($row['EMAIL_ADDR']) . '</td></tr>';
echo '</table>';
echo '<p>Is this correct?</p>';

mysql_close($GLOBALS['DB']);
?>
```

Command Injection

Related to SQL injection is command injection. This is when your script makes a system call with improperly escaped arguments. PHP offers several program execution functions: `exec()`, `passthru()`, `shell_exec()`, `system()`, and the backtick (`` ` ``) operator. Each of these will accept an argument and attempt to execute it on the command line. The results are either returned directly to the output buffer or to the script as a string. It's best to avoid these functions if possible for several reasons; the most important reason is for portability. Still, there are times when they are useful.

Consider the following code for `exploit_04.php`:

```php
<?php
// Assume $_GET['file'] has been filtered appropriately to prevent
// directory traversal and stored as $file

echo '<p>Information about the requested file:</p>';

echo '<pre>';
echo shell_exec('ls -hl --color=never ' . $file);
echo '</pre>';
?>
```

This code intends to display the attributes such as the file owner and size for a selected file using the unix `ls` command. The fact that there is a serious directory traversal exploit just waiting to happen should be obvious, but I've intentionally used an exaggerated sample for the sake of instruction. Please assume the incoming file name has already been filtered correctly to prevent traversing outside the appropriate base directory.

Although `$file` has been filtered (as we are assuming) to prevent a directory traversal attack, it is still being provided to `shell_exec()` unescaped. As with SQL injection, a malicious user can insert commands to be executed with the same account privileges held by the Apache web server. A semicolon is used to separate multiple commands on the same line, so `;cat filename` would result in source of a file being sent to the browser. This is shown in Figure 12-5.

```
ls -hl --color=never ;cat file
```

This is a rather mild example. In fact, if the server had sufficient permissions to do so `;rm -f filename` could possibly delete the file!

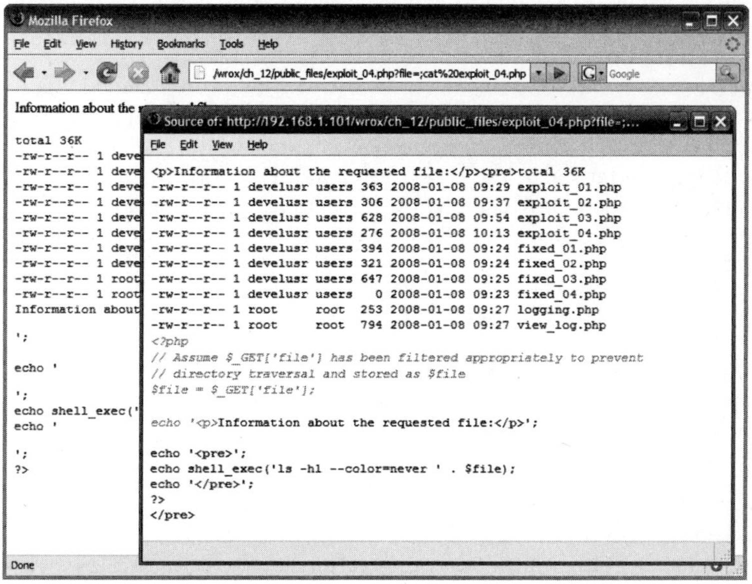

Figure 12-5

The `escapeshellarg()` and `escapeshellcmd()` functions are used to escape characters that have special meaning to the shell, such as the semicolon. `escapeshellarg()` operates on a single argument while `escapeshellcmd()` does so on an entire command string. You should use these to help protect yourself when using `exec()`, `passthru()`, `shell_exec()`, `system()` or the backtick (`) operator is unavoidable.

```php
echo escapeshellcmd('ls -hl --color=never ' . $file);

// or also
shell_exec('ls -hl --color=never ' . escapeshellarg($file));
```

Weak Authentication

Weak authentication practices can lead to exploits just as serious as those I've already discussed thus far, although sometimes it may be more difficult to spot these vulnerabilities than the others. Weak authentication is exploitable when a malicious user can obtain another user's login credentials or privileges either through monitoring network traffic or brute-force password hacking. Oftentimes this is harder to detect because the attacker logs in as if he were the other user, so any actions look like they are legitimate.

Depending on your design requirements, you may want to apply the non-standard `autocomplete="off"` attribute to `input` elements. It was originally introduced by Microsoft for Internet Explorer but is observed now also by Mozilla-based web browsers. The attribute instructs the browser to prevent the caching of previously entered values in the field. With such caching, a user can sit down at a shared computer, place the cursor in the text field and press the down-arrow key to see a list of previously entered values. Although this may be insignificant in itself, it is one additional step in an overall plan for increased security.

Many of the Internet's early protocols seem to be designed with the expectation that users were honest. `Telent`, `FTP`, `POP3`, `IMAP`, `HTTP` and others all pass information — including login credentials — in plain text across the network. Sadly, all users are not honest and it is easy to configure a machine's network card to observe all the information being passed through the network. Many protocols have since been augmented to support encryption. To protect your users from eavesdroppers watching the wire with the intent to steal passwords, it is also a good idea to require all login (and other sensitive) information to be passed using `HTTPS`.

```
<form action="https://www.example.com/login.php" method="post">
 <div>
   Username: <input type="text" name="name" autocomplete="off"/><br/>
   Password: <input type="password" name="password"/><br/>
   <input type="submit" value="Login"/>
   <input type="hidden" name="submitted" value="true"/>
 </div>
</form>
```

The Secure Sockets Layer (SSL) protocol was designed as a way to easily use asymmetric encryption to establish a secure connection between two computers. `HTTPS` is `HTTP` transacted over an SSL-secured connection. It calls for two computers to authenticate themselves through cryptographic means and then establishes a secure connection between two computers over which symmetrically encrypted data is passed.

The server must be configured to accept and correctly handle the incoming connections securely. `HTTP` uses port 80 by default, and 443 is the default port for `HTTPS`. You may require an SSL certificate for `HTTPS`. For publically used sites it is a good idea to purchase certificates from a well-known vendor such as Verisign (`www.verisign.com`) or GeoTrust (`www.geotrust.com`). This certificate typically contains a serial number, encryption keys, the server's domain name, company name, address, the expiration date of the certificate, and the details of the certification authority who issued the certificate.

Certificates can be expensive, however, so for personal sites or development environments you may want to use a self-signed certificate generated with OpenSSL. OpenSSL is a commercial-grade open-source SSL toolkit available online at `www.openssl.org`.

There is another drawback to strong cryptography in that it can fall under various legal restrictions depending on which part of the world you are in. To quote the disclaimer from the OpenSSL project's website:

> *Please remember that export/import and/or use of strong cryptography software, providing cryptography hooks or even just communicating technical details about cryptography software is illegal in some parts of the world.*

So if you're reading this book in a country in which all this is illegal, forget I said anything. I'm too young/busy/whatever to go to jail.

Encryption will protect information as it passes through the Internet but it doesn't prevent brute-force password hacking attempts. This is where the attacker simply tries to guess what the password can be and keeps trying until he is successful. To protect against this type of attack you may wish to track login attempts and disable the account after 3 to 5 incorrect login attempts have been made. A more modern approach is Multi-Factor Identification (MFI).

The three main recognized ways to verify an individual is in fact who he claims to be are:

❑   By something the user *has*, for example a bank card or key fob

❑   By something the user *knows*, for example a password or PIN number

❑   By something the user *is* or *does*, for example fingerprints, DNA and signatures

But there are other less common ways as well. For example:

❑   By *where* the user is, for example, at a particular computer terminal

❑   By *when* the user is, for example, during a certain hours during the day

❑   By *who else knows* the user, for example, social networks

MFI combines two or more authentication metrics to verify an individual. When you go to an automated teller machine (ATM) to withdraw money from your bank account you are actually participating in MFI — you provide the ATM card (something you *have*) and your PIN number (something you *know*). You can mix and match various methods to incorporate MFI into your site.

Logging

If an attacker successfully obtains the necessary information to log in to someone else's account, then any actions they perform look like they are legitimate even though they are not. At best with careful logging and monitoring you may be able to identify and stop some of these attacks in their tracks. At worst, hopefully you have enough information in your logs to roll back any changes an attacker made. Logging is important. It doesn't have to be complex to be effective, either.

The following code can be used to record database updates to a log file:

```php
<?php
// specify log file
define('LOGFILE', '/srv/apache/example.com/logs/database.log');

// define group and record separator characters
define('GS', chr(0x1D));
define('RS', chr(0x1E));

// begin or continue session
```

(continued)

(continued)

```
session_start();

// write the provided message to the log file
function write_log($message)
{
    $fp = fopen(LOGFILE, 'a');
    fwrite($fp, date('Ymd\THis') . $_SESSION['username'] . GS . $message . RS);
    fclose($fp);
}
?>
```

Log entries are separated by an end of record character (RS, character code 0x1E). Each entry starts with a fixed-width character string, which represents a timestamp in ISO-8601 format followed by the username of the person who issued the call. The timestamp will always be 15 characters in length but the length of the username can vary so the group separator (GS, character code 0x1D) is used to terminate it. The final entry of the record is the log message (which will be the SQL statement executed by the user).

Depending on the complexity of the SQL statement I may break it up onto separate lines. My style is to write simple queries that have one or two conditions in its WHERE clause as one line but more complex ones that use JOINS or several Boolean comparisons in the WHERE clause spanning multiple lines. Consequently, a new line or carriage return would not be a suitable record delimiter and is why I chose character code 0x1F.

To use the function, include it in your project's lib/functions.php file or another file that is included into the script that makes INSERT, UPDATE, and DELETE queries. Then pass the query string to the function before issuing it to the database. Here's an example:

```
<?php
include "../lib/common.php";
include "../lib/db.php";
include "../lib/functions.php";

session_start();

$query = sprintf('DELETE FROM %sUSER WHERE USER_ID = %d',
    $_POST['userid']);

write_log($query);
mysql_query($query, $GLOBALS['DB']);
?>
```

A resulting log entry might look like this:

```
20071220T153217tboronczyk↔DELETE FROM WROX_USER WHERE USER_ID = 1▲
```

It can sometimes be difficult to find the right balance between speed, readability, and space requirements as log files can fill up quite fast on busy sites. Representing the log in this type of format preserves all the important information while saving space. The same entry in XML, for example, which is often touted for its readability, is actually slower and bloated:

```
<entry>
<datetime encoding="iso-8601">200712201<datetime>
<username>tboronczyk</username>
<message>DELETE FROM WROX_USER WHERE USER_ID = 1</message>
</entry>
```

The first entry is comprised of 66 characters and the XML representation is 157. That's over a 237 percent increase in required disk space just to store the XML entry!

It is not that difficult to parse the log file. The file can be read in one character at a time until the record separator character is encountered which acts as a signal that the entire record has been read into memory. Then the record is split on the group separator into two pieces — the first is the timestamp and username and the second is the log message or SQL. The first piece is split further using substring() into the 15-character timestamp and the username. The whole processed until the end of the file has been reached.

Here is some example code, which I have saved as view_log.php. Figure 12-6 shows the processed log file.

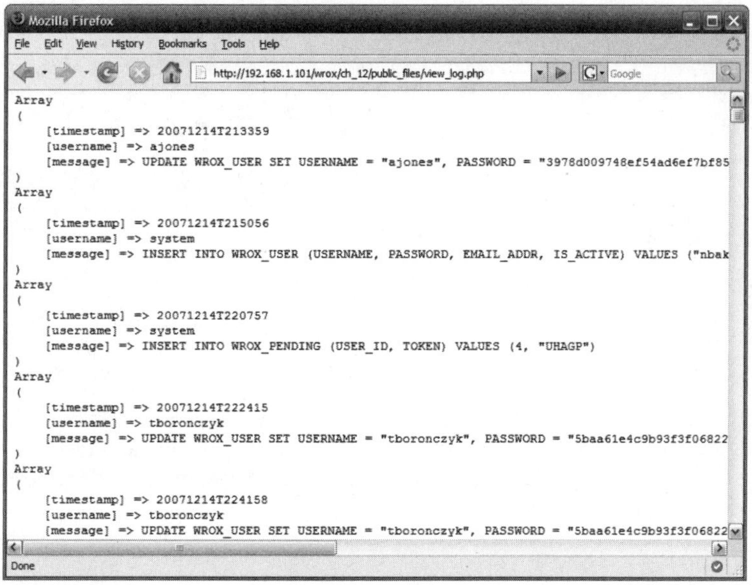

Figure 12-6

```php
<?php
// specify log file
define('LOGFILE', '/srv/apache/example.com/logs/database.log');

// define group and record separator characters
define('GS', chr(0x1D));
define('RS', chr(0x1E));

echo '<pre>';
$fp = fopen(LOGFILE, 'r');

// read in record until the record separator is encountered
while (!feof($fp))
{
    $c = '';
    $line = '';
    while ($c != RS && !feof($fp))
    {
        $line .= $c = fgetc($fp);
    }

    // split the line on the group separator
    $tmp = explode(GS, $line);

    $record = array();

    // timestamp is 15-characters long, the remaining is the username
    $record['timestamp'] = substr($tmp[0], 0, 15);
    $record['username'] = htmlspecialchars(substr($tmp[0], 15));

    $record['message'] = htmlspecialchars($tmp[1]);

    print_r($record);
}
fclose($fp);

echo '</pre>';
?>
```

Alternatively, the logic discussed here to write to and read from the log file can be encapsulated into a custom stream wrapper. Such a wrapper is nothing more than a class that abstracts the logic behind a scheme name. For more information writing a stream wrapper see the PHP documentation at www.php.net/stream_wrapper_register.

Preventing Accidental Deletes

Murphy's Law states whatever can go wrong will go wrong. So even with the appropriate logging and monitoring measures in place accidents are bound to happen. Even with warning and confirmation screens a legitimate user can still delete information they didn't really intend to. The problem with DELETE statements is that they are irrecoverable.

One suggestion to prevent the unintentional deletion of data stored in a database is to add a new field to the records named IS_DELETED or something similar which works much the same way as the IS_ACTIVE field in the user registration project discussed in Chapter 1. The field is a TINYINT(1) which contains either a 0 or 1 to denote if the record is considered *deleted*. Your application would not issue any actual DELETE queries, rather it would set the field value to 1. It's trivial to change the value of the field to restore the record in case of an accident.

Depending on the type of application you are developing, you may not want to have stale data in the database. To prevent deleted records from accumulating in the table you can write an administrative script that can run weekly (or even nightly) from cron or Scheduled Tasks to actually delete the records. The code below shows a script that I use.

A SHOW TABLES query is issued to retrieve a list of all tables in the database. For each table name that is returned, the column names are retrieved with a SHOW COLUMNS query and scanned to find any names that are named IS_DELETED. If so then a true DELETE query is issued otherwise the script moves on to analyze the next table.

```php
#! /usr/bin/php
<?php
include '../lib/common.php';
include '../lib/db.php';

// retrieve list of tables
$table_result = mysql_query('SHOW TABLES', $GLOBALS['DB']);
while ($table_row = mysql_fetch_array($table_result))
{
    // retrieve list of column names in table
    $column_result = mysql_query('SHOW COLUMNS FROM ' . $table_row[0],
        $GLOBALS['DB']);
    while ($column_row = mysql_fetch_assoc($column_result))
    {
        // if the table has an IS_DELETED field then delete old records
        if ($column_row['Field'] == 'IS_DELETED')
        {
            mysql_query('DELETE FROM ' . $table_row[0] . ' WHERE ' .
                'IS_DELETED = 1', $GLOBALS['DB']);

            // break out to process next table
            mysql_free_result($column_result);
            break;
        }
    }
    mysql_free_result($column_result);
}
mysql_free_result($table_result);
mysql_close($GLOBALS['DB']);
?>
```

Summary

This chapter focused on different issues related to security and logging. The points discussed here will help you prevent the misuse of your application in a way that could compromise data or even the system itself and minimize the effects if such a compromise were to happen. You have learned about XSS, path traversal, command injection, and weak authentication. You have also learned how to conveniently log various activities and prevent the accidental deletion of records by adding an IS_DELETED field.

This is the final chapter in the book and I sincerely hope you have enjoyed reading this book as much as I enjoyed writing it. But more importantly I hope that the ideas, reusable components, and basic applications awaken your creativity and serve you well in whatever projects you work on.

Index

Symbols and Numerics

& (bitwise-and operator), 33–35
@ symbol to suppress warning messages, 18
| (bitwise-or operator), 33–35
12-hour vs. 24-hour clocks, 121

A

ACCESS_TIME, 242
accidental deletes, preventing, 330–331
account management (mailing lists), 73–79
ACTION property (VALARM), 131
add_forum.php, 47
add_post.php, 43
addslashes(), 3
administrative interface (search engine),
    91–97
Advanced Bash-Scripting Guide, 295
Ajax, applying with JavaScript
    (shopping cart), 217
Ajax file manager application
    client-side functionality. See client-side
      functionality (Ajax file manager)
    code, 142
    design of, 137–138
    Java Script and Ajax, 138–142
    main interface, 143–147
    overview, 137
    public_file/js/ajax.js code, 139–140
    public_files/index.html code, 144–147
    public_files/process.php code, 168–174
    public_files/upload.php, 161–162
    server–side functionality. See server–side
      functionality (Ajax file manager)
    XMLHttpRequest object, 139–142
alarm component (calendar), 131
Apple QuickTime format (MOV), 177–178
arguments, command-line (shell scripts),
    295–297

asymmetric encryption, 326
Asynchronous JavaScript And XML(AJAX).
    See Ajax
authentication, weak, 325–327
autocomplete="off" attribute, 326
avatars (community forum), 31, 56–59
AVI video format, 191

B

backtick (`) operator, 324–325
bar charts (web site statistics), 248–252
BASEDIR constant, 174
BBCode (Bullet Board Code) markup tags, 59–62
bitwise operators, 33–35
blog system application
    comments, adding, 285–288
    database tables, 265–266
    overview, 265
    posts, adding, 267–277
    posts, displaying, 282–284
    public_files/admin.php code, 271–273
    public_files/fetch_admin.php code, 276
    public_files/fetch.php, 287
    public_files/js/blog_admin.js code, 273–276
    public_files/js/blog.js code, 285–287
    public_files/post_admin.php code, 277
    public_files/post.php code, 287–288
    public_files/rss.php code, 278
    public_files/view.php code, 283–284
    RSS, generating, 278–281

C

caching thumbnails (online photo album),
    192–193
calendar application
    calendar.public_files/month.php code,
      118–119